John Richard Burton

A History of Kidderminster

With short accounts of some neighbouring parishes

John Richard Burton

A History of Kidderminster

With short accounts of some neighbouring parishes

ISBN/EAN: 9783337428747

Printed in Europe, USA, Canada, Australia, Japan

Cover: Foto ©ninafisch / pixelio.de

More available books at **www.hansebooks.com**

A HISTORY

OF

KIDDERMINSTER,

WITH SHORT ACCOUNTS

OF SOME

NEIGHBOURING PARISHES.

BY THE

REV. JOHN RICHARD BURTON, B.A.,

HEAD MASTER OF KIDDERMINSTER SCHOOL.

"*Deo juvante, artes et industria floreat.*"

LONDON
ELLIOT STOCK, 62, PATERNOSTER ROW, E.C.
1890.

PREFACE.

NCOURAGED by the favourable reception of the *History of Bewdley*, I have attempted a similar production illustrating the rise and progress of Kidderminster. Excepting some account of the town in Nash's *Worcestershire* (1782), an interesting lecture by the Rev. B. Gibbons, and a few chapters of a history by the Rev. Dr. McCave, which appeared in the *Kidderminster Sun* newspaper—all of which are now very difficult to obtain—there is no publication to tell the story of the past.

This Work is derived largely from manuscripts which have never before been published. Next to the Saxon Charters in the British Museum, the most valuable portion of our earlier history is contained in a copy of the Maiden Bradley Chartulary lent to me by the late Rev. William Hallen, and bequeathed by him to Lord Foley. The Borough archives elucidate the progress of municipal and social life in the dark ages: my thanks are due to Mr. James Morton, the Town Clerk, for permission to inspect and copy them—a task rendered easier by a transcript previously made by the experienced antiquary, Mr. de Gray Birch. In searching the Public Records I received valuable help from the late Mr. Walford D. Selby. To Mr. W. H. St. John Hope I am indebted for permission to consult the Habingdon and Prattinton MSS. belonging to the Society of Antiquaries. Through the kindness

(iv.)

of Mr. and Mrs. Fenwick, I have had access to the valuable MSS. of the late Sir Thomas Phillipps, Bart., of Thirlestaine House, Cheltenham. The Rev. T. W. Greenall has provided me with several excellent photographs for illustrations. My thanks are also due to the Rev. J. F. Kershaw, and Messrs. J. Amphlett, M. Tomkinson, J. Brinton, Everard Barton, T. F. Ivens, W. H. Talbot, J. H. Hooper, W. M. Roden, R. Grove, C. E. Flowerdew, and others for help in various ways.

Several lists of names are given with the object of helping those who may wish to trace local families; and I have also introduced more general information than is wanted by many readers, because I find that our artisans take a keen interest in the history of their native town and its neighbourhood.

BONTDDU,   J. R. B.

August 30th, 1890.

LIST OF SUBSCRIBERS.

LIBRARY EDITION.

(Fifty Copies Printed.)

1. Abergavenny, Most Hon. the Marquess of, K.G., Eridge Castle, Sussex.
2. Adam, Mr. Peter, Cairndhu, Kidderminster.
3. Amphlett, Mr. John, Clent House.

4. Barton, Mr. Everard, Warstone House.
5. Baldwin, Mr. Enoch, The Mount, Stourport.
6. Beauchamp, Right Hon. the Earl, Madresfield Court.
7. Blencowe, Rev. C. E., Marston S. Lawrence Vicarage.
8. Blencowe, Canon A. J., West Kirby Rectory.
9. Burton, Mr. George H., Markby, Stamford.
10. Burton, Mrs., Woodfield.
11. Burton, H. J. Chandos, Woodfield.

12. Crane, Mr. John H., Oakhampton.
13. Crowther, Mr. W. E. A., The Spennels.

14. Fisk, Rev. T., Highcliffe.
15. Fletcher, Mr. Tom, Falling Sands.
16. Foley, Right Hon. Lord, Ruxley Lodge, Esher.
17. Foley, Mr. P. H., Prestwood.

18. Gibbons, Rev. B., M.A., Waresley House.
19. Grosvenor, Mr. G. W., B.A., D.L., Broome House.

20. Harvey, Mr. J. J., The Grove.
21. Howard, Mr. Henry, Stone House, near Kidderminster.

22. Jenkins, Mr. R., Mill Street.

23. Morton, Mr. E. J., Heathfield, Wolverley.

24. Norris, Mr. W., The Mount, Tenbury.

25. Salisbury, Very Rev. the Dean of, The Deanery.

26. Tempest-Radford, Mr., Beveré Manor.
27-36. Tomkinson, Mr. M., Franche Hall.

37. Walcot, Rev. John, Bitterley Court, Shropshire.
38. Walcot, Mr. Owen C., St. Leonards.
39. Walcot, Capt. R.N., H.M.C.S. *Protector*.
40. Wilson, Mr. Jas., Birmingham.

(vi.)

Adam, Mr. W., Linden Avenue.
Addenbrooke, Mr. E. H., Mill Street.
Antiquaries, Society of, London.
Attwood, Mr. C., M.A., Carlsruhe, Malvern Wells.
Awdry, Mr. W. C., The Bank.
Ayscough, Rev. T. A., M.A., The Vicarage, Tenbury.

Baldwin, Mr. A., Wilden House.
Baldwin, Mr. J. Gough, Stourport.
Baldwin, Mr. E. Arthur, Astley Town.
Baldwyn-Childe, Mrs., Kyre Park, Tenbury.
Barlow, Mr. John, Crescent Villa.
Barrington-Ward, Mr. M. J., M.A., Worcester
Barton, Mr. Everard, Warstone House.
Barton, Mr. Charles T., The Hill, Wolverley.
Barton, Mrs., Astley Hall. (2.)
Bathe, Rev. Stephen B., Rushbury Rectory.
Beach, Mr. T., Areley Kings.
Beddoe, Mr. H. C., Hereford.
Bennett, Miss C. E., High School for Girls.
Bennie, Mr. John, Oak Grove.
Binnian, Mr. James, Blakebrook.
Bradley (the late), Rev. E., Lenton Vicarage.
Brinckman, Mrs. William, Ribbesford House. (2.)
Brinton, Mr. John, Moor Hall. (2.)
Boughton, Sir C. H. Rouse, Bart., Downton Hall, Ludlow.
Broadfield (the late), Mr. E., Post Office.
Broome, Mr. E. A., Areley Kings House.
Bucknall, Mr. T. S., Summer Bank.
Burcher, Mr. F., Kidderminster.

Carter, Mr. H. G., Chester Road.
Carter, Mr. Henry, Lorne Street.
Cawood, Rev. John, Bayton Rectory.
Chesshire, Rev. J. L., Wribbenhall Vicarage. (2.)
Claughton, Rev. Canon, The College, Worcester. (2.)
Cobham, Right Hon. Viscount, Hagley Park.
Cole, Mr. Moses, Farfield House.
Collins, Mr. Sam., Franchise Street.
Cooper, Mr. S. Jehu, Bewdley Street.
Cooper, Mr. T., Wollaston Street, Stourbridge.
Corbet. Mr. Miller, Swan Street.
Cornish Brothers, Birmingham.
Cotton (the late), Mr. W. A., Bromsgrove.
Cowell, Mr. Albert, Broomfield.
Coxon, Alderman, Kidderminster.
Crowther, Mr Clement, Green Hill.

(vii.)

Davies (the late) Mr. D. Lloyd, Wyre Court, Bewdley
Day, Mrs., The Woodlands. Habberley.
Dixon, Mr. H. Jecks, Kidderminster.
Dougall, Mr. A., Blakebrook.
Downing, Mr. J. Marshall, Dowles. (2.)
Downing, Mr. W., Birmingham. (2.)

Elkington, Mr. F., Sion Hill, Wolverley.

Fawkner, Mr. W., Avenue House.
Fenwick, Rev. J. E. A., Thirlestaine House, Cheltenham.
Finch, Rev. W., The Monks, Chaddesley Corbett.
Flowerdew, Mr. C. E., School of Art.

Gabb, Mr. L. A., Bewdley.
Gibbons, Rev. B., M.A., Waresley House. (5.)
Gibbs, Rev. W. C., M.A., Hagley Rectory.
Godson, Mr. A. F., M.A,. M.P., Westwood Park.
Goodwin (the late), Mr. D. W., The Elms. (3.)
Goodwin, Mr. J. R., The Laurels.
Grant, Mr. Charles, Roden Avenue.
Grazebrook, Mr. H. Sydney, Chiswick.
Green, Mr. W. Howe, Blakebrook.
Greenall, Rev. T. W., M.A., Bishampton Rectory.
Grindon, Miss, Comberton Road.
Grosvenor, Mr. G. W., D.L., Broome House.
Grove, Mr. R., sen., Church Street.
Grove, Mr. R., jun., Church Street.
Guest, Mrs. Bird, Blakebrook.

Harvey, Mr. J. J., The Grove (2.)
Hall, Lieut. F. R. N., R.N., Broadway.
Hallen, Rev. Cornelius, Alloa, N.B.
Haycock, Mr. Harry E., Manchester.
Hemborow, Miss, Woodfield.
Hepworth, Mr. Benjamin, Comberton Villa.
Herring, Mr. Henry, Yew Tree House.
Hill, Mr. T. Rowley, St. Catherine's Hill, Worcester.
Hodgson, Rev. John, F.S.A., Kinver Rectory.
Holdsworth, Mr. G., Kidderminster.
Holland, Mr. John B., Farfield.
Hooper, Mr. J. H., M.A., Diocesan Registry, Worcester.
Homfray, Mr. Alfred, Broadwaters House.
Hughes, Mr. Edward, Town Carpet Mills.
Hughes, Mr. F., Trimpley.
Hughes, Mr. Fred., Trimpley.
Hughes, Mr. Thos. W., Lorne Street.

Ingram, Rev. E. H. Winnington. M.A., Ribbesford Rectory
Isaac, Mr. Charles, The Limes.
Ivens, Mr. T. F., Comberton Road.

James, Rev. Alfred, M.A., Burwarton Rectory.
Jenkins, Mr. R., Mill Street. (10.)
Jobson, Mr. Howard C., Summerhill.

Kershaw, Rev. J. F., M.A., St. John's Vicarage.
Killingbeck, Mr. John, Lark Hill.
Knight, Mr. J., Ettingshall, Wolverhampton.
Knight, Sir F. W., K.C.B., Wolverley House.

Landon, Mr. Whittington, Bewdley.
Lane, Rev. C. A., Forest Gate, E.
Lea (the late), Venerable Archdeacon, Droitwich.
Lea, Rev. F. Simcox, M.A., Tedstone Delamere Rectory.
Lea, Rev. T. Simcox, M.A., Tedstone Delamere.
Lea, Rev. Josiah T., Far Forest Vicarage.
Lea, Mr. J. W. Birmingham.
Lea, Mr. Thomas, M.P., The Larches.
Lea, Miss Isabella, Whitville.
Lloyd, Mr. S. Zachary, Areley Hall.
London Library, St. James's Square, S.W.
Lymington, Right Hon. Viscountess, Hurstborne Park, Hants.

Manby, Mr. Cordy, Wassell Wood.
Mark, Mr. T., Brookfield. (6.)
Mayne, Mrs., Oaklands.
Meredith, Mr. J. T., Bank Buildings.
Moore, Rev. O. A., M.A., Sumner Place.
Morton, Mr. E. J., M.A., Heathfield, Wolverley. (2.)
Morton, Mr. James, Dalrymple.
Mottram, Rev. C. P., M.A., Doverdale Rectory.

Ouseley (the late), Sir F. G., Bart., St. Michael's College, Tenbury.

Penny, Mr. W., Church Street.
Phillipps (the late), J. O. Halliwell, F.R.S., Hollingbury Copse, Brighton.
Phillips, Rev. Sidney, M.A., The Vicarage. (2.)
Phillips, Miss, The Infirmary.
Pritchard, Mr. C. A., Upper Norwood, S.E.
Purdey, Mr. W. B., Kidderminster.

Robertson, Rev. D., M.A., Hartlebury Rectory. (2.)

(ix.)

Robinson, Mr. Brooke, M.P., Barford House, Warwick.
Ryland, Mr. J. W., Rowington, Warwick.

Sanders, Rev. Canon S. J. W., LL.D., Northampton.
Sharpe, Rev. John, D.D., Elmley Lovett Rectory.
Shaw, Mr. Edwin, The Newlands.
Simpson, Rev. G. A. K., M.A., Sutton Coldfield.
Smith, Mr. W. H., Hagley.
Southwell, Mr. T. Martin, Bridgnorth.
Spencer, Mr. W. F., Spring Grove.

Taylor, Mr. W., Mus. Bac., Church Street.
Tempest-Radford, Mr. T., Beveré Manor, Worcester.
Thompson, Mr. R. J., Park Lane.
Tomkinson, Mr. M., Franche Hall. (10.)
Tucker, Mr. W., Franche Road.

Vawdrey, Rev. D., M.A., Areley Kings Rectory.

Waddell, Mr. A. R., M.D., Kidderminster.
Wadely, Mr. W., F.C.O., Blakebrook.
Warner, Rev. C., M.A., Clun Vicarage.
Watson, Mr. John, Waresley Court. (2.)
Watson, Mr. R. Talbot, Honeybrooke. (2.)
Whitcombe, Mr. R. H., Bewdley.
Whittall, Mr. A., Kidderminster.
Wilding, Rev. C. J., M.A., Arley Vicarage.
Wilson, Rev. J. Bowstead, M.A., Knightwick Rectory.
Wilson, Mr. James, Birmingham.
Woodward, Mr. Robert, M.A., Arley Castle.
Woodward, Mrs. H. Toye, Franche Court.
Worcester, Right Rev. the Lord Bishop of, Hartlebury Castle.
Worcester, The Public Library.

CONTENTS.

	PAGE.
CHAPTER I.	
THE MONASTERY	1
CHAPTER II.	
THE VILLENAGE	9
CHAPTER III.	
THE BARONAGE	28
CHAPTER IV.	
THE BOROUGH	54
CHAPTER V.	
THE CHURCH	86
CHAPTER VI.	
THE NONCONFORMISTS	134
CHAPTER VII.	
THE SCHOOLS	141
CHAPTER VIII.	
THE CHARITIES	146
CHAPTER IX.	
THE CELEBRITIES...	150
CHAPTER X.	
THE MANUFACTURES	171
CHAPTER XI.	
THE NEIGHBOURHOOD :—	
CLENT ...	189
WOLVERLEY	193
HAGLEY	195
STONE ...	197
CHADDESLEY CORBET	198
HARTLEBURY	201

APPENDIX.

DOMESDAY BOOK (Latin)...	203
CHARTER OF HENRY II. (Latin)...	203
THE PARISH REGISTERS	204
BAILIFFS, HIGH STEWARDS, RECORDERS, &C. ...	222

LIST OF ILLUSTRATIONS.

Map of Kidderminster (1753), by John Doharty, Jun.	... *Frontispiece.*
Map of Land near Bewdley Heath (1704) ...	*Faces p.* 16
Memorial Brass of Maud Harmanville, Sir John Phelip, and Walter Cokesey	,, 40
Monument of Sir Hugh Cokesey and Wife...	,, 40
Monument of Thomas Blount and Wife	,, 40
Monument of Sir Edward Blount and his Wives ...	,, 40
View of Kidderminster (1780) } ... *Between pp.* {	80
View of Kidderminster (1890) }	81
Tower of All Saints' Church...	... *Faces p.* 88
All Saints' Church—North Side	,, 89
Richard Baxter ...	,, 120
The Right Rev. T. L. Claughton, Bishop of St. Albans	,, 124
St. George's Church—North Side ...	,, 128
St. John's Church—S.W. View	,, 132
The Grammar School ...	,, 141
Sir Ralph Clare ...	,, 152
Sir Rowland Hill	162

(xii.)

ADDENDA.

As an illustration of the system of frankpledge (p. 56), the following is of interest :—" In 30 Henry II. (1184) the villata of Kideministra was fined two marks, because it concealed before the Justices what was afterwards found out." (Madox: *Firma Burgi*, p. 57 h.)

The remnant of the mediæval churchyard cross has been moved to a more eastwardly position, and is replaced by a massive one with the following inscription :—" In piam memoriam Patris Matris Majorum Cognatorum intra sacros hos fines quiescentium Signum Fidei Spei Salutis æternæ Crucem jampridem labefactatam Filius reficiendam curavit. A.D. MDCCCLXXVI."

LOWER MYTTON.—The population of the parish in 1881 was 4997, the acreage 2106, and value of benefice £600 with residence. The flagon, two chalices, and two patens were presented by the Rev. Charles Turner Farley. The handsome lectern was given by the Rev. B. Gibbons.

INCUMBENTS.

[1193]	..	Philip.	1779	..	John Grubb.
1552	..	W. Spytull.	1781	..	Francis Baines.
1663	..	Timothy Kirk.	1782	..	David Davies, M.A.
1669	..	Edward Thomas.	1829	..	Charles Wharton, M.A.
1671	..	John Brown.	1850	..	Stephen Rd. Waller,
1692	..	Nathaniel Williams, B.A.	1861	..	Benjamin Gibbons, M.A.
1694	..	Jonathan Cotton.			

CORRIGENDA.

Page 34, line 21, for " Suffold " read *Suffolk*.

Page 82, line 15, for " 1828 " read 1830.

Page 85, lines 9, 10, correct census returns appear to be :—
1851. Borough, 17,033; Foreign, 3,819: total, 20,852.
1861. Borough, 13,978; „ 3,932; „ 17,910.

Page 126, line 1, for " Rectors " read *Vicars*.

Page 128, last line, for " Heming " read *Hemming*.

Page 157, line 6, for " *vimamus* " read *vivamus*.

CHAPTER I.

The Monastery.

IT is believed that Kidderminster may lay some claim to British origin; and that Roman forts existed at Sudwale (near Sutton) and at Wribbenhall, on the "Portway," a road leading from Worcester to Wroxeter, the ancient *Uriconium*. *(Hardwick Add. MSS.,* British Museum, No. 31,003.) "Wal" in a place-name is often an indication of Roman occupation. The "Portway" ran through Upper Arley, and in Wulfrune's Saxon grant to the Canons of Wolverhampton it is called "The Street." In Arley Wood, near this path, a vast Roman Camp, square and treble-ditched, is yet remaining. *(Nash,* vol. ii., app. i.) Another Roman road out of Salop passes Stourbridge, Hagley, Clent, Bellington House in Chaddesley, and through part of Kidderminster parish, towards Worcester. *(Ib.,* app. cviii., and *Midland Antiquary,* vol. ii., No. 6.) Some ancient querns or millstones, supposed to be Roman, were dug up in 1879 under the floor of an outbuilding of the "Three Tuns," about 30 yards from the Stour. In the same place was found a Roman coin of the Emperor Constantine II. (A.D. 337-340). Sepulchral urns containing calcined bones were also found in Dowles brick-yard in 1882, and a coin of Tiberius at Button Oak about 1780. These are indications that in Roman times a civilised people had already taken up their abode in this neighbourhood.

A

After the departure of the Romans came the struggle between the Britons and the Saxon invaders, which was especially fierce on the Severn Valley. By the battle of Deorham in A.D. 571 the West Saxons were able to penetrate up the Severn as far as Shrewsbury; and for several miles along the river side their course would be through the district afterwards included in the great parish of Kidderminster, then chiefly consisting of woods, swamps, heather, and gorse. Perhaps on their way the Britons made a stand at the old entrenched camp near Trimpley, still bearing the name of Wassell or Wars-hill. In A.D. 626 various tribes of Saxons and Angles who had come more recently to our shores were united under Penda in the last of the Saxon kingdoms, the *Mercia* or boundary kingdom which afterwards stretched from the Fens to the Severn, and from the Thames to the Humber. The greater part of Worcestershire (including Kidderminster), and parts of Gloucestershire and Warwickshire, formed the subordinate province of the *Wiccii* or *Hwiccas*. Mercia was the last of the Saxon kingdoms to embrace Christianity. In A.D. 635 Penda, its heathen king, was defeated by Oswald of Northumbria at Winwood. His successor, Peada, married a daughter of the Northumbrian King, and was baptized by Finian and brought back four priests to evangelise his Mercians. Two Wiccian princes were baptized in A.D. 661, and before A.D. 675 religious buildings were founded in the principality, at Deerhurst and Tewkesbury. In A.D. 680 Bosel was consecrated first Bishop of Worcester, his jurisdiction extending over all the ancient province of the Wiccas, until Henry VIII. founded the Bishopric of Gloucester. The Christianity of the Midlands was consequently derived from Lindisfarne and Iona, not from Canterbury.

Amongst a people rude and violent in character, destitute of all learning, almost ignorant of agriculture, and whose heaven was supposed to be a perpetual hunting-ground, the religion and manners of the Christian teachers worked a most beneficent change. Green *(Conquest of England,* page 8) speaks of "the revolution which was wrought by the planting of a Church on the soil with its ecclesiastical organization, its bishops, its priests, its court, and its councils, its language, its law, above all the new impulse given to political consolidation by the building up of Britain into a single religious communion. From the cradle to the grave it forced on the Englishman a new law of conduct, new habits, new conceptions of life and society. It entered above all into that sphere within which the individual will of the freeman had been till now supreme, the sphere of the home; it curtailed his powers over child and wife and slave; it forbade infanticide, the putting away of wives, or cruelty to the serf. It proclaimed slavery an evil, war an evil, manual labour a virtue. It met the feud face to face by denouncing revenge. It held up gluttony and drunkenness, the very essence of the old English feast, as sins. It interfered with labour-customs by prohibitions of toil on Sundays and holy-days."

The Kings of Mercia soon saw how good it was for their people that centres of religion and learning should be planted throughout their dominions; and so it came to pass that on the banks of the Stour, amid the tangled woods, the homes of wolves and other wild animals, there was heard the sound of the axe, and a little wooden church arose—the mother church of Christianity in this district. Rude houses clustered around it, with gardens and open field, the *felled* part of the woods; and thus originated the monastery of Ceadde or Cedd, of which all the traces here have long been swept away, except only the name Kidder-minster, which has survived to tell the story.

The monks in those times, like many missionaries in our own day, did not disdain to wield the axe and follow the plough; they built bridges; they set up mills; they were the best gardeners and farmers; they knew something of medicine and painting; and some of them could read and write. At their head were often to be found princes and princesses and men of noble birth. Men and women who longed for the higher life of religion and peace in a turbulent age found within them an asylum and shelter.

Of course, before the minster was founded this wild district must have had some other designation, derived from its natural features. It was on the Stour (probably the Celtic *Ys*, flowing, *Dwr*, water). But as the Stour is 30 miles in length, some further appellation must be added to denote the locality, and this was supplied by a succession of large pools, now called "Broadwaters," through which a brook passes. This the Saxons called Us-mere *(Us=Ouse,* flowing water, and *Mere,* a pool or lake). In the time of William the Conqueror in a deed describing the boundaries between Kidderminster and Wolverley, the "Broadwaters" is called Us-mere. There is also a house near Hurcott still called "Ismere House."

The original name, then, was "at-Sture-in-Usmere," and in the British Museum (Vitellius C 9, fol. 126) there is fortunately preserved for us a Saxon deed which throws a clear light on the origin of our town. It runs as follows:—

"I Ethelbald, by the gift of the Lord, King not only of the Mercians but of all the provinces which are called by the general name of South-Angles, for the benefit of my soul, do grant to the possession of the Church a certain portion of land, to wit ten cassats, to my venerable Earl Cyniberht to build a monastery in the district of the Husmers, near the river which is called Stour : so that as long as he lives he shall have the power of holding it, or of giving it up to any one he wishes whilst he lives, or at his death. And the aforesaid land is on both sides of the above-named river having on the north a wood which they call Cynibre [? Kinver], and on the west another called Moerheb [perhaps Eymore] of which the greatest part belongs to the said land.

"But if anyone shall be tempted to violate this gift let him know that he shall render a terrible account to God for his tyranny and presumption. This charter is written in the year from the Incarnation of our Lord Jesus Christ 736 and in the 4th of our reign.

"I Æthelbald the King subscribe, confirming my own donation
"I Wor Bishop agree and subscribe
"I Wilfrid Bishop [4th Bishop of Worcester]
"I Æthelric Subregulus of Aethelbald
"I Ibeacsi unworthy abbot
"I Heardberht brother and duke of the aforesaid King

"Ebbella   Ovoc *comes*   Cusa
"Bercol   Sigebed   Pede
"Oba   Ealduuft." *

Power was given in the above charter to Earl Cyniberht to leave the property to whom he would ; and about forty years later (A.D. 775) we find that his son Abbot Ceolfrith devised to the Church of Worcester, "where presided the venerable Bishop Milred" (5th Bishop, 743—775), twenty manses at a

---

* Printed in *Heming,* vol. ii., p. 555 ; Dugdale *Monas.,* i., 121. The readings are somewhat different.

famous place called Heanberi, together with fourteen cassats at Sture in the province of Usmere. (*Dugdale*, i., p. 608; also in *Heming*, and Kemble's *Codex Diplomaticus*.)

Another charter, beautifully written on vellum, and preserved in the British Museum (Tiberius A 13, fol. 106), tells of the settlement of a dispute six years later between King Offa and the Bishop of Worcester concerning lands at various places, including Stour-in-Usmere. It may be translated thus:—

" + In the name of God most high. Times succeed to times, and through constant changes it comes to pass that words spoken long ago become in vain unless we confirm them by writings. Wherefore I Heathored by the dispensation of God the suppliant (*supplex*) Bishop of the Huiccii, most diligently inquiring jointly with the consent and advice of my whole household, which is founded in Huugerna city, have thought and examined concerning its peace and ecclesiastical state. We have had indeed a dispute with Offa King of the Mercians and our most dearly beloved lord. For he said that we without any hereditary right unjustly kept the inheritance of his relation to wit King Aethelbald that is in a place which is called *at Beathum* xc manses and in many other places, that is at *Stretforda* xxx cassats, at *Sture* xxxviii. In like manner he claims at *Sture in Usmere* xiv manses, at *Breodune* xii, in *Homtune* xvii cassats. But the aforesaid cause of contention was settled in a synodal council held in a place which is called at *Bregentforda*. We have therefore restored to the aforementioned King Offa that very celebrated monastery *at Bathum* without any dispute to hold or to assign to any one be should think proper & to be enjoyed for ever by his proper heirs: and we have also added on the South side of the River which is called *Eafen* (Avon) xxx cassats, land which we purchased for a fair sum of Cynewulf King of the West Saxons. Wherefore the aforesaid King Offa, in satisfaction of this compensation made to him, & for unanimity of the strongest peace, hath granted the aforementioned places *at Stretforda, at Sture, at Breodune, in Homtune, at Sture in Usmere*, beyond all cause of controversy, with that liberty to our abovementioned church that is in *Uugerna* city, that they shall not be subject to any greater cess than the obligation of the building of forts, the constructing of bridges, and pasturage for the King and his attendants.

" Now therefore I Offa by the grace of God have subscribed with my own hand the sign of the most sacred Cross of Christ, for assurance of its being confirmed, Iambertus Archbishop sitting with me, and all the Bishops Abbots & Princes have consented & subscribed to the same.

" This deed is written at *Bregentforda* in the year of the Incarnation of Christ DCCLXXXI.

" *Offa* King of the Mercians
" *Iaenberht* Archbishop

6   A HISTORY OF KIDDERMINSTER.

"*Berhtwald, Brorda,* Princes
"*Eadbald, Esne, Eadbald, Eadberht,* Presbyters
"*Eadberht, Hygeberht, Aethelmod, Ecgbald, Ceolwulf, Diera, Aethelwulf, Heardred, Heathoredus, Gisthul, Eadberht, Aldberht,* Bishops."[*]

It is not easy to reconcile the King's conduct in now laying claim to Sture-in-Usmere with his previous approval of Ceolfrith's bequest; but from other sources we know that he was a violent, unscrupulous man with whom "might was right," and that this act was quite in keeping with his character.

Under the rule of the Bishops of Worcester for 40 years the monastery must have prospered; and many spots of waste land were reclaimed, forming the "tons" or enclosures for farm buildings that we find in Domesday Book, such as Wanner-ton, Mede-ton, Sud-ton, Olding-ton, Bristi-ton, Pokels-ton, &c.

If Kinver Wood was the boundary on the north, the old district of Sture-in-Usmere must have included Wolverley and Cookley, which were also being settled. On the other extremity Ribbesford and Wribbenhall (including the land whereon Bewdley now stands) formed part of this extensive domain.

In A.D. 816 Deneberht, Bishop of Worcester, made an exchange with Kenulph, King of Mercia. In return for liberties at *Huuitinton, Speaclcahtun, Teolunaldicotau, Weogornea-leage,* and *Ceaddes-leage* the Bishop assigned to the King xiv. manses in two allotments at a place called "at Sture." We may feel a certain doubt as to whether this refers to Kidderminster from the omission of the "In Usmere." But, as Dr. McCave well puts it, "we are satisfied with Bishop Tanner that it is Sture-in-Usmere. On the one hand the land in question belonged to the Church of Worcester, and Deneberht was resigning it for liberties in four places, one of which was neighbour to Sture-in-Usmere, *Ceaddesleah* or Chaddesley. On the other hand, the amount of land was precisely *fourteen* manses; and fourteen at Sture-in-Usmere had been granted by Abbot Ceolfrith to the Church of Worcester; fourteen under the same description had been confirmed to Worcester diocese by King Offa. These fourteen, according to Kenulf's charter, were in two allotments,

---

[*] Also printed in *Heming*, pp. 224-227; Kemble, *Cod. Dip.*, i., p. 170. See also *Dugd. Monas.*, i., p. 138.

'duobus in curtis'; and similarly Ethelbald's grant at Sture-in-Usmere consisted of *two allotments*, ten original cassats near the river Stour with additional land in Moerheb Wood." If further confirmation is needed, we find that Wolverley and Kidderminster henceforth appear as Crown property. In A.D. 854 Burhred, King of Mercia, gave the Wolverley portion to Bishop Aelhun; William I. gave Cookley (Culleclive) "a certain member of Wolverley" to St. Wulstan; and Kidderminster itself remained Royal demesne till the time of Henry II.

For more than 200 years from A.D. 854 there is almost a complete blank in our history, and these two centuries are more sad than any that England passed through since she became a nation. The country was devastated by hordes of heathen Danes, who especially wreaked their vengeance on the religious buildings and their occupants. There is no express mention of Kidderminster, but we can easily conjecture its fate from what befel its neighbours. Nearly all Mercia lay prostrate at the feet of the Danes; and Burhred the King and Werefrith the Bishop both fled the country in despair. Everywhere the monasteries were destroyed and their inmates murdered. But this is a matter of general history. Coming nearer home we read in the *Chronicles of Worcester Church (Heming*, ii., p. 406), " Meanwhile the Countess Godgiva [the famous Lady Godiva of Coventry] hearing of S. Wolstan's goodness, loved him exceedingly, and assisted him in the divers needs of this age; and at her entreaties her husband, to wit Earl Leofric, gave the church of Worcester two estates called Blakewell and Wolverley, which heretofore the Danes and other adversaries of God had seized upon with violence, and had totally alienated from the said church." Again, *(Heming*, p. 251), " In the time of King Ethelred Clifton, Ham, Eastham, Burford, Tenbury, and Kyre, with all the surrounding districts, were subject to our church of Worcester. But when this province had been plundered and most mercilessly devastated, and the Danes had taken and violently kept possession of nearly all that province: Earl Hacun and his soldiers invaded the aforesaid lands and many others with cruel violence, and kept them when seized for their own property. But finally his wife Gunhilda, seeing that it had been done unjustly, instead of the service of the land, caused to be made for us a certain gilded image of St. Mary. But nevertheless even until now the lands have been alienated from sacred uses." A further extract from *Heming* (i., p. 256) refers to one of the Domesday hamlets of Kidderminster itself :—" The Danes took away by violence from the monastery the village of Ribbesford, whose villeins were required to provide us with fishing nets and hunting implements as often as we required them." Ribbesford apparently had not changed its owner with the rest of the manor; for in about A.D. 1002 it was given by Bishop Wulfstan the " Reprobate " as part of the dowry of his sister for her life.

We see that Wolverley and Ribbesford were devastated during the Danish invasion, and we may wonder why no mention is made of Kidderminster, which lay between them, and which undoubtedly shared the same fate. But the omission is a natural one. The monkish historian is writing the annals of his own monastery ; and we have seen above that in A.D. 816 Kidderminster (Sture) was given to the King; consequently the monastery had no further interest in its fortunes. If as this work proceeds the reader is inclined to think an undue proportion of it is devoted to ecclesiastical matters, he should remember that we are indebted to the clergy for nearly all we know about the ancient history of our country ; and that they would naturally write most about matters coming under their own observation or concerning themselves.

Tanner in his *Notitia Monastica* catalogues the monastery of Sture (Kidderminster) as a " destroyed monastery." Its destruction was without doubt wrought by the Danes — a destruction so thorough that we never again meet with a single line to tell us the monastery had ever existed. Where the building stood we know not ; what scenes of horror were perpetrated here when it perished we know not ; but the minster that lay a heap of ruins nearly 1000 years ago has left a name behind it now known throughout the world.

CHAPTER II.

The Villenage.

DURING the three centuries which elapsed between the foundation of the monastery and the Norman Conquest many of the most fertile spots in the wild district *at-Sture-in-Usmere* had been brought into cultivation, and had received those distinctive place-names which we know so well. The minster as paramount in importance naturally gave its name to the whole parish.

The etymology of the word Kidderminster is a moot point. It is markworthy that the letter *R* in the second syllable does not appear earlier than the time of Henry III.* The most probable conjecture is that it denotes the minster either of St. Chad or his almost equally famous brother St. Cedd. Both were the great Apostles of the Midlands, the former being 1st Bishop of Lichfield (A.D. 665), the latter afterwards Bishop of London (A.D. 664). In Somerset, Chedesforda (Domesday) has become Kittisford. The Saxon form of Chad was Ceadde, and the letter *C* being pronounced hard, the name would sound as Keaddeminster. The neighbouring parish of Chaddesley was formerly spelt Ceaddesley, but the initial letter has been softened. In Domesday Book, where the name first occurs in a written form, it is Chideminstre, but *Ch* was used by the Norman scribes to express the *K* sound, *e.g.*, Chent (Kent), Chenfare (Kinver), Chemesey (Kemsey), &c. Another supposition is that Earl Cyniberht the founder gave his name to the monastery, which was thus called Cyniberts-minster. Others again go back to

---

* In Great Roll of 30 Henry II., *Kideministra*. 11 John, *Kideministre*, 17 Henry III., *Kidaministr'*. Not till 54 Henry III. (1270), *Kidraministr*.

the Celtic *Kid*, a hill, and *Dwr*, water; whence we get "the minster on the hill near the water."

About 800 years ago the curtain is drawn aside for a moment, and we have a most interesting peep at Kidderminster under its new name. In A.D. 1086 the Domesday Book was compiled by order of William I., and the original is still preserved at the Chapter House, Westminster. As this is by far the most valuable record of our past history, the exact Latin text will be given in an appendix. The translation runs as follows:—

> "King William holds Chideminstre in demesne with sixteen Berewicks: —Wenvertun (Wannerton), Trinpali (Trimpley), Worcote (Hurcote), Frenesse (Franche), and another Frenesse, Bristitune (Puxton?), Harburgelei (Habberley), Fastochesfelde, Gurbehale (Wribbenhall), Ribeford (Ribbesford), and another Ribeford, Sudtone (Sutton), Aldintone (Oldington), Mettune (Mitton), Teulesberge (Agborow?), and Sudwale.
>
> " In these lands there are, together with the manor, 20 hides. This manor was all waste. There is one plough in demesne, and 20 villeins, and 30 bordars with 18 plough-teams, and 20 ploughs more may be employed there. There are 2 serfs and 4 serving women, 2 mills of 16 shillings, 2 salt works of 30 shillings, and a fishery of 100 pence. A wood of 4 miles.
>
> "The Reve holds the land of a Radknight in this manor, and has a pleugh of five oræ. One house in Wich (Droitwich), and another in Worcester, rendering ten pence, belong to this manor; the whole of which paid 14 pounds rent in the time of King Edward. It now pays 10 pounds 4 shillings by weight. The King has afforested the wood belonging to this manor.
>
> " William holds one hide of the land of this manor, and the land of a Radknight, and has one villein there and eight bordars having four ploughs and a half It is worth eleven shillings. Aiulf holds a virgate of the same land. There is a plough and two serfs. It is worth two shillings."

King William the Conqueror was the owner of nearly all the parish. His land contained 20 hides, that is about 2400 acres of arable land, together with extensive commons and four miles of wood. The rental of the land was £10 4s. by weight annually—just one penny per acre. This rental was derived from a number of tenants who were in the condition of bond servants, and attached to the soil, but in different degrees of servitude. The money payment formed but a small part of the lord's dues. The villeins held their land on the obligation of working for the lord so many days each week, according to the custom of the particular manor. In the King's demesne or home farm, which probably comprised the present borough of

THE VILLENAGE.

Kidderminster, as distinct from the "foreign," was only one plough-team. But there were 20 villeins and 30 bordars, having amongst them 18 plough-teams. Each villein or bordar had his own piece of land, and was also expected to plough, harrow, sow, and reap the lord's demesne.

The Provost, Reve, or Bayliff was the head man of the village, and under the direction of the lord's steward he regulated the work due from the villeins on the lord's estate. At Kidderminster he held as a special privilege the land of a Radknight, an officer whose duty was to ride in attendance upon his lord when he went from manor to manor. It was easier, when roads were bad, for the lord to move with his retinue from place to place, and stay at each till he had consumed the year's produce of the land. William son of Ansculf, Lord of Dudley, had about 160 acres cultivated by one villein and eight bordars with four and a half plough-teams. Aiulf had 30 A. with a ploughteam and two serfs. The exact enumeration of *ploughs* (carucæ) was made on account of a tax called *Carucagium*, levied on every plough. Under the liability to such a tax there must have been a temptation to conceal the real number of ploughs employed. Hence the surveyors are careful to note that " 20 plough-teams more may be employed there." *(Hale.)* It is strange that we have no mention of a church or priest, though less than 100 years after this we find a rector here with considerable endowment, and Kidderminster giving its name to a very extensive Rural Deanery. There were two bondmen and four bondwomen, who were of the lowest scale in social position : they were at the arbitrary disposal of their lord, only their lives and limbs being under the protection of the law. Some were slaves by birth ; others, who could not pay the *wer* or damages awarded against them, or criminals whose lives were forfeited, became slaves to escape the punishment of death. A valuable appendage to the manor was a house at Droitwich, and this will help us to understand the mention of " 2 salt works of 30 shillings " included in the manor. It is not likely that the salt works were at Kidderminster ; and we have three similar instances in Domesday of Burgenses of Wich attached to distant manors. Another tenant was allowed to live in Worcester for the purposes of trade, but he still remained a member of the manor of

Kidderminster. Mills were of the first necessity in a manor, and were a source of revenue to the lord, by whom they were sustained for the common benefit, and in return enjoyed the monopoly of grinding for the manor. Heavy penalties were exacted for any breach of this rule. In olden times the miller was next in importance to the lord and the rector. One of the mills mentioned was undoubtedly our Town Mill, which after grinding by water power for 1000 years, has lately called in the more powerful aid of steam ; the second was probably the mill at Mytton. If Domesday Book gives a complete list of the households of Kidderminster in 1086, we may make a guess at the population. We have—

Radknights 2, suppose an average of 4 in household ... 8
Villeins 21,   ,,   ,,   ... 84
Bordarii 38,   ,,   ,,   ...152
Servi 4,   ,,   ,,   ... 16
Ancillæ 4,   ... 4
                              ───
                              264

Winter roots and artificial grasses were then unknown in England, so the valuable fertile meadows regularly watered by the Stour were kept exclusively in the lord's hands, and became the " borough," while portions of the outlying district or " foreign " were assigned to the villeins. Our Mill Street and Church Street were probably the first to be settled, and the Town Bridge would be a necessity to connect the Mill with the district on the other side of Stour. To this centre the main roads would converge.

As Royal demesne Kidderminster in very early times enjoyed various privileges, and its tenants were " quit of toll, pannage, murage, stallage, carriage, picage, lastage, pontage, and passage throughout our whole realm of England, and to be quit of contributions of the expenses of knights coming to our Parliaments, and ought not to be placed in assize, juries, or recognizances, except only in those which ought to be made in the courts of the manor." As a counterbalance to the power of the great nobles, the Kings of England fostered the growth of towns, especially those in their own domains ; and the mere production of a copy of Domesday Book by Queen Elizabeth's Treasurer of the Exchequer in 1586, wherein it was recited "King William holds Chideminstre in demesne," was considered as satisfactory proof that all these privileges belonged of right to the town.

After Domesday Book there is a complete blank in our history for 70 years. The manor, administered by a steward and bailiff, descended in turn to William II., Henry I., and Stephen; and as this district was not apparently disturbed by the civil wars, the population would be gradually increasing, and more of the waste land would be taken into cultivation. In 1154 Henry II. came to the throne, and soon afterwards he granted a charter conveying the manor of Kidderminster to one of his faithful followers, Manser Biset, his Dapifer, Cupbearer, or "Gentleman Sewer." The original charter, on vellum, is still in the possession of the Corporation of Kidderminster, and reads thus:—

TRANSLATION.

"Henry the King, Duke of Normandy and Aquitaine, Earl (of Anjon), to the Archbishops, Bishops, Earls, Barons, Sheriffs, Ministers, and all his faithful ones of France and England greeting. Know ye that I have given (and) granted (in fee) and inheritance to Manser Bysett, my steward, for his service, in Worcestershire, Kidderminster for £20; in Wiltshire, Combe for £26; in Gloucestershire, Wikewood for £10; in Hampshire, Dounreston for £8; and the Burgage of Rokebon with the Hundred and with all its appurtenances for £41, and the appurtenances of Lechedesham. And furthermore I have given him Wadersey, which used to pay to my mother yearly 20 sh. to wit, in Wichenford. Wherefore I will and firmly command that the same Manser and his heirs have and hold these lands aforesaid of me and my heirs, well and in peace and honourably and hereditarily, in wood, in plain, in meadows, pastures, in ways and paths, and in all places, with soke and sake, and toll and theam, and infangthief and outfangthief, and with all liberties and free customs wherewith any of my Barons of England holds best, and most quietly, and most honourably. Witness me myself, Thomas the Chancellor, Reginald Earl of Cornwall, William Earl of Leicester, Henry of Essex the Constable, R. de Ham, Robert de Lacy, Warine son of Bernard, Josceline Baret, Robert de Dunstable. At Canterbury."

The privileges conferred on Manser Biset by this charter are very extensive. *Soke* and *sake* authorised him to administer justice within his lordship, to try causes arising among his tenants and vassals, and impose fines on them for their offences.

Tol gave liberty to buy and sell within the precincts of the manor, and to charge a duty for passage, buying, and selling in it; and also freedom from toll in other markets. *Theam* gave him power to try bondsmen and villeins in his court, and to dispose of them, their wives and goods, at his pleasure. *Infangthief* and *outfangthief* permitted him to punish thieves committing theft in his liberty, whether they resided in it or not.

The first witness of the charter next to the King is Thomas the Chancellor, that is the famous Thomas à Becket, who held the office from 1155 till 1162, when he resigned on becoming Archbishop of Canterbury. This fixes the date within a narrow compass.

The reader will have noticed in Domesday Book that " the King has afforested the wood belonging to this manor." More was implied in this than the mere preservation of the game. " The common law ran only where the plough ran. Marsh and moor and woodland knew no master but the King, no law but his absolute will." *(Green.)* This was a serious limitation to the lord's power, so in 11 John (1210) we find that Henry Biset, a successor of Manser, stood charged £100 to the King for having his wood of *Borlese* (Burlish); and that that wood and his manor of Kedeministre might be de-afforested, as they were perambulated by the view of H. de Nevill and knights of the county. (*Maj. Rot.* 11 John, rot. 6 b. See *Nash*, Introduction lxix. f.)

Leaving a more detailed account of the Biset family for another chapter, we will follow the fortunes of the town and its people. Henry Biset, son of Manser, before A.D. 1200, granted to Ralph de Auxeville, probably a Norman knight, " one hundred shillings worth *(solidatas)* of land, to wit 14s. from my lord's mill of Kedemynstre, my whole mill of Mytton, the whole vill of Oldyngton, and the whole vill of Comberton, to be held by him and his heirs of me and my heirs, by rendering annually one Hostorium-scer or 5s.; and it shall rest in the choice of the aforesaid Ralph to pay which of the two he prefers. Witnesses: Geoffrey Talbot, Hugh de Augere, Robert de Brinkworth, &c." (*Wanley MS.*, page 166.)

Manser Biset in his lifetime had founded a convent for

leprous women on his wife's property at Maiden Bradley, in Wiltshire; and we shall see how, through what was at first only a slender thread, the monks gradually gained a firm hold in Kidderminster, and ultimately owned nearly half the parish. Their first acquisition was from the above-named Ralph de Auxeville of "one Native, with his sons, daughters, house, land, tenement, and appurtenances." The Kidderminster man who was thus transferred with all his belongings was named William de Acheborne, and the convent in return was to pay 2s. 8d, a year to Ralph de Auxeville. *(Wanley MS.)*

A time of peril soon came to the lord of Comberton and Oldington. Either in John's wars with the French or in the quarrel with the Barons, Ralph was imprisoned and threatened with death. The leprous sisters and monks of Maiden Bradley came to the rescue, and provided him with the ransom of 100 marks, and in return for this kindness he made the following grant:—

"Know all men present and to come, that I Ralph de Auxeville have given to the Leprous Sisters of Bradley and to the Brethren serving God there, one virgate [30 acres] of land in Oldington which Thomas the son of Gilbert and William the Turnur held, and another virgate of land in the same vill which Edred and Brien held; and moreover two virgates of land in the same vill which Esebern and Osbert his brother, and Osbert Wade and William de Freinsh held. And also at Comberton one virgate of land which Edred and Reginalda the widow held; and 14s. to be received annually from the Great Mill of Kideminstre, and the whole Mill of Mytton with its appurtenances. And the aforesaid Leprous Sisters shall have these lands and rents, with the men holding the lands and their services, by rendering thence to me and my heirs one pound of cumin annually at the feast of S. Michael or twopence; and to the Lord of Kideminstre 5s. And in return for this my donation the aforesaid Leprous Sisters and Brethren have given to me 100 marcs sterling to redeem my body from prison and from death." *(Wanley MS., pp. 51-53.)*

A portion of Comberton and Oldington still remained to Ralph de Auxeville; but soon these acres followed the rest, and in 1227 we find a further grant:—

"I Ralph de Auxeville have given to God and the Blessed Mary and the Leprous Sisters of Bradley one virgate of land in Comberton which Geoffrey de Freinsh and Osbert son of Orderic held, and half a virgate of land in the same vill which Edwin son of Edwin held; and one virgate of land at Oldington which Thomas the son of Edwin held, and one virgate which Ivo held in the same vill, and one virgate which William and Edred Snel held, and, half a virgate at Comberton which William the Smith held, &c., for the soul of my lord Henry Biset, and for my soul, and for the souls of all my ancestors and heirs. Witnesses, Hugh de Ang., Henry de Ribelf., William Chaplain of Beverel, Hugh Mustell, Calixtus, Dean, Adam de Hurecot, Adam Penstant." Endorsed : " This Charter was enrolled in the presence of Stephen de Segrave and his fellow Justiciaries at Worcester. In the reign of H. son of King John xi." *(Madox ; Form. Anglic.* p. 255.)

Upon this follows the confirmation of Walter de Auxeville, brother and heir of the aforesaid Ralph.

After this short tenure of the unfortunate Ralph de Auxeville, Comberton, Oldington, and the Mill of Mytton were the property of Maiden Bradley convent, and so remained for more than 300 years. The monks appear to have managed their property well, and it was probably for the convenience of their tenants that previous to A.D. 1214 there was founded the chapel of S. Michael at Mytton. One of the brethren would be present on S. Michael's day to pay the lord's rent, and this would enable him also to attend the dedication festival at the same time.

Shortly afterwards other portions of Oldington came into the hands of the monks :—

" I Nicholas son of Ivo de Oldington have released to Sir John Prior of Maiden Bradley, &c., all that messuage which Nicholas Balle held of me in the vill of Oldington, as it is enclosed with a wall and a ditch, also that house in Oldington which Goditha the widow held, &c."

On Aug. 1, 1226, King Henry III. visited the town ; and again in 1233, June 3, he was here, and issued an order in which he commanded the Sheriff of Hampshire to cause a wainscotted chamber in his palace of Winchester to be painted with the same figures it had been ornamented with before. Where he lodged we do not know. Probably at the Hall between Hall-street and the church.

In A.D. 1235 an agreement was made between William, Prior of Maiden Bradley, and Geoffrey Stertwine, of Nether Mytton : " The Prior and Convent delivered to Geoffrey their mill at Mytton on the Stour with a portion of Oldington and a portion of Comberton at a rent of one mark of silver. But Geoffrey shall make the whole mill fit for work, and keep it in repair at

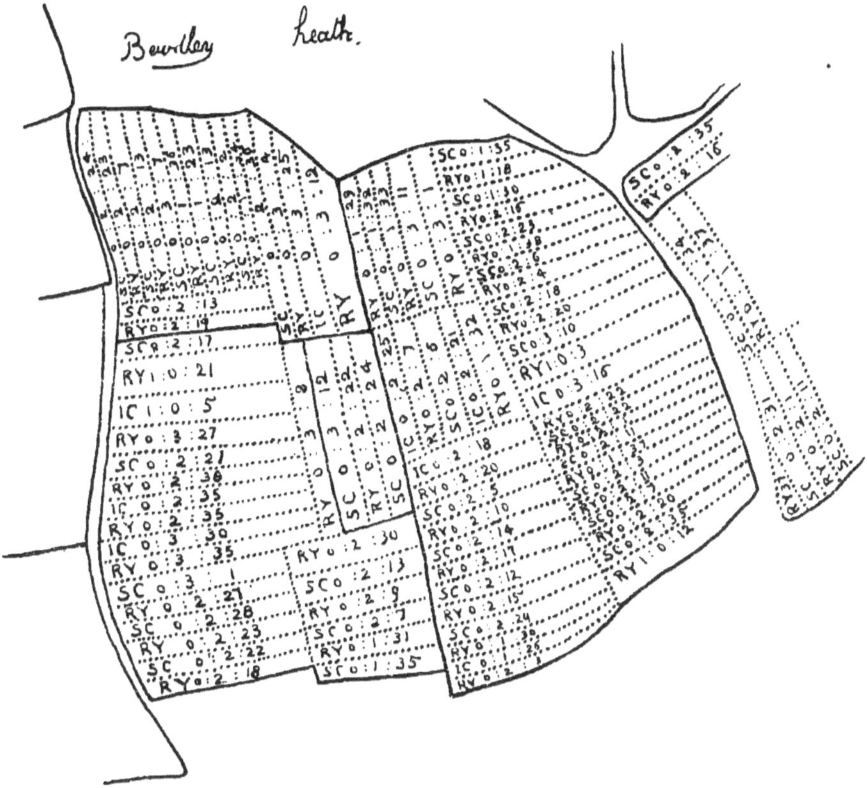

Bewdley heath.

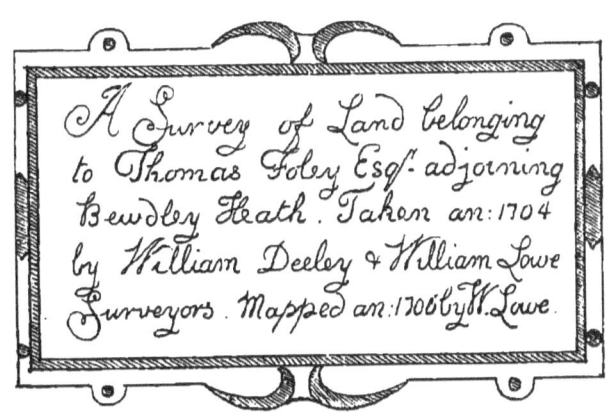

A Survey of Land belonging to Thomas Foley Esqr. adjoining Bewdley Heath. Taken an: 1704 by William Deeley & William Lowe Surveyors. Mapped an: 1706 by W. Lowe.

his own expense, being assisted by the men of the convent when it is necessary, as has been the custom."

Another deed without date shows that the convent had acquired an interest in a different part of the parish. "Know all, that we Brother John, Prior of Maiden Bradley, &c., have given to Thomas Biset all the land which was formerly William Becke's at *La Horeston*; an 1 3 acres of land situated at *Henleghe* which were formerly John de la More's, &c., for an annual rent of 3s. 5d."

In 22 Henry III. (1238) John Biset obtained a charter of free warren in all his demesne lands at Kidderminster, and a fair yearly for two days, viz., on the eve and day of St. Bartholomew. Other fairs have been granted for Ascension-day (now changed) and Corpus Christi. Fairs and markets were valuable acquisitions in these times; and the privilege was eagerly sought for by the lords of manors on account of the tolls which they were able to exact from traders. Thus Kidderminster was steadily rising in importance, and was beginning to acquire a considerable share of self-government. Between 1237 and 1241 the town succeeded in maintaining its independence from all authority of the Sheriff of the county except "attachment of the Crown, when occasion shall arise." The charter of Walter de Beauchamp, Earl of Warwick, written on vellum, is still preserved in the archives of the Corporation. It is to this effect :—

"Know present and future men, that I Walter de Beauchamp, have enquired by men worthy of credit, that no Sheriff hath entered into the manor of Kidderminster to hold the Sheriff's turn there, or to take any money in the name of the turn of his Shrievalty there, before the time of William de Cantilupe the elder who was Sheriff of Worcester for the Lord King [1202—1215]. And therefore I have released to John Biset and his heirs as his right, for me and my heirs, or any one who shall be our Sheriff for the time being, to enter into the manor of Kidderminster, to hold the Sheriff's turn there, or to take any money by name of the turn of his Shrievalty, as is aforesaid, there: nor will I Walter, nor my heirs, nor any Sheriff for the time being, enter in the manor aforesaid, to make any attachment there, or to take distress there, which belong to the Sheriff, except attachment of the Crown, when occasion shall arise. And for this release and quit-claim the aforesaid John has given to me 16 silver marks. And that the present writing for ever may obtain the strength of confirmation, I have strengthened the same with the impression of my seal. These being the witnesses Lord Walter Bishop of Worcester, Lord Richard Abbot of

c

Evesham, Roger le Power, Peter de Wike, William de Corbett, Geoffrey de Warm', Alexander Dapitot, Thomas de Stoke, Robert de Parco, and many others."

Leaving the development and organization of the " borough " for future consideration, we will now examine some records which, with the aid of Seebohm's valuable book on *The English Village Community*, enable us to form a notion of the system of husbandry then almost universal in England. From the annexed tracing of a map (belonging to Mr. T. F. Ivens) made in 1704, and showing a portion of Lord Foley's estate, we see that the land is cut up into a number of little narrow strips. The strips vary more or less in size and shape, but each has an area of rather more than half-an-acre. The ancient form of the acre was " 40 rods in length and 4 in breadth " (33 Edw. I.), and it was thus set out for convenience in ploughing—in the first instance by using an actual rod. " The furlong is the ' furrow-long,' *i.e.*, the length of the drive of the plough before it is turned ; and this by long custom was fixed at 40 rods. The word ' rood ' naturally corresponds with as many furrows in the ploughing as are contained in the breadth of one rod. And four of these roods lying side by side made the acre strip in the open fields, and still make up the statute acre." *(Seebohm.)*

Two or three furrows were left unploughed between each half-acre division, forming boundaries of turf called *balks*. At the ends of the strips was another larger piece of turf called a *headland*, where the ploughs could turn. " When a hill-side formed part of the open field the strips were made to run horizontally along it ; and in ploughing, the custom for ages was always to turn the sod of the furrow downhill, the plough consequently always returning one way idle. The result was that the strips became in time long level terraces one above the other, and the balks between them grew into steep rough banks." *(Seebohm.)* These banks are generally called *lynches* or *linces*, and some may be seen in this neighbourhood, notably at Hartlebury and Abberley, near the road from Stourport to the Hundred House.

Lord Foley's estate in 1704 at Wribbenhall, Oldington, Hoarstone, High Habberley, and the Lea was divided into these half-acre strips ; and this survival from remote ages is a valuable guide to the right understanding of our old records, since by the Enclosure Acts of 1774, &c., the ancient system of open fields was swept away for ever.

In 1086 there were apparently (except perhaps the Radknights) no free men in Kidderminster. The villeins, who were the highest class of serfs, made up 30 per cent. of the population, the bordars or cottars were 54 per cent., and the slaves 11 per cent. All of them were bound to join in cultivating the lord's demesne or home-farm of nearly 1000 acres, forming " the borough." But each villein had a virgate (or yard-land) of 30 acres, or a bovate of 15 acres, in his own occupation, on which he could work when not on duty for the lord. These virgates or bovates were not all in one piece, but scattered through the outlying hamlets or " foreign " in half-acre strips. Except the mill at Mytton, and a house or two at each of the sixteen berewicks or enclosures for farm produce, the people probably lived in the town, partly for mutual protection and partly to be on the spot for the lord's work. Ploughing was then done by teams of four or eight oxen ; but as no one villein was rich enough to possess a team of his own, each tenant of a bovate contributed one ox to the team, and had his proper proportion of the land when ploughed. The acre was the quantity that a plough-team could get through in the morning's work. At first the ownership of the strips varied from year to year, but in time became fixed to each individual. When a slave or a cottar was raised to a villein, his lord usually provided him with his ox, a cow, six sheep, and seven acres sown on his virgate, so that the " heriot " at his death would be originally a return to the lord of his own " outfit." The Smith and the Carpenter, who appear in the list of villeins, had their strips ploughed free in return for keeping the ploughs and harrows in working order. The cottars held a similar holding—usually a house and a few acres of land ; and as they had no plough or oxen, they were more like our day-labourers. The services required from all the tenants were (1) *weekly work* at ploughing, reaping, carrying, usually for two or three days a week, and most at harvest-time ; (2) *precariæ*, special or extra services when the lord required them; and (3) payments in kind or money at specified times, *church shot*, &c. *(Seebohm.)* The best husbandman each year was chosen by the villeins as *Præpositus*, Provost, or Bailiff. He was to regulate the work due to the lord; and his office has been handed down, amid all the silent social changes, through perhaps a thousand years to our present Mayor. The title of Bailiff as Chief Magistrate was retained down to A.D. 1835.

The arable land was generally divided into three fields representing the rotation of crops, viz.—(1) Tilth-grain; (2) Etch-grain (oats or beans sown in spring); and (3) Fallow. In Lord Foley's map of Wribbenhall we find the "Over Field," "Middle Field," and "Lower Field." Thus each villein would have yearly 10 half-acre strips of wheat or rye, 10 of oats or beans, and 10 would lie fallow. When all the corn was housed, the tenants could let their cattle feed at random over the open field, where there were no hedges, only balks or narrow strips of turf. On Lord Foley's map there are "Running Doles;" these were similar strips of meadow land, which could be grazed in common after Lammas Day (August 1).

The earliest list of any Kidderminster tenants with their holdings is contained in Ralph de Auxeville's grant (p. 15), where each tenant holds half a virgate. In his second grant (p. 15) Thomas and Ivo each hold a virgate, and the rest is in half-virgates. The date of the latter deed is 1227.

In the Maiden Bradley chartulary is a list of the tenants of Oldington some years later. This is interesting as containing the first direct mention of a *free* man holding land in the manor.

FREEMEN.

Nicholas holds one virgate of land by charter, and pays iiis.

RUSTICI OR VILLEINS.

Richard Balle, Bailiff, holds a messuage and half a virgate and pays iis. viiid.

Other tenants holding a messuage and half a virgate, and paying 2s. 8d., are Robert Balle, Osbert Wade, William Gamulde, Roger le Lay, Thomas Wade, Algar Wade, Thomas

Hupshulle, Walter Snel, Thomas Black or Blake *(Niger)*, and Osbert Balle. Thomas Wade also holds a fishery at a rental of 6*d.*, Roger le Lay a fishery at 3*d.*, and Osbert and Robert Balle a fishery at 3*d.*

The cottars were Philip Muller and Petronilla daughter of Edwin, each having a house with three acres of land and a small piece of meadow at 2*s.* rental; Margery daughter of Godiva a house at 8*d.*; and Nicholas Hidde a house with six acres of land at 1*s.* 6*d.*

The whole land in Oldington contained in this list amounts to $6\frac{1}{4}$ virgates with 12 acres and some meadow. This agrees almost exactly with the 7 virgates given to Maiden Bradley by Ralph de Auxeville. Taking the virgate at 30 acres, there would be 210 acres in cultivation at this time, divided amongst 16 tenants, at a total rental of £1 19*s.* per annum, or rather more than 2*d.* an acre. In 1704 Lord Foley was owner of Oldington. The acres under cultivation had increased in the 500 years to 328, with only nine tenants; but there were still 264 acres in Oldington Common, much of which is now "Oldington Wood," skirting part of the road between Kidderminster and Stourport.

The chartulary at the same time gives the names of two tenants at Mytton (Mutona):—

William de Stour holds one Corn-Mill *(Blarecum)* and one Fulling-Mill *(Folcrecum),* and pays xiiis. ivd.

John le Brile holds one messuage and half a virgate of land and pays iiis.

In the Public Record Office *(Exchequer Ministers' Accounts* $\frac{193}{21}$), there is fortunately preserved a more complete list of the villeins of Kidderminster made some 20 or 30 years after the preceding. It is undated, but from the handwriting appears to be of the time of Edward I., and is endorsed

CUSTUMAR' ET REDDITA DE KEDEMINYSTER.

Villani Prime Excanbie.

	s. d.
HABERLEGH (Habberley)	
Henry le Proude holds 1 virgate .. .. per annum	5 8
Editha de la Hulle holds one house and one noke	2 2*d.*
Hugh Bedellus holds 1 messuage and half a virgate..	3 10¼ *l.*

A HISTORY OF KIDDERMINSTER.

POKELESTON (Puxton)

		s.	d.
Henry Black *(Niger)* holds 1 messuage and half a virgate.. .. .. per annum	..	3	4
Thomas Godrih holds 1 messuage and half a virgate	,, ..	5	3
Roger de la Grave holds 1 messuage and half a virgate..	,, ..	3	10¼
William Pokel holds land	,, ..		2

SOTTON (Sutton)

		s.	d.
William Thorkil holds 1 messuage and half a virgate	,, ..	3	10¼
Henry Chancellor *(Cancellarius)* holds 1 messuage and half a virgate	,, ..	3	10¼
Walter Tekle holds 1 messuage and half a virgate..	,, ..	3	10¼
Robert Cortys holds 1 messuage and half a virgate..	,, ..	3	10¼
Margery de Ris, daughter of Robert de Ris, holds 1 messuage and half a virgate ..	,, ..	3	10¼
——— holds land of Richard de Smalbroc, 1 messuage and half a virgate ..	,,	3	10¼

AGBERUE (Agborow)

		s.	d.
Adam son of Petronilla holds 1 messuage and half a virgate	,, ..	3	10¼
Henry de Holie holds 1 messuage and half a virgate	,, ..	4	0

LEA

		s.	d.
Henry de la Lee holds his mansion.. ..	,,	1	6
Muriele holds a certain meadow at Schireneware..			12d
Juliana relict of Robert le Bercher holds 1 messuage and half a virgate	,	3	10¼

NETHERTON

		s.	d.
Robert Hawis holds 1 messuage and half a virgate..	..	3	10¼
William le ———, land and messuage of Succus	,, ..	4	0
Richard de Grange, 1 messuage and half a virgate..	,, ..	3	10¼
William Agemon, 1 house and curtilage ..	,, ..		8d.
Richard Smith *(Faber)* holds one butt, and suit of court, and pays four horseshoes with the nails.			

THE VILLENAGE.

WRODDENHALE (Wribbenhall) — s. d.

Henry de Eldenhale, 1 house and 1 croft .. per annum	..	10d.
John de la More, 1 messuage and half a virgate..	,, ..	4 3¾
William Colemon, 1 messuage and 1 noke..	,, ..	5 9¼

FRAINIS (Franche)

Henry Drin, 1 messuage and 1 virgate ..	,, ..	6 10¼
Maude de la Grave, 1 messuage and half a virgate..	,, ..	4 4½
Walter Red, 1 messuage and 1 virgate ..	,, ..	6 10¼

TREMPEL (Trimpley)

Thomas Young *(Juvenis)*, 1 messuage and half a virgate..	,, ..	3 7¼
Richard Hervi, 1 messuage and half a virgate..	,, ..	4 3¼
Agnes Hereward, 1 messuage and 3 nokes..	,, ..	6 0¼
Robert de la Pucce, 1 messuage and half a virgate..	,, ..	7 0
Editha Godrih, mansion	,, ..	20d.
Thomas Carpenter, mansion and 1 croft ..	,, ..	20d.
———— holds land of Elwald	,, ..	3 0
John Wicliug, 1 croft	,, ..	4d.

COMBERTON

Richard Scherewind, 1 messuage and half a virgate..	,, ..	7 3
John le Kay, 1 messuage 1½ virgates ..	,, ..	5 9
Robert Smith *(Faber)*, 1 house	,, ..	3
————, 1 messuage and half a virgate	,, ..	5 9
Simon de Arderne, 1 messuage and half a virgate..	,, ..	5 9
Robert de Winkleover, 1 messuage and half a virgate	,, ..	5 9

MUTTON (Mytton)

William de Sture holds one mill and pays..	,,	1 mark and homage and suit.
Richard de le Bole, 1 messuage and half a virgate, and pays	,,	.. 3 0 and suit.
Thomas Balle, 3 acres at Simareshert	,,	.. 3d.

OLDINTON

Robert Young, 1 messuage and half a virgate.. .. .. 3 0
homage and suit.

			s.	d.
Wife of Richard Ball, 1 messuage and half a virgate		per annum	3	10
Nicholas le Kay (? Lay), 1 messuage and half a virgate with a weir		,,	4	1
John Hill *(de Monte)*, 1 messuage and half a virgate..		,,	3	10
Thomas le Challoner, 1 messuage and half a virgate..		,,	3	10
Galfrid son of Thomas, 1 messuage and half a virgate..		,,	3	10
William Snel, 1 messuage and half a virgate..		,,	3	10
Algar Wade, 1 messuage and half a virgate.		,,	3	10
Thomas Wade, 1 messuage and half a virgate..		,,	4	4
Juliana Wade, 1 messuage and half a virgate..		,,	3	10
Osbert Ball, 1 messuage and half a virgate.		,,	3	11½
Henry Ball, 1 messuage and half a virgate.		,,	3	11½
Editha Goumill, 1 messuage and half a virgate..		,,	3	10

COTTARII

		s.	d.
Alicia Molloc, 1 mansion, 6 acres, with 1 rood of meadow	,,	2	0
Henry son of Nicholas Ball, 1 mansion and "witebut," 6 acres with witebut ..	,,	2	9
Petronilla daughter of Edwin, 1 mansion, 6 acres, 1 rood of meadow ..	,,		22½d.
William le Smocare, 1 mansion	,,		10d.
Robert le Troyere, 1 house of Robert Young, rendering annually for having warranty	,,		2d.

By comparing this list with the previous one, it is seen that William de Stour is still occupying the mill at Mytton at the same rent. Algar Wade, Thomas Wade, and Osbert Ball are still at Oldington, but their rental is increased from 2s. 8d. to 3s. 10d. The 6d. extra paid by Thomas Wade is no doubt in consideration of his fishery, though it is not specially mentioned. Robert Ball is dead, Henry Ball now shares the fishery with Osbert, so each pays 1½d. additional rent on that account. Nicholas le Kay (? Lay) has succeeded to the fishery of Roger le Lay. The "weir" for catching fish is fully described in *Seebohm* (p. 152). Walter Snel has been succeeded by William; and Richard Ball's widow now holds by courtesy the acres formerly cultivated by her husband. Of the cottars, only the aged Petronilla daughter of Edwin still holds her mansion and bit of land, while her son Adam has become a villein and has his half-virgate at Agberow. Comparing the latter lists with that of Ralph de Auxeville's tenants, the growing use of surnames may be noticed. By a comparison with the Domesday record we find that the slaves have disappeared, the cottars have decreased from 38 to 5, while the higher class of villeins has increased from 23 to 59, and, as already noticed, there is a freeman holding book-land. The rental has increased, but this is probably owing to the substitution of money payments for some of the more burdensome obligations due to the lords, and is a step towards complete freedom.

From the following summary of the tenants and rentals of these hamlets, it is noteworthy that the property of the monastery in Oldington, Comberton, and Mytton has been so well developed that the rental is nearly equal to the total of the 11 other hamlets. The manor of Hurcott at this time belonged to the Rector of Kidderminster, and does not appear in the list.

| | Tenants. | Rent. |
		£ s. d.
Habberley	3	0 11 4¼
Puxton	4	0 12 7¼
Sutton	6	1 3 1½
Agborow	2	0 7 10¼
Lea	3	0 6 4¼
Netherton	5	0 12 4½
Wribbenhall	3	0 10 11
Franche	3	0 18 0¾
Trimpley	8	1 7 6¾
Comberton	6	1 10 6
Mytton	3	0 16 7
Oldington	13	2 10 0
Cottarii	5	0 7 7½
Total	64	£11 14 11

The lists of tenants given above belong to a period before the terrible Black Death (1349) wrought such ravages in England. More than one-third of the population died, and in many places the corn lay rotting on the ground for want of reapers, while cattle and sheep roamed over the country for want of herdsmen. Three Archbishops of Canterbury died in one year, and a large proportion of Worcestershire parishes lost their incumbents. The demand for labour was much greater than the supply, the labourers were masters of the situation, and a death blow was given to the old system of villenage. The "Statute of Labourers" ordered them to work for the same wages that had been paid before the Plague, viz., 1d. per day, with extra allowance in harvest time; but this ordinance could not be enforced, and many of the landowners were impoverished. We have no particulars of this sad time as it affected Kidderminster; but in 1351 John le Bottiler handed back to Prior Thomas of Maiden Bradley all his life interest in "one toft which adjoins a tenement of the said Prior near the church of Kedermynstre, and 11 acres of arable land in the open field between the church and Hurcote." *(Wanley MS., p. 171.)*

About the time of Richard II. the monks have left us another rent-roll, and it is of interest as showing that all the villeins and bordars had now developed into liberi or free-men; and also that "new land" had been taken into cultivation :—

"In the vill of Comertone are 4 virgates of land of old feoffment, and one of new land which contains 48 acres with its appurtenances.

"FREE MEN.

"Richard Derewynde holds one messuage and half a virgate of land, and 6 acres of new land by charter, to wit that land which Nicholas son of Edwin of Cumerton formerly held and pays thence per annum 7s. 3d."

Twelve other free tenants are named, and "the sum total of the rents of Oldington and Cumerton are £4 19s. 10d."

In "Kidemester Borough" the Prior and Convent make the following payments to the lords of Kidderminster :—

"For Oldington and Comberton 5s. [This payment was reserved by Henry Biset when he made the grant to Ralph de Auxeville. (See page 15)]

"For new land near Burlase, 5s.

"For 2 Woodcrofts and a Grove 2s.

"For 2 Tenements, and for Liberty of the Borough; 2 capons or 4d.; and 2 pairs of gloves, or 2d.

"To Henry de Caldwell for new land near Burles, a half-penny.

"To Master Henry de Kent for a Tenement, formerly Reginald Tugge's, near the Mill, 4*d*.
"To Thomas Chaumpeneis for the tenement of John de Horspole 3*s*. 1*d*.
"To Thomas Balle of Mytton for 3 acres of land near Merdene 1*d*."

From their tenants in the borough the Prior received as follows:—

"The Lady Lucy [probably the wife of Sir John Attwood, who founded Trimpley Chantry] holds a certain tenement which was Robert de Alvedeleghe's, 6*s*.
"The said Lucy pays for a certain land called Cranesmore 1*d*.
"The said Lucy pays for an oven situated between the house of Henry Pitt and a new house built by Robert de Alwedeleghe 1*d*.
"The same pays at the Feast of S. Michael a half penny for a curtilage which is near La ——, and a half penny which Aldyne son of Osanne used to pay.
"Roger Lowe holds a burgage and pays 2*s*.
"William Wheelwright holds a house with a little place and pays 2*s*.
"Simon de Kent holds a burgage, and pays 2*s*., and for the enlargement of his house on the other side 12*d*."

The "mansion" of the villein in these times was a thatched one-roomed building of wood, with its crevices plastered up with clay. Glass was an unknown luxury, and there were no windows. Chimneys were not used, and the fire was in the middle of the room against a hob of clay, and the smoke escaped through the door, or where it could. The floors were of bare earth, strewn with rushes and dried herbs, which became a receptacle for bones and filth. "A few chests were ranged round the walls, the bacon-rack was fastened to the timbers overhead, and the walls of the homestead were garnished with agricultural implements. Sometimes there was an upper storey of poles reached by a ladder. Close by the door stood the mixen, a collection of every abomination—streams from which in rainy weather polluted the stream." (Rogers' *Six Centuries of Work and Wages.*) The oxen generally lived under the same roof as their owner. Such were the "good old times" of 600 years ago.

The Baronage.

THE family of Biset came over with the Conqueror, and was settled in Nottinghamshire. Manser Biset, son of William Biset, was a faithful adherent of Henry Fitz-Empress before his accession to the throne. Under the title of *Dapifer* he was witness to a deed of gift made by Henry to Randle Earl of Chester in 1152 (Sir Peter Leycester's *Cheshire*); in 19 Stephen he was witness to the accord made between Henry and Stephen touching Henry's succession to the Crown; and in reward for his services he received the royal manor of Kidderminster, with estates in Hampshire and Gloucestershire soon after Henry's II.'s accession (page 13). Manser married Alice heiress of Bradley in Wiltshire, and his wife's home became his principal residence. There he founded a convent for Leprous Women, to which he gave the Rectory of Kidderminster. He was succeeded in the lordship of Kidderminster by his son Henry; and in 1st John another Henry, nephew of the foregoing, became his heir (Dug. *Bar.*, i., 632, a) and gave to the King 500 marks for livery of the lordships of Kidderminster and Sandhurst. *(Ibid.* Oblata 1 John, m. 23.)

After him it appears that William Byset died seised of the barony of Byset (Madox, *Baron. Aug.*, 52); and to him succeeded John Biset (Dug. *Baron.*, i., 632, a), who in 4 Henry III. was charged with £100 for his relief, for the lands and tenements which William Byset, his brother, whose heir he was, held at the day of his death. John Biset married Alice daughter and co-heiress of Thomas Basset of Headendon, Oxfordshire, and had three daughters, Margaret, Ela, and

Isabel. He obtained charters for free warren and a fair in Kidderminster (1238). In 1241 he was made Chief Forester of England, and attended the Grand Tournament held at Northampton at Easter in that year, occasioned by Peter of Savoy, Earl of Richmond, against Earl Roger Bigod. *(Matt. Paris,* 550, n. 30.)

Shortly afterwards he died, and in a plea between the Abbot of Roucester and Albreda de Basingbourne in 27 Hy. III. (1243), Albreda called to warrant Margery, Ela, and Isabella, daughters and heirs of John Biset. Margery was of full age, Ela and Isabella under age, and in the custody of John de Plessetis. (Thoroton's *Nottinghamshire. Pl. de Ban. cor. Rob. de Laxington et Soc. Pasch.* 27 *Hy. III., rot.* 1 *and* 2.)

Margaret Biset (perhaps a sister of John) gave to the Leprous Women of Bradley 6s. 8d. yearly rent in Kidderminster. *(Mon. Ang.* ii., 409.) Matthew of Paris (635, 30) tells us that in 1238, when an assassin came in at midnight through the window at Woodstock with a drawn dagger in his hand to kill the King, one of the Queen's maidens, Margaret Biset by name, saved his life "For she was holy and devoted to God, and by chance was awake, singing her Psalter by candle light, and at her terrible cries the royal servants rushed in." She died in 1242— " of an illustrious family, more illustrious by her character." *(Ib.,* 786, 46.)

After the death of John Biset his property was divided in equal shares between his daughters; and consequently the manor of Kidderminster was broken up into three portions. John de Rivers, lord of Burgate in Hampshire, married the eldest daughter Margery. He gave in 1267 to Brother John, Prior of Maiden Bradley, all the lands which Hugh in the Grove formerly held, and the said Hugh with his whole retinue, &c. Witnesses — Walter Scammel Archdeacon of Berkshire, Sir Hugh de Plessetis, John de Wotton, Hugh Attwood, Henry de Caldwell, William de Eymore.

Sir John de Rivers, kt., lord of Ongar, Essex, granted a rent of 13s. 4d. to John Stacy, clerk, in 1329. (Morant's *Essex* i., 128, b.)

Either by gift or purchase the one-third share of Kidderminster falling to Rivers was soon acquired by Maiden Bradley. The monks had before this received a grant from Sir John of the advowson of the church.

Isabel, the second daughter, married Hugh de Plessetis. He was son of John de Plessetis, who in 1242, in consideration of 200 marks, obtained a grant of wardship and marriage of the heirs of John Biset, and was in such favour with the King (Dug. *Bar.*, 772, a. b.) that he forced Margery, sister and sole heir of Thomas Earl of Warwick, to marry him. Hugh was son and heir by a former wife Christian, daughter and heir of Hugh de Sandford, lord of Stoke Norton, Oxon, and at the death of his father (1263) was 26 years old. He died 1291, leaving issue Hugh his son and heir, 25 years of age. *(Dugdale.)*

Another one-third part came to John de Wotton and Ela, which John died seised of Kidderminster of inheritance of Ela Biset in 28 Edw. I. *(Inquis.* 28 Edw. I. in *Nash*, vol. ii., app. lxxvi.) John de Wotton and Ela had a son who took his mother's name, and as John Byset was charged for his relief 31 Edw. I. *(Hil. Fin.,* &c., p. 52, c. 1, l. 1.)

In 33 Edw. I. an exchange of land was made between Thomas, Prior of the Convent of Brommore, and Sir John Byset, kt., to which Sir John de Riveres, kt., was a witness. (Madox: *Formul. Angl.,* n. cclxxiv.)

There was an office held 35 Edw. I. in which John Biset held within the manor of Kidderminster the moiety of one messuage with a close, the moiety of one water-mill, 10 acres of meadow, 160 acres of land, and two woods. (*Nash* ii., 236, b.) By the title of "Sir John Byset, kt., lord of Kidderminster, together with the community of the whole borough," a chaplain was presented to the chantry of the chapel of the Blessed Virgin Mary of Kyderministre in 1305. (Ry. Geynes in *Nash* ii., 57.) Sir John had a daughter Margaret, who in 1324 was a minor in the King's custody. (Hutchins' *Dorset,* ii., 458, b.) She was married to —— Romsey, and died in 1374, leaving a son, Sir Walter Romsey, kt., who inherited from his mother a certain manor in Kidderminster which heretofore was but a third part of the said manor of Kidderminster whole. [*Walterus de Romeseye chivaler, filius Margaretæ filiæ cujusdam Johannis Biset, filii et heredis Johannis de Wotton et Elæ Byset. (Hil. Fin. 17 Rd. II., rot. 5 in Madox: Baron. Angl. 53, a. 37.)*] The said Walter did homage and fealty to the King Feb. 22, 47 Edw. III., the estate being held *in capite*. (*Hil. Fin.*, p. 51.) He paid part of his relief for it in 17 Rd. II., another part in 3 Hy. IV., and died in 1404. (Hutchins' *Dorset* ii., 458a.)

In 1385 and 1386 (see "Final Concords") Sir John Beauchamp of Holt, a favourite of King Richard II., became possessed of so much of Sir Walter Romsey's estate in Kidderminster that when on 10 Oct., 1387, he was BY PATENT (being the first instance of the kind) summoned to Parliament, he took the title of Lord de Beauchamp, Baron of Kidderminster. This Sir John Beauchamp, son of Richard Beauchamp of Holt, succeeded his father in 1327, being then eight years old. He served in the French wars, was an Esquire of the King's Chamber, received Knighthood in Scotland, was Justice of North Wales, and subsequently (1387) Steward of the King's Household. He married Joane daughter and heir of Robert le Fitzwith. (Dugdale's *Baronage*, and "New Peerage" in *Genealogist.*) In the Corporation archives is an inspeximus on vellum by Henry VIII., 1530, of a charter of Richard II., 1386, previously inspected by Henry VI., 1427:—

"Richard by the Grace of God, &c.

"Know ye that we have granted and by this our charter have confirmed to our beloved and faithful Knight John Beauchamp of Holt and Joan his wife and his heirs free chace as well in vert and venison as in all manner of other things which appertain to a free chace within the manor demesne and fee of Kedermestre, and infangthief and outfangthief and the chattels of felons and fugitives, &c., and let all his tenants and residents therein be quit of toll, panage, and murage, throughout the whole of our realm, &c.

These being witnesses R. Bp. of London, J. Bp. of Durham our Treasurer, W. Bp. of Winchester, W. Bp. of Coventry and Lichfield, keeper of our privy seal, Thomas Bp. of Chichester, J. Bp. of Hereford, Edmund Duke of York and Thomas Duke of Gloucester our very dear uncles, Robert de Veer, Marquess of Dublin, Thomas de Mowbray, Earl of Nottingham, Edward de Courtenay Earl of Devon, Michael de la Pole Earl of Suffolk, our Chancellor, John de Montacute, Steward of our Household, and others. Given at Osney 7 August in the 10th year of our reign, A.D. 1386."

A HISTORY OF KIDDERMINSTER.

A few months after his elevation to the Peerage the Baron of Kidderminster was attainted by the " Wonderful " Parliament, and beheaded on Tower Hill. He was buried in Worcester cathedral, 1388, and left a son, John de Beauchamp, ten years of age, who, by the reversal of the proceedings of 11 Rd. II. in 1398, became second Baron of Kidderminster. In 1399 he accompanied the unfortunate King into Ireland ; and when in 1400, under Henry IV., the proceedings of 11 Rd. II. were re-affirmed, his honours again became forfeited. He was, however, Escheator of Worcestershire 1406. He died in 1420, leaving only a daughter Margaret, who married firstly John Pauncefort, and secondly John Wysham. Thus the Barony became extinct, after having been for 20 years under attainder. *(The New Peerage.)*

PEDIGREE OF BISET.

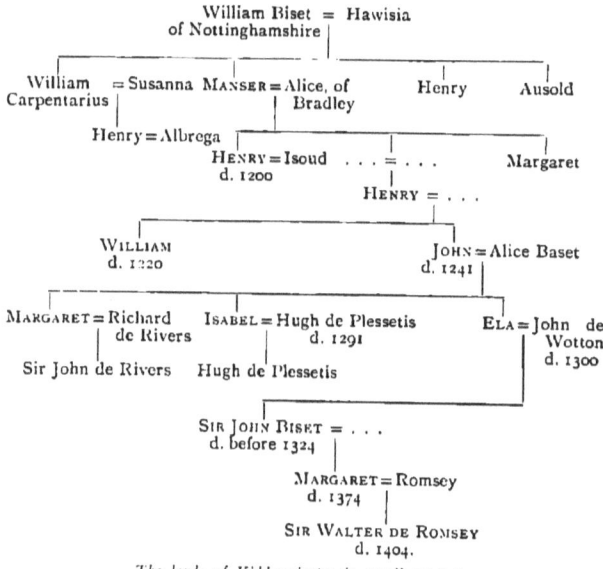

For some reason, of which I have not yet met with any explanation, one-third of Kidderminster had in the time of Edward I. come into the possession of the Burnells. It could not be the *Rivers* portion, for this had fallen into the hands of Maiden Bradley. It could not be the inheritance of John de Wotton and Ela, for this was possessed by their descendant Sir Walter Romsey in the time of Richard II. It would seem then that Hugh de Plessetis, who succeeded to his portion in 1291, and of whom we hear nothing afterwards, alienated it almost immediately, for in 1292 Robert Burnell, Bishop of Bath and Wells, died seised of part of Kidderminster manor. *(Inq. p. Mort.*, 21 Edw. I., n. 50, cal. p. 115.) The Bishop was a trusted adviser of the "English Justinian," Edward I., and resided at Acton Burnell in Shropshire, where the famous Parliament was held. He was not of noble birth, and his chief ambition was to found a great baronial family; he " added field to field," and at his death was in possession of estates in 19 counties, and the holder, in whole or part, of 82 manors. He died at Berwick, and was conveyed to Wells cathedral for burial. Philip Burnell, the Bishop's nephew, was his heir, and did homage to the King for all the lands and tenements which his uncle had held *in capite*. He rapidly wasted his uncle's hastily gotten patrimony, and was one of the first to suffer by the facilities for recovering traders' debts which the statute of Acton Burnell had afforded. *(National Biography.)* His wife was Maud daughter of Richard Earl of Arundel, and he had a son, Sir Edward Burnell, who succeeded to the estates in 1293. *(Inq. p. Mort.* 22 Edw. I., n. 45, cal. p. 120.) During his minority he was in the wardship of Maculinus de Harle. He served in Edward's Scottish campaigns (1311—1314), and is said to have always appeared in great splendour, attended by a chariot decked with banners of his arms. He was summoned to Parliament as Lord Burnell from the 5th to the 8th year of Edward II.

In 1313 King Edward II. gave licence to Edward Burneley to grant 160 acres of wood, with the appurtenances, in the manor of Kidderminster, to the Prior and Chapter of Worcester, and confirmed the donation. *(Heming* ii., 547, and *Nash*, lxxv. a.) The said Chapter had power from the King to charge their manor of Quinzehides (?) with the payment of £10 yearly rent to Edward Burnell and his heirs ; and the King's charter for 100 acres of land, 3 acres of meadow, 10 acres of pasture, and 60 acres of wood in Kyderminster ; and also another for one carucate of land, 20 acres of meadow, 10 acres of pasture, one weir *(gurgitem)*, and 3s. rent in the manor of Kidderminster. [This land is still in the possession of the Dean and Chapter of Worcester.]

Lord Burnell married Olivia daughter of Hugh le Despencer, and died 1315 without issue, leaving Maud, his sister and heir, then 24 years of age. She was wife of John de Handlo, of Tishmersh, Northants, who died in 1346 seised of the manor of Kidderminster. Their son Nicholas Handlo assumed his mother's name of Burnell, and having served in the wars with France, was summoned to Parliament as a Baron (Lord Burnell) in 1350. He died in 1383, and was succeeded by his son, Hugh Lord Burnell, aged 36. He was Governor of Bridgnorth Castle 1386, and was one of the Lords who received the abdication of Richard II. in the Tower of London. In 1406 he was made a Knight of the Garter. He married (1) Philippa daughter of Michael de la Pole, 2nd Earl of Suffold, (2) Joyce Baroness Botetourt, who died in 1406, and (3) Joan Dowager Baroness Fitzwalter. In his time the Prior and Convent of Worcester had the King's charter for what they held in Trimpley. *(Nash,* lxxviii. b.) The figure of his second wife was formerly in a window of Kidderminster church, having on her mantle *or, a saltire engrailed, sable ;* and also a shield of those arms supported by two angels, and these words written over them : " Yes ben Bottowrt Armes."

In 1417, his only son Edward being dead, he made an arrangement for the marriage of his grandchild Margery with Edmund Hungerford, son of Sir Walter Hungerford, kt. He then prepared a beautiful alabaster tomb for Joyce and himself in the choir of Hales Abbey, Salop ; assigned portions of his large estates to his three grand-daughters, Joyce, Katharine, and Margaret, and gave the rest, which included Kidderminster, to Joane de Beauchamp, Lady Bergavenny. (Dug. *Bar.,* ii., 62.) He died 27 Nov., 1420, and the Barony of Burnell fell into abeyance.

THE BARONAGE.

PEDIGREE OF BURNELL.

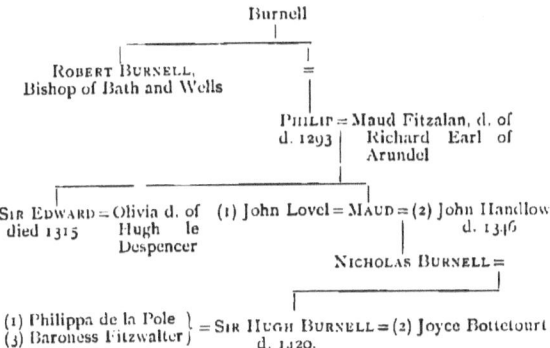

The lords of Kidderminster in small capitals.

Joan Baroness Bergavenny was daughter of Richard Fitz-Alan Earl of Arundel, who was beheaded by Richard II. Her brother, Thomas Earl of Arundel, was a zealous partisan of Henry IV., and as Governor of the Tower of London had the custody of the captive King. Lord Burnell, as we have seen, belonged to the same party, and there was also a distant relationship between them, his great-grandmother being a daughter of another Richard Earl of Arundel. But Kidderminster-Burnell was not the first possession of the Bergavenny's in this manor. In 1403 Joan's husband, Sir William de Beauchamp, Lord Bergavenny, 4th son of Thomas Earl of Warwick, presented to the Chantry of S. Mary in Kidderminster. He had probably received part of the estates of his namesake, John de Beauchamp 2nd Baron of Kidderminster, after his attainder in 1400. He died 8 May, 1411, and was buried at the Black Friars, Hereford. His widow was then 36 years of age, and held the Castle of Abergavenny and his other estates in dower; and presented to the Chantry of Kidderminster in 1420, 1422, 1424, and 1435. In 1428 (by record in Scaccar, *Nash* lxix.) she held that part of a knight's fee in Kidderminster which Nicholas Burnell before held, and died 14 Nov., 1435.

36   A HISTORY OF KIDDERMINSTER.

Their son Richard Beauchamp was 14 years old when his father died in 1411, and in 1420 was created Earl of Worcester. He married Isabel Le Despencer, daughter of Thomas Earl of Gloucester, was mortally wounded at Meaux, in France, and was buried at Tewkesbury 1422.

His only child was the Lady Elizabeth Beauchamp, born at Hanley Castle Dec. 16, 1415. She carried the estates and title of Lord Bergavenny to her husband, Sir Edward Nevill, 6th son of Ralph 1st Earl of Westmoreland, and died 18 June, 1447, aged 32. Her husband survived her, and died 18 Oct., 1476, seised by courtesy of the manors of Kidderminster-Biset and Kidderminster-Burnell.

Their son, George Nevill 4th Lord Bergavenny, was the next heir, and constituted William Lord Hastings steward of Kidderminster. About 1485 the Prior of Maiden Bradley, owner of one-third of the manor, complained to Lord Bergavenny of the high-handed conduct of his officers in Kidderminster, and received a very fair and straightforward answer. *(Wanley MSS.)*

"*Peticio Domni Prioris ad Dominum de Bergaveny,*

"To my Good and Gracius Lord George Nevil Lord of Bergevenee, Shewith unto your Good Lordeship William Priour of the Church of oure Lady of Mayden-Bradley in the Countie of Wiltshyre, That wheras one John Byset was seysed of a maner of Kedermynstre with a Lete and a Wareyn in a Wast Grounde, Parcel of the same Maner appendant, with the appurtenances in the Countie of Worcetur, in his demeane as of Fee : and so seysede had Issue Three daughters ; That is to say Margery, Elizabeth and Ela. Which Margery took to Husbounde one John de Ripariis : Elizabeth toke to Husbounde one Hugh de Plessetes : and Ela toke to Husbonde one Rondolfe Nevile. And after the seid John Byset gave one parte of the seide Maner, divided in Three Partes by Metes and Boundes (except the seid Lete, Warreyn, and the Wast Grounde, and the Grounde of the Comyne High-Weyes within the Precincts of the seid Maner remayning unparted) to the seide John de Ripariis and Margery, To Have to theyme and to ther Heyres in Fee : And in like wyse gave another Parte of the said Maner to the said Hugh of Plessets and Elizabeth his Wyffe and their Heyres in Fee : And aftur, gave the residue of the same Maner to Rondolfe Nevil and Ela his Wyffe, and ther Heyres in Fee. By Force whereof the said John de R. and Margery his Wyffe, Hugh de P. and Elizabeth his Wyffe, and Rondolphe Nevile and Ela his Wyffe, were eche of them severally seysede of ther Partes of the said Maner in Form abovesaide : and of the said Lete, Wareine, Wast Ground and Highe Weyes in Comyne, Undividede. The Estate of wiche Hugh de Plessets and Elizabeth, Rondolphe Nevile and Ela your Lordeship now hath : and the estate of wiche John de Ripariis and Margery his Wyfie the seide Priour now hath, and he and his Predecessours of long time have had. There your Bayliffes and Officers of your partes of the seid Maner have of late Distourbed, Lettede, and Denyede the seid Priour and his Officers to Take and Felle the Woodes growinge one his parte, as is aforeseid Dividede of the Maner ; and to have perceyve and take his parte of the Wayfes, Strayes, Fynes, and Amerciaments of Blode-shedinge, Affrayes, and other Profetts commynge in the Hie wayes and the Ground wich your seide Lordship and the Priour holden in comyne : And over that, your seid Bailiffs and Officers distreyneth the Tenants of the same Priour uppon ther Tenures of the Parte of the seid Priour of the seid Maner, to come and appere in your Court of your Burgh of Kedermynstre to answere there to Playntes and other processes, when as Ye have no Jurisdiction uppon theme, Contrary to Right and Good Conscience. For Reformacion whereof Please it your seid Lordship in consideration that the seid Priour and his Bretheren bene men of Religion, and Bounden to the Service of God, and unable to Sue for ther Ryght ageyne your seyd Lordship by the Law of the Londe ; that it wolde Please your same Lordeship to sett such Direction in this Premissis, as Right and Good Conscience in that Behalfe shal Require. And thei shal dayly pray to God for the prosperous Contynuance of your same good Lordship."

"*Copia litere misse a Domino de Bergeveny ad Ballivum suum ibidem per Petitionem Domni Prioris.*

" Trusty and wel-beloved I grete you welle ; letting you witte that it showed unto me by the humble peticion of William Prioure of the churche of our Lady of Mayden-Bradeley in the county of Wilteshire, which in the right of his seid Churche is seised of the third parte of the Maner of Kedermynstre, with certayne Libertees and Franchesis unto his seid thirde parte belonging ; How that ye and oder myne Officers there have of late letted and denyed the said Prioure and his Officers to Take and Felle their woods growing in his parte of the seid Lordship ; and also to perceyve and take his part of the Wayfes, Strayes, Fines and Amerciaments that He there accordinge unto the old Customarie ought of right to have, by reason of his seid thirde part of the seid Maner ; and moreover how that ye distrayne the Tenaunts of the same Prioure upon there Tenures of the seid Thirde parte of the seid Maner, to come and appere in my Court of the Borow of Kedermynstre, and to answere thereto Pleynts and other Processe, where ye ought not so to do, as I am enformed by my Councill Lernede. Wherefore I will and also charge you, as ye intende to do me Pleasure or to have my Good Lordship, that ye from hensforth suffre the seid Priour and his Officers to Felle ther Woodes there without any Lett or Disturbance ; and also to have and Perceyve his parte of such Wayfes, Strays, Amerciaments, and other casuelleties and Profights as he ought of Right to have ; and also that ye Distreyne not his Tenaunts to answere to any Pleynts otherwise than the

Law Requireth. For I wolde be loth to Kenne in the censures of the Church, to mayntenne or Favour you or any other of mine Officers to Hurt, Prejudice, or Wronge Hym or any other Person; otherwise than may stond with my Right, the Lawe, and Good Conscience. Yeven under my Signet and sign Manuelle, at London, the 13th day of May.

"SUBSCRIPTIO LITERE.

"*To Thomas Forest Bayly of my Maner of Kydermynstre.*

In 1530 Henry VIII. inspected the charter of Richard II. (see p. 31), and ratified and confirmed anew all the privileges therein granted "to our beloved and faithful George Nevyle, knight, Lord Bergavenny, now tenant of the aforesaid manor demesne and fee of Kedermestre, and to his heirs. Witness me myself at Westminster the first day of February, in the 21st year of our reign." To the charter is appended an impression of the second great seal of Henry VIII. in dark green wax.

Kidderminster continued in the descendants of this Lord Abergavenny until John the 10th Baron parted with some of it by sale to Richard Foley, of Stourbridge, 12th Dec., 1660. *(Hardwick.)* In Lord Foley's Map of Wribbenhall, made in 1706, part of the land is still marked as belonging to "me Lorde Aburgavenny." Space will not permit of a detailed account of this illustrious family, which, including the Burnell relationship, had a large interest in the town for more than 400 years. From it there sprung six Earls of Westmoreland, two Earls of Salisbury and Warwick, an Earl of Kent, a Marquess Montacute, Barons Ferrers, Latimer, &c., one Queen, an Archbishop of York, five Duchesses, and many Countesses and Baronesses. *(Camden.)* It is now represented by William Nevill 21st Baron, 5th Earl, and 1st Marquess of Abergavenny, of Eridge Castle, Kent.

The Bisets, Burnells, Beauchamps, and Abergavennys, as we have seen, were in their turn lords of Kidderminster; but they all had large estates in other counties, and it does not appear that any of them resided here except occasionally, and none were buried here. But as early as 1347 a knightly family was settled near the town, and had acquired the sub-manor of Caldwell, where a moated castle was built, of which some portions still remain. In the Book of Aids, 20 Edw. III. *(Nash* ii., 37, a), Hugh de Cokesey is said to hold lands in Kidderminster which John Biset formerly held; and in 1357 he died seised of Kidderminster and Kaldewell. *(Nash* ii., lxxvii., b.) By an inquisition it was found that he held at the day of his death within the manor of Kidderminster one messuage, half a yardland (virgate), two acres of meadow, with appurtenances. *(Nash* ii., 47.) He was a younger son (Dugdale *Warwicks.*, i., 359) of Sir Walter Cokesey, of Cokesey, kt., and married Dionysia, eldest daughter of William le Boteler, of Wemme, and co-heir to her brother Edmund. His figure, with that of his wife, was formerly in the fourth N. window of Kidderminster church, with " *Orate pro Animabus* . . . *Cokesey et Dionisie*," subscribed to their arms—*Argent, on a bend azure between two cotises dancette gu. three cinquefoils or ;* impaling *gu. a fess counter compony arg. and sa. between six crosses formée or.* He lived in the time of the Black Death, and presented to the Chantry of S. Mary in 1349 and 1350; and departing this life 1356, " lies buried under an arch in the N. wall of the church in a raised tomb whereon is his effigy with the legs crossed. The arms on his breast show him the same Cokesey as in the window: the brisure denotes him a younger brother." *(Hayley.)* The tomb thus described is no doubt that engraved in *Nash* (appendix, p. 50), having an arch with elegant Decorated tracery; but, sad to say, during the last 90 years it has entirely disappeared. Our 19th century zeal for " restoration " has much to answer for! Dionisia, surviving her husband, presented to the Chantry twice, and died in 1376 seized of Kidderminster and Caldwell. *(Inquis.* in *Nash,* lxxviii., a.)

Sir Walter de Cokesey, kt., presented Hugh de Caldwell to the church of Witley in 1287, which looks as if he had some connection with Caldwell at that time. *(Hayley.)* Sir Walter bequeathed his body to be buried with the Friars Minors in Worcester. *(Dugd.* i., 359.) " To the said Friars I leave ten marks of silver in place of all my arms borne with my body, and these arms shall remain entirely to my son Walter; but the horse conveying my body and arms shall belong to the said Friars." (Dug. *Warw.,* ii., 930.)

After the death of Dionisia, the manor of Caldwell only appears among the local possessions of Cokesey. Maculinus de la Mare presented to the Chantry in 1391, 1395, and 1400 ; and in 1402 Alice wife of M. de la Mare died seised of Kidderminster.

Walter Cokesey, son and heir of Hugh and Dionisia, was under age at his father's death, but in 1365, making proof of his age, had livery of his inheritance (Dug. *War.*, i., 359), and being a knight in 1375, married Isabel, daughter and heir of Sir Urian St. Pierre, kt. According to Habingdon, his portrait with gilded spurs, and that of his wife, were in the same window with that of his father, with "*Orate pro animabus Walteri Cokesey et Dominæ Isabellæ,*" and his arms (without cotises) impaling *arg., a bend sa. with a label of three gu.* His arms were also in the great W. window of Worcester cathedral, and subscribed "Monseur Walter de Cokesey." He died 1405 seised of the manor of Caldwell, and leaving Walter his son and heir of full age. In the same window of Kidderminster church, with the foregoing, were likewise the portraits of this last-mentioned Walter and his wife, with "*Orate pro animabus Walteri Cokesey et Matildis Uxoris ejus,*" and his arms (as before) impaling *or, two bars gu.* He died *(Inq. Nash.* lxxix., b) 8 Henry IV., and his widow Matildis was married to Sir John Phelip in or before 1409 ; for in that year John Phelip, as lord of Witley—a lordship belonging to the Cokeseys—presented to that church. Consequently, in the same window, her figure appears again by the side of her second husband, and her arms impaled with his : *quarterly, gu. and argent, in the first quarter an eagle displayed or.*

Sir John Phelip is said by Dugdale *(Bar.,* ii., 212) to have been a valiant soldier under Henry V. In Rymer's *Fœdera,* ix., 646, is a safe conduct granted Nov. 13 by John Duke of Bedford, Protector, for Alexander de Carnys, attended by eight men and eight horses, to come from Scotland into England to pay the ransom of James Douglas, lately a prisoner of Sir John Phelip, deceased. Sir John was present at the siege of Harfleur in 1415, and died ten days afterwards, probably of the dysentery which was so fatal to the English at that place. His seat was at Dennington, in Suffolk, but having married Walter Cokesey's widow, he probably lived at Caldwell, and his body

BRASS IN KIDDERMINSTER CHURCH,
REPRESENTING MAUD HARMANVILLE AND HER TWO HUSBANDS,
SIR JOHN PHELIP AND WALTER COKESEY.

MONUMENT OF SIR HUGH COKESEY AND WIFE
IN KIDDERMINSTER CHURCH
From Nash's Worcestershire

MONUMENT OF THOMAS BLOUNT AND HIS
WIFE MARGERY.
(From Nash's *Worcestershire*.)

MONUMENT OF SIR EDWARD BLOUNT AND HIS
TWO WIVES

From Nash's *Worcestershire*

was brought to Kidderminster church for burial by the side of his wife and her first husband. All three are buried in the chancel under a flat stone inlaid with portraits and inscription in brass. The engraving of this memorial is taken from Nash's *Worcestershire*, but it is not very correctly drawn, especially as regards the lady's head-dress. The letters on the belt are I.P., the initials of John Phelip. The first shield is gone, but must have borne the arms of Phelip, which are impaled with Harmanville on the second shield. The third shield bears Harmanville, the fourth Phelip impaling Harmanville, the fifth Cokesey, and sixth Cokesey impaling Harmanville. The inscription beneath reads thus:—

> MILES HONORIFICUS, JOHN PHELIP SUBJACET INTUS:
> HENRICUS QUINTUS DILEXERAT HUNC UT AMICUS:
> CONSEPELITUR EI SUA SPONSA, MATILDIS, AMATA,
> WALTERO COOKESEY, PRIUS ARMIGERO SOCIATA.
> AUDAX ET FORTIS APUD HARFLEU JOHN BENE GESSIT
> ET BARO VI'M MORTIS PATIENS MIGRARE RECESSIT
> MC QUATER XV OCTOBRIS LUCE SECUNDA.
> SIT SUUS, ALME JESU, TIBI SPIRITUS HOSTIA MUNDA.

By his first wife Juliana, daughter of Sir Thomas Erpingham, who died 1383, he had a son, Sir William Phelipp, Lord Bardolph, K.G., who was with him in the French campaign, and fought at Agincourt, being afterwards appointed Captain of Harfleur. Matildis was his second wife, and he had yet a third wife: for Henry V., "who loved him as a friend," granted the manor of Michelhampton, Gloucestershire, the lordship of Grovebury or Leyghton Busard, Bedfordshire, and the manors of Nedding and Ketchbarston, in Suffolk, to John Phelip, kt., and Alice his wife. She was daughter of Sir Thomas Chaucer, kt., son of Sir Geoffrey Chaucer, the famous poet. Lady Phelip married secondly Thomas Montacute, Earl of Salisbury, and thirdly William de la Pole, Duke of Suffolk. This aged Duchess survived her first husband 60 years, and was buried at Ewelme, Oxfordshire.

Sir John Phelip was a benefactor to Worcester cathedral in setting up the fourth and most noble window of the E. cloister. *(Thomas.)* In it were his arms and those of Nevill Lord Furnivall (whose daughter was married to his stepson), with the

F

inscription, "*Orate pro anima Domini Johannis Phelipes Baronis de Donyngton, qui hanc fenestram fieri fecit.*" Here, as well as on the brass, he is styled Baron, and a sort of coronet encircles his helmet in the effigy.

Walter Cokesey, who lies buried under the brass, had a son, Sir Hugh Cokesey, who was the last heir male of this family. He had two wives—(1) Joan daughter and co-heir of Thomas Nevill, Lord Furnivall, by his second wife Ankaret, daughter of John Lord Strange, of Blackmere ; and (2) Alice . . . . who survived her husband, and died in 1459. A Walter Cokesey, perhaps a younger brother of Sir Hugh, died in 1425 seised of a messuage in Kidderminster called Purchas and 6 acres of land. Sir Hugh died Dec. 15, 1445, without issue, leaving Joyce his sister and heir. He was *probably* buried by the side of his first wife in the chancel of Kidderminster church, and the monument with their effigies is still in existence, though it has suffered mutilation. In right of his grandmother, Isabel daughter and heir of Agnes, sister and heir of George Braose (or Brewes), he quarters their arms with his own. The engraving represents the tomb as it was 100 years ago ; Sir Hugh's legs have disappeared in the interval! Habingdon describes "a lady in a mantle faced with three rows of ermine, on several parts whereof were painted Cokesey's arms, kneeling before the Virgin and Child, and praying thus, '*Pia Mater, miserere mei,*'" which was high on the wall above this monument.

Joyce Cokesey, sister and heir of Sir Hugh, married (1) . . . . Beauchamp; (2) John Grevill, of Campden, Gloucestershire ; (3) Leonard Stapleton ; and under her courtesy title of Lady Joyce Beauchamp presented to the Chantry of our Lady at Kidderminster in 1468-9, and afterwards by name of Joyce Beauchamp, widow, in 1473. In 1469 she is said to have founded the Chantry of S. Katharine in Kidderminster church, and her effigy in a beautiful, though much mutilated, monument is inserted in the upper part of the wall of the S. side of the church. A very poor drawing of this monument is given in *Nash*, Add. p. 50. She died in 1473, leaving a son, Sir John Grevill, kt., who inherited his mother's estates, and presented to the Chantry in 1479. He died 1480, leaving Thomas his son and heir 26 years of age. Thomas assumed his grandmother's name of Cokesey, and was one of the Knights of the Bath created at the coronation of Henry VII. He died in 1498, without issue, whereupon Robert Russell and Robert Winter, being his cousins and heirs, had livery of his lands. Caldwell came to Winter, and was in the possession of his family when Leland visited the town in 1539. George Wintour, of Hodington, who descended from Robert, sold it to the Clares, in whose family it remained till 1777.

PEDIGREE OF COKESEY.*

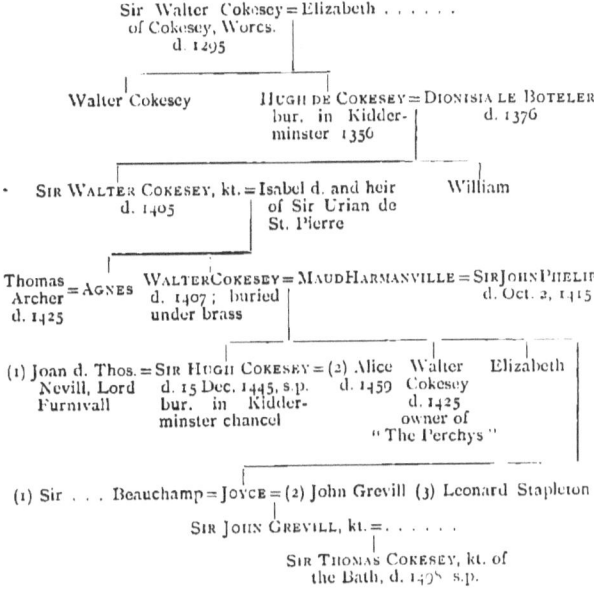

* The pedigree in *Nash* ii., 50, is very inaccurate.

Simon Clare married Margaret Rice *(Nash* i., 260), daughter and heir of Simon Rice, who was a great benefactor to Kidderminster, and built the Chantry of S. Mary at the east end of All Saints' church. He was a citizen and merchant of London, and the arms on the wall (now obliterated) were supposed to be those of the Merchant Adventurers with three ears of rye—an allusion to the name of the founder. On the middle part of the body of the church was a figure on a brass plate, with this epitaph :—" Of your charity pray for the souls of Thomas Rise and Margery his wife, and their children's souls, the which Thomas deceased 31 Dec., 1494." This Margery was one of the co-heirs of the ancient family of D'Abitot, of Croome, and through the marriage with her granddaughter, a large part of Croome D'Abitot came to the Clares of Caldwell. Simon Clare presented to Croome living in 1545, and Francis Clare in 1577. Their interest in Croome was purchased by Sir Thomas Coventry in the reign of James I. Simon Clare's second wife was Agnes daughter of Sir Thomas Blount : after 33 years of married life the wife died July 29, 1580, only six days after her husband. The pedigree of the family is appended, but Sir Ralph Clare played such a prominent part in the history of the town that we must reserve a further account of him for the " Celebrities." Sir Ralph, says the Herald's Visitation, died a bachelor in 1670. On the other hand Nash speaks of his great-grandson Francis Clare, who died at Kidderminster in 1777, aged 86. Most likely the descent is from Sir Ralph's brother Francis, a Captain of Foot in the service of Charles I., who died 1680. Another mistake appears in Sir Thomas Phillipps' additions to the Visitation, where he assigns a daughter to Captain Clare, who married John third son of Charles Acton, of Elmley Lovett. The Registers record the marriage (Feb. 5, 1602) of Mr. John Acton to Mrs. (we should say " Miss ") Anne Clare : but this took place eight years before Captain Clare's birth. She was really daughter of Sir Francis (born Feb. 28, 1584), and *sister* of Sir Ralph and Captain Francis. " Lady Anne Acton, of Elmley, widow," and Ralph Clare dealt with the advowson of All Hallows, Worcester, in 1622. *(Midland Antiquary,* ii., 31.) The arms of Clare, which appear to have been adopted as the groundwork of the borough arms, are given

THE BARONAGE.

in the Herald's Visitation (1682) :—*Quarterly, 1 and 4, Or, three chevronells Gu. within a bordure engrailed Az. ; 2, Argent, a chevron between 3 spear heads Gu. on a chief Az. three martlets Or ; 3, Or, two lions passant the one in chief Gu. the other Az. within a bordure of the second.*

PEDIGREE OF CLARE OF CALDWELL.

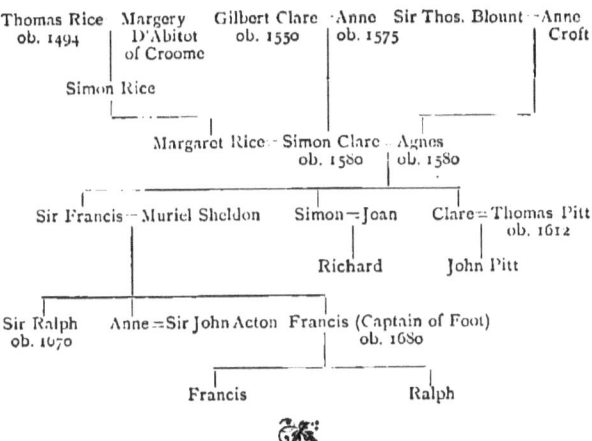

During the Middle Ages, as we have already seen, the ownership of the manor by a single baron had been breaking up ; but speaking roughly, we may say that the tripartite division of the parish, which was made in 1241, remained intact till 1546. Two-thirds had descended to the Lords Abergavenny, and one-third, together with the larger part of the Rectory, to the convent of Maiden Bradley. When the monasteries were suppressed in 1536-40, by far the largest portion of their property was shamelessly distributed among the avaricious courtiers of Henry VIII. Maiden Bradley fell to one of the most grasping of these plunderers, John Dudley, best known by his latest title of Duke of Northumberland. His father was the notorious lawyer Dudley, who so skilfully extorted money from the people to fill Henry VII.'s coffers and his own pockets. John Dudley, Lord Lisle, had a grant of the

Maiden Bradley property 21 Dec., 37 Henry VIII. *(Patent Roll Hy. VIII., pt. 16.)* This included the one-third of the lordship of Kidderminster, Oldington, Comberton, Hurcott, the patronage of the church, and all the great tithes that the monastery had been able to get hold of. Thus the best part of the tithes and church property fell into lay hands, and has remained so to this day. The sacrilegious plunder which this Lord Lisle appropriated to his own use was enormous—20 abbeys, colleges, and monasteries, besides chantries. At Kidderminster he seized upon two chantries, and at Bewdley he got another belonging to a guild which was a sort of friendly society of that time. He was raised to the Earldom of Warwick by Henry VIII., and created Duke of Northumberland by Edward VI. But he did not live long to enjoy his hastily and ill-gotten wealth, for in August, 1553, he was condemned for high treason, and lost his head by the executioner's axe on Tower Hill. As an attainted person his property fell to the Crown, and was soon distributed among various families.

For the sum of £454 9s., paid by Thomas Blount, of Kidderminster, Queen Elizabeth granted him the manor and advowson of Kidderminster Feb. 1, 1560, in as ample a manner as John Duke of Northumberland, then lately attainted, or any Prior of the late Priory, had held it, &c. But the Blounts had been living in the town for at least 20 years before this purchase. We find from the parish registers that in 1539 William Blount was buried here; and in 1541, Feb. 5th, Joyce Blount was married to John Combes, of Stratford-on-Avon, from whose family Shakespere purchased 127 acres of land. (Halliwell-Phillipps, *Outlines*, pp. 128, 151.)

In an altar tomb on the N. side of the choir lies the figure of Thomas Blount in armour, his head under his helmet, a ruff about his neck, by his side a gauntlet, and a lion at his feet. On his left hand his wife with a book in her joined hands, and two sons, two daughters, and a child in swaddling clothes standing against the back of the arch with the initials of their names in scrolls. The arms are Blount impaling Cornwall of Kinlet. On the side of the tomb is Waryn impaling Poney. The inscription round :—" Hic jacet Thomas Blount Armiger et Margaria Uxor ejus qui quidem Thomas obiit Die 28º Novemb⁵ A.D. MCCCCCLXXX prædicta Margarita obiit Die 2º Novemb⁵ A.D. MCCCCCLXXXXV. R.I.P."

Close to the tower entrance of the church on the left is the monument of Sir Edward Blount in armour leaning on his elbow, and on his left his two wives. This stood formerly on the S. side of the chancel under a beautiful arch which, together with the lower portion of the tomb, has been " restored " away. Nash describes it as it was 100 years ago :—" On the top of the arch stands an angel holding a shield with *Barry nebulé of 6 Or and Sable*, Blount On the tomb were shields Blount, impaling *Gu. on a saltire Arg. a rose of the first*, Nevill ; Blount, impaling *Sa.* 3 *greyhounds current Arg. collared Or*, Wigmore. On another, quarterly 1. 4. Blount 2. *Arg. a lion rampant Gu. crowned Or, within a border Sa. besantee.* 3. *Or*, 3 *chevrons Gu.* impaling quarterly 1. Nevill (2) *Or fretty Gu. in a quarter per pale Ermine and Gu. a ship Sa.* 3. *chequé Or. and Az.* Warren 4. *Or* 3 *chevrons Gu.* Clare 5. Quarterly *Arg. and Gu. fretty Or a bendlet Sa.*, Le Despencer 6. *Gu. a fesse between 6 cross crosslets Or.* Beauchamp." The inscription (now gone) :—" Hic jacet Edwardus Blount eques auratus, hujus loci quondam dominus, antiquo et perillustri sanguine oriundus, matrimonio bis junctus : priorem duxit uxorem Mariam Neville baronis Abergavenii sororem ; alteram Mariam Wigmore antiquo stirpe atque nobili creatam. Vir fuit dotibus animi eximiis, acri semper et vivido ingenio, prudentia singulari, quem privatæ vitæ amor a negotiosis honoribus ad laudabile otium pertraxit ; rei familiaris nec parcus nec prodigus, domi elegans, in suos munificus, in pauperes liberalis ; quem appetebant summi, colebant infimi, amabant omnes. Beatam vitam felici morte conclusit die 13º Novembris, A.D. 1630, ætatis 76. R.I.P."

Sir Edward Blount, in 1601, and for some years later, was lessee of the Crown lands at Bewdley, and as such was engaged in much litigation with the town. From the *State Papers* (vol. ccxli.) we learn that in 1592 a bill was brought into the Court of Exchequer by John Taverner, surveyor of woods S. of the Trent, against Edward Blount, of Kidderminster, for felling wood for eight years past in Wyer Forest, and converting timber worth £100 to his own use; also firewood worth £100 and underwood worth £50; and request for a writ of subpœna to summon Blount to appear and answer to the premises.

Sir Edward Blount resided at the Hall close to the churchyard—the last remnants of which have been recently pulled down. When the Savings Bank in Hall Street was built the workmen found extensive vaults or crypts of solid masonry below, but all was covered up again without investigation. In 1606 Sir Edward settled his estate upon Charles Lord Mountjoy, of Devonshire, and died in 1630. On May 6, 1635, Lord Mountjoy, Earl of Newport, for £8650 sold part of the property to Edmund Waller, the famous poet. In 1643 the " English Tibullus " was detected in a plot to deliver up London to Charles I., and was brought to trial by the Parliament. After a year's detention in the Tower he was fined £10,000, and released " to go travel abroad." His estates were sold to raise the money: Comberton was bought by Adam Hough, whose name appears on the Court Rolls of Bewdley in 1655 as steward of the manor; and was sold by his descendant Adam Hough, about 1777, to Mr. Steward. Hurcott was bought by George Evelyn, who in 1648 disposed of it to his famous brother John, author of *Silva* and the well-known Diary. John Evelyn soon afterwards sold it to Colonel John Bridges for £3400. About 1670 Colonel Bridges sold the patronage of the church to Thomas Foley, in whose family it remained till the whole Foley estate here was purchased by Lord Ward in 1838.

The old Hall had been bought in 1635 by Daniel Dobbins, a London merchant, afterwards elected Member for Bewdley in Barebone's Parliament. Dobbins lived in Kidderminster for some years, and there are several entries of his family in the registers. He sold the " capital mansion house near the almshouses adjoining to Stower side, the Vicarage meadow, and a meadow on the W. side of Stower, also one suite of arras containing 5 pieces," to Sir Thomas Rouse, of Rouse Lench, for £1200. His son, Richard Dobbins, sold to Capel Hanbury, of Hoarstone, the tithes of Wribbenhall and Trimpley, Sept. 4, 1680, for £692; and Capel Hanbury conveyed them to Thomas Foley in 1689.

PEDIGREE OF BLOUNT OF KIDDERMINSTER.

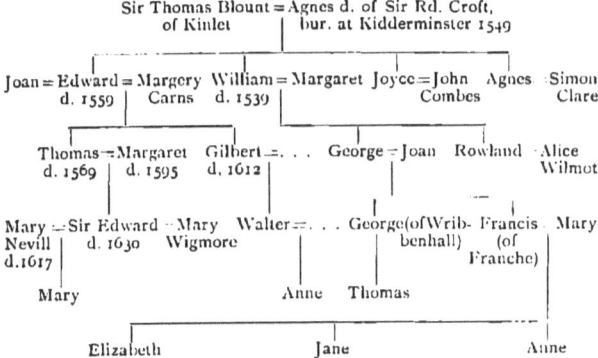

The romantic story of Richard Foley, of Stourbridge, who by enterprise and skill restored the prosperity of an industry which was languishing from foreign competition, is told in Smiles' *Self-Help*, p. 207. By his energy he conferred immense benefits on his native county, and laid the foundations of a large fortune for his own family. His son, Thomas Foley, was Sheriff of Worcestershire in 1655, and Member for Bewdley in 1660 and 1673. Baxter, who was Sheriff's Chaplain, and preached the sermon, says:—" I will mention the great mercy of God to the town of Kidderminster and country in raising up one man, Mr. Foley. Being a religious, faithful man, he purchased among other lands the patronage of several great places, and among the rest of Stourbridge and Kidderminster, and so chose the best conformable ministers that could be got ; and not only so, but placed his eldest son's habitation in Kidderminster, which became a great protection and blessing to the town, having placed two families more elsewhere of his two other sons, all three religious, worthy men. And in thankfulness to

G

God for his mercies to him, built a well-founded hospital near Stourbridge to teach poor children to read and write, and endowed it with about £500 a year." The Foley motto, " *Ut prosim* " (That I may do good) is most appropriate in this case. His magnificent educational foundation has been of great benefit to thousands of poor boys, and is still so well administered that it is carrying on its good work to an extent that the founder little dreamed of. The present Lord Foley takes much interest in the institution, in which Kidderminster, Bewdley, Stourport, Dudley, and other places have a share. The annual value of the endowment now is about £5000, and the buildings have been enlarged to accommodate 160 boys, instead of the original number of 60. Thomas Foley died in 1677, and is buried in Witley church, where a marble monument commemorates his many virtues. The accompanying pedigree will show the division of this family into the three main branches of Witley and Kidderminster, Stoke Edith, and Prestwood. Paul Foley, of Stoke, was a member of the Convention Parliament, 1688, and in 1695 was chosen Speaker of the House of Commons. Thomas Foley, grandson of the founder of the hospital, was Member for Stafford, and on 31 Dec., 1711, was made BARON FOLEY OF KIDDERMINSTER. He married Mary daughter and heir of Thomas Strode, serjeant-at-law, and died 22 Jan., 1732, leaving a son, Thomas second Lord Foley, High Steward of Kidderminster, and five other children. All died *sine prole*, when the Barony became extinct. The estate was left by will to Thomas Foley, of Stoke Edith, who by a new creation was made Baron Foley of Kidderminster, May 20, 1776. His wife was Lady Grace Granville, daughter and co-heir of George Lord Lansdowne. One of his sisters, Anne, was married to Sir Edward Winnington, from whom descend the Winningtons of Stanford and the Ingrams of Ribbesford.

The Barony of Foley of Kidderminster has descended in unbroken line to Henry Thomas, fifth Lord, who succeeded to the title in 1869, and resides at Ruxley Lodge, Esher, Surrey; but the Witley and Kidderminster estates were sold by Thomas Henry, fourth Lord, to the trustees of Lord Ward in 1838.

THE BARONAGE.

PEDIGREE OF BARON FOLEY OF KIDDERMINSTER.

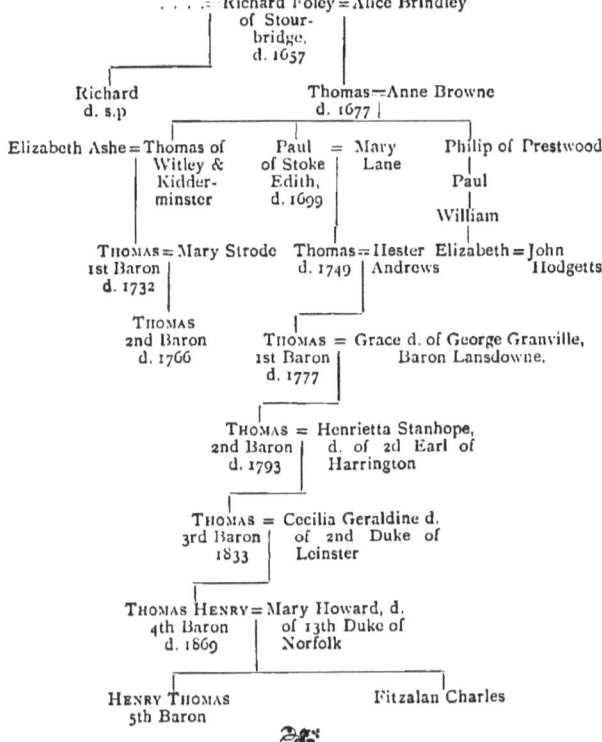

William, 11th Baron Ward, succeeded to the title on the death of his father in 1836. He was descended from Humble Ward, created Baron Ward of Birmingham in 1644, and his wife Frances Sutton, in her own right Baroness Dudley. In 1860 he was created Earl of Dudley and Viscount Ednam. He married first Selina Constance daughter of Hubert de Burgh, Esq., and secondly Georgiana Elizabeth daughter of Sir Thomas Moncrieffe, 7th Baronet, and had four sons and a daughter. Lord Dudley has left a name which will live for many generations in the town of Kidderminster and the county of Worcester. For at a time when it seemed as though the carpet trade of Kidderminster must be annihilated, Lord Dudley generously came to the rescue, and the manufacture was started on a more successful career than before. The Church, the Infirmary, the Schools of Art and Science, and many other useful institutions, were benefited by his help. Lord Dudley died 1885, and was succeeded by his eldest son, William Humble, 2nd Earl of Dudley and 12th Baron Ward, elected High Steward of Kidderminster in 1888. In recognition of the many benefits conferred on the town by the late Lord Dudley, a public memorial was erected, which took the form of a cloister to the parish church, with inscription on a brass plate:—

"To the Glory of God and in memory of William Earl of Dudley, 11th Baron Ward, this cloister was built, partly by subscriptions and partly by a donation from Thomas Tempest-Radford, Mayor, in the Jubilee year of the reign of Her Majesty Queen Victoria, as a remembrance of his many gifts to this church, of which he was patron, and also of his generous efforts to benefit the trade of the town, of which he was High Steward.

"First Stone laid by Canon Claughton, then Vicar, July 1, 1887.

"Dedicated by Henry Lord Bishop of Worcester, Feb. 1, 1888.

"FREDERICK BURCHER, } Borough
"THOMAS F. IVENS, } Churchwardens.

"MICHAEL TOMKINSON, Mayor, } Foreign
"E. F. WHITEHOUSE, } Churchwardens.

"R. J. THOMPSON, Builder."

In place of the one hall for the lord, and the 60 mud houses for the serfs, mentioned at the beginning of the previous chapter, we have now hundreds of dwelling-houses in the parish, with which, for convenience and comfort, the ancient baronial halls could not for a moment compare. The Earl of Dudley owns by far the larger part of the old parish, but many smaller estates would be worthy of record if space allowed.

Some pedigrees of families connected with this neighbourhood may be found in the *Worcester Visitation*, 1682 :— Burlton of Sandbourne, Clare of Caldwell, Foley of Witley and Stourbridge, Oldnall of Stone, Solley of Lickhill and Wribbenhall, Spicer of Stone, Townshend of Elmley Lovett, Toye of Kidderminster, Vernon of Caldwell, Wilde of Belbroughton, Wilmot of Kidderminster; and in the British Museum *(Additional MS.* No. 31,003) Crane of Habberley, Hurtill of Trimpley, Soley of Sandbourne, Seabright of Wolverley, Jewkes, Steward, Wannerton, and Pardoe of Kidderminster.

CHAPTER IV.

The Borough.

IN 1241 a charter was obtained for two fairs yearly at Kidderminster. Before 1333 fairs and markets were a regular institution in the town, though when the charter for the *market* was first obtained I have not met with any evidence. Most likely it was founded when the town was the King's private property. But as early as 23 Edward I. (1295) Kidderminster took its place as one of the leading towns in the county, and returned two burgesses to Parliament. In the Parliamentary Reports (page 6) their names are recorded—"Walter Caldrigan and Walter Lihtfot — Kidderminster Borough." Besides Worcester county and city, there were also representatives from Droitwich, Dudley, Evesham, and Pershore, but in a few years all these towns renounced their privilege except Worcester and Droitwich. The members of Parliament received daily wages, and thus the representation of a town laid a burden on its inhabitants from which they were glad to be delivered. Kidderminster, as being ancient demesne of the Crown, was relieved from contribution to the wages of the knights of the shire.

In our list of husbandmen holding land in the "foreign" we found only one solitary freeman; but there are indications that in the borough this class was well developed in the 13th century. In 1230 a certain man of *free condition* of the manor of Kidderminster recovered common pasturage at Witfield, pertaining to the manor of Wolverley, before the itinerant Justices at Worcester. (Annal. Eccles. Wigorn. in *Ang. Sacr.*, i., 488.) In the British Museum *(Egerton MSS.,* 456) is an original deed

THE BOROUGH.

in Latin of the time of Edward I., containing a grant by Henry Thomas, of Fraynshe, to Robert Troke, clerk, of Kydcrminster, of land in Wytefeld. Witnesses: Hugh Mustell, Robert Attwood *(de Bosco)*, John de Kent, Richard Brid (Bird), and Richard Pitt *(in Puteo)*. Though this deed is contemporaneous with the list of villeins given in Chapter II., the names are all new, and give evidence of the rise of a new class, *libere tenentes*, or copyholders within the borough. In a Taxation Roll for Worcestershire belonging to Sir E. Lechmere *(Hist. MSS. Report*, v., p. 304), Kidderminster ranks fourth among the towns. There are 58 names, contributing £9 5s. 4d. Worcester paid £82 11s. 6d., and Droitwich £27 13s. 2d. The growth of freedom in the town is obscure, but the borough is fortunate in the possession of a record of proceedings which took place at a Court held here 557 years ago. It shows how tenaciously the burgesses clung to the privileges they had already gained, and how far self-government had advanced.

"In the Court holden on Monday next after the feast of St. Michael the Archangel, in the 7th year of the reign of King Edward the third from the Conquest.

"It was required by John de Costone, Steward *(Senescallus)* of John Bissett in what way and in what manner and by what title the Commonalty of the Burgesses of the Town of Kidderminster ought to elect Bailiffs on Monday next after the feast of St. Michael *and not the lord;* and why the said Bailiffs ought on the days of fairs and markets to be fed out of the lord's toll; and why the Provosts or Bailiffs ought to gather the toll and not render an account: and why all the Burgesses tenants and inhabitants in the Borough have not come twice in the year to the view of Frankpledge held upon the Hill *(super Montem)*.

"The Reply by Edmund, Lord of Hagley, Clement Lord of Dunclent, Robert Atwood *(de Bosco)*, John de Hethey, John de Kent, and by all the Burgesses and the whole community of the Town of Kidderminster. And they said that in ancient time of a certain King, whereof there exists no memorial, the said Burgesses elected one Bailiff on the aforesaid Monday to serve the King, namely, to gather the said toll and place the said toll in a certain box, and render it without an account. And the said Burgesses on the said Monday ought to elect one Catchpoll to make all the attachments and well and faithfully gather the money of the pleas and perquisites of the court, and render an account when he shall be required by the lord's ministers for the time being. And for the labours and services of the said Bailiffs for the time being, upon the days of the courts, fairs and markets, they ought to be fed with the lord out of the lord's toll. And the said Bailiffs ought to elect six Burgesses and not more, and to send them to the view of Frankpledge, twice during the year, namely, on Wednesday next after the feast of St. Michael, and on Wednesday next after Hockday. [The Tuesday in the third week after Easter.]

" Custom allowed and may be held for law. And the said John Coston allowed this reply, because it was allowed in former time whereof there is no memorial."

Under the system of frank-pledge all the freemen residing in the same "tithing" were pledged to the King for the good conduct of each other; and if any one of them did wrong all the rest were bound to secure his arrest, or pay the penalty. The "view of frank-pledge" was a sort of roll-call, testifying to the fact that the frank-pledges were in full efficiency, and that every one belonged to such a body. Some interesting cases, showing the practical working of this system in Worcestershire, were contributed to *Berrow's Journal* in November, 1889, by Mr. J. B. Matthews.

Among the records of the town is " The Composition of the Manner and Burrow of Kethermister A.D. 1102." It sets forth that " In the tyme of King Henry the Firste was the Burrow of Ketherminster gyven and Assured by the same Kyng unto Master Bissett his gentleman Shoure with all freedomes, customs and priviledges as ffreelie and as honorablie as Any Noble Manne off England Inioyed the same." The document is written on vellum, and is very old, but there are two palpable mistakes in it. Henry the *Second* was the donor, not Henry I.; and the date is really about 1330, as Edmond Lord of Hagley, Clement of Dunclent, Robert Atwood, John a Heathey, and John a Kent are among the jury.

Business was transacted in or around the Market Cross, which from Leland's description must have been a beautiful Gothic structure. It stood in the High Street, and is shown in Doharty's map (1753). A boundary was marked out by the Worcester Cross, Proud Cross, Barriers in Church Street, and Dakebrooke (Daddlebrook) in Blackstar Street, and if any trader had dealings within these limits and failed to pay his lawful toll, he was mulcted in the large sum of 6os. and a purse to the lord.

The Court-House, where the lord resided when in the town,

was close to the church. Its "Grange," "Barn," and "Orchard" have left their names on our modern map. Near it on "The Hill" were held every year in the open air the two Courts Leet. As the lords of Kidderminster had their chief houses in distant places, and only visited the town occasionally, much power naturally fell into the hands of the local authorities. When men gained the "freedom" of the borough they were enrolled, after payment to the lord, into a community, by the "Twelve" and the "Twenty-four" men, the germ of our Aldermen and Town Councillors. On the Monday after Michaelmas Day the Twenty-four Burgesses elected the High Bailiff, and he then chose for himself an "Assistance" or Low Bailiff, and two "Catchpolls" or constables, for his year of office. At the two great "Leetes Courts" the Bailiff gave a dinner at his own cost to the Low Bailiff and his wife, the Town Clerk and his wife, and the Twelve men and their wives. In important matters "for the prince and the lord," the Bailiff was to send his "Assistance" to fetch at least three of the eldest of the Burgesses to ask their advice. The Bailiff had also a Gaoler, who was required to deliver up his prisoner to the Constable at Worcester Cross when the term of his imprisonment expired. The Catchpolls had to gather up all the amercements for their year, and account for them to the lord's auditor, and they received 12d. each felon for their trouble. They also received fees of meal, salt, old clothes sold, of mercers and wheelwrights, of bread wanting weight, of proclaiming of beasts, &c. Any one who did "lvell cawle or yvell intreate" the Bailiff or Catchpolls was to be grievously punished. The lord of Kidderminster had the power of life and death in the manor, and it was his duty to provide the halter *(Collistrigium)*, a Goomstool for the ducking of scolding women, the Pillory, and Stocks. Once a month the Bailiff was to weigh bread both white and brown: if it lacked the assize the baker was to be put in the pillory and the bread given to the poor. Butchers who exposed for sale any "messled brawne" or leprous meat must cover the same with a linen cloth and put salt upon it, as a sign of its unsoundness. Unless this were done, the Catchpoll might seize it, and the Bailiff *give the same to the poor!*

No artificers called Tencers, the Burgesses excepted, could occupy their "Syences" without the consent of the Bailiff. All measures were to be sealed with the Bailiff's seal, viz., the bushel, the half-bushel, the peck, the half-peck, the tolled dish, the pottel pot, the quart, the pint pot, and the half-pint. The standard weights and measures of the statute of Winchester were in his custody: one iron ell, one brazen pound, half-pound, and quarter-pound, one iron seal for leather, one for pots, one for yards, and one for strikes and lesser measures. If the Burgesses did not at all times assist the Bailiff and his officers they could be disfranchised of their "Burges shipp."

All the Burgesses might fish freely in the Stour between the mouth of Blake brook and the mouth of Wannerton brook; but if they fished to sell they must make a fine with the lord. The fishponds at the Mill and the Sluice were reserved. The Burgesses could also fish in the Severn up to the middle of the water. All the meadows alongside the Stour were common after mowing and raking, but if any "waif or kemelyng" came into the demesne it was to be seized for the lord. A woman after her husband's death was to have his land, but only during her good behaviour. If a waif or kemelyng came into the borough it was to be proclaimed thrice at the fairs and markets, and thrice in the church. If claimed the owner must prove possession before the lord's officers at third hand, and find pledges for a year and a day in case of a counter claim. If not claimed within a year and a day it was to be parted between the lords. If the waif was found in the foreign, it was assigned to the lord on whose land it was found; if on the highway it was divided between the three lords, as the roads were considered to be their joint property. Swarms of bees were treated as "waifs and kemelyngs."

Each lord was to have heriots and reliefs from the free tenants in his demesne, except the Burgesses of Kidderminster. Also each lord was to have after the death of a customary tenant (*i.e.*, a villein) the best heriot, a two-horse cart iron bound* the half *(rustarum?)*, the half of the pigs, the half of the

---

* Iron was expensive, and many wheels were made of solid wood by sawing a tree at right angles to its length.

cloths not assysed, and the horses, but not the mares. "The customary tenants in the land remaining in the lord's hand shall make a fine with the lord in full court, three proclamations having been made, and he who is of nearest kin to the deceased man, according to the custom of the manor, shall have the best besides (?)"

No lord nor rector might have a dead heriot while there was a live heriot. If there was only a pig it was to be parted between the lord and the rector: if below the value of 6d. the lord was to have the whole.

No tenant could make a sub-tenant in the manor without his lord's permission under penalty of forfeiture of his tenure.

Tenants were not permitted to make "Stakings" for catching fish in the Stour and Severn without licence of the lords.

On fair days and markets the Burgesses might set up stalls and tables in front of their houses, but were to remove them afterwards on account of the danger to strangers passing through the town by night. Outsiders were to pay for each stall 1d. to the lord and ½d. to the Low Bailiff.

As a precaution against fire, every householder was required in dry weather to have a vessel full of water near his doorway. He was also forbidden to make a pile of brushwood, hay, or straw in the borough near the houses, under a penalty of 40d., half to the lord and half to the church. The same penalty was inflicted on those who allowed their swine to wander in the streets without a keeper.

"Regrators" were not allowed to come early to market and buy up the goods to "make a ring." No one could traffic till the bell was tolled, and he ought not to buy more than was required to supply his house from one fair day to another, under a penalty of 40d., half to the lord and half to the church. The brewers of the town had to pay 6d. twice a year, and minute precautions were taken to ensure the townsmen a "good glass of beer." "If a man or woman buy a gallon of beer dearer than the assize, that buyer may go immediately to the Bailiff and make complaint, and shall have of the lord one farthing for his pains."* But this was not all. There were certain official beer-tasters who were required to present twice in the year " both how many there are who make weak beer, and who do not make wholesome beer, and who do not invite them to taste the beer as often as they brew it."

The tolls payable to the lord were :—For a horse or mare, buyer 2*d*. and seller 2*d*.; for an exchange, double tolls ; for an ox or bullock, 1*d*. from each dealer ; for four sheep, the same ; for a load of fish, herrings, corn, &c., 2*d*. from each ; for a horse load of anything, ½*d*. ; for the load of a man or woman, ¼*d*. If the purchaser lived in the town he was free from these tolls, unless he bought the goods to retail them. If a " Native " of the lord bought anything, he was freed from toll, and made affirmation upon the book before the Bailiff with the thumb upwards as a sign.

On the eve of the Ascension the Bailiff and Burgesses perambulated the town. From Ascension-tide till Michaelmas the Bailiff had to see that a watch went three times nightly over the demesne. Also on fair or market days the Bailiff, attended by three Ancient Burgesses and Catchpolls, went round the town " to see the peace kept in good order." They likewise appointed a Borough Herdman to keep the cattle in the lord's waste, and a Borough Swineherd for the pigs who went for " pannage," or acorns and beech mast in the lord's wood.

Some regulations for the making of woollen cloth and kerseys will be deferred to another chapter.

Lastly we meet with an ordinance which shows vividly with what a far-away time we are dealing :—

" Also wee will that the bayleeff may keep a grayhound or a gray Bitch and a fferret for the tyme off his office, and 3 dayes in the weeck to huntt ffor to kill two cowple of Rabbitts or Connies within your warrant and nott Above in payn of xxs.

" Also we will that the burgesses shall and may keepp one gray hound or gray Bitch for to huntt the hare ffox, Roe Red dear or fallow deare.

---

* When barley was 2*s* a quarter 4 gallons of beer was to be sold for a penny. Hops were then unknown in England.

THE BOROUGH.

"Also wee will that your Burgesses may comming throw your warrant with his bow bentt nott going outt of the high way may kill a Conney and so to bear hir away uppon the end off his Bow, and shall nott kill Above one in payn off xxs., and that no tencer shall kill any within your warrant in payne of xxs."

The Park ran close up to the town from which it was separated by Park-lane; and as late as 1753 (see Doharty's Map) this lane was bounded only by palings and hedges on both sides as far as Caldwell. A track ran across the Park towards Bewdley, and all the space between Kidderminster and Wribbenhall, including Wood Street, the Workhouse, Spring Grove, &c., was a preserve for game. Leland in 1539 went "from Kidderminster to Beaudly, two miles, by a *fayre downe*, but somewhat barren." In the Act passed in 1774 for enclosing waste lands the following are enumerated :—" Upper and Lower Witchells, Rocum otherwise Rockham, the Long Coppice, the Yew Tree Coppice, the Spread Coppice, the Crofts, Dobyn's Sling, Black Brook Common, Ferney Bank, Oldington Common, Kidderminster Upper and Lower Heath, Burlish Common, Pools called the Slashes, &c." By this Act it was expressly forbidden to cut down the clumps of firs on the hill called the Sheep-rack or on Mount Pleasant, as being trees of ornament; and the roads to be laid out must be 60 feet wide.

On the flat piece of land between Mill Street and Park Lane were the Park Butts, where the Burgesses gained such skill in the use of the bow that, "not going out of the highway," they could shoot conies; and most likely some of them acquired here the deadly precision which 12 years afterwards made such havoc amongst the French at Cressy. Skill in archery was much fostered by the laws. In Edward IV.'s reign it was enacted that every Englishman should have a bow of his own height, and that butts for the practice of archery should be erected near every village, where the inhabitants were obliged to shoot up and down on every feast day under penalty of being mulcted a halfpenny. In 12 Edw. IV., cap. 2, it was ordered that four bowstaves should be brought into this realm for every ton of merchandise; and in 22 Edw. IV., " Whosoever shall sell a long bow of yew above 3s. 4d. shall forfeit 20s." Again in 1 Rich. III., cap. 2, " Ten bowstaves shall be brought into this realm for every butt of Malmsey." A "ring" of Lombards had raised the price from £2 to £8 the hundred.

It is not easy to put all our information about a locality in olden times into a continuous narrative, and yet every authentic scrap of such knowledge which has survived the lapse of five or six centuries is worthy of record. The following original deeds are in the British Museum:—

"Grant by Henry de Feckenham of Kidderminster to John son of Margery Atte Malpas of land called Oldefelde near Fraynsh. Witnesses: Henry de Waresleye clerk, Wolston de Kent, Geoffrey Oky, Simon de Bromesgrove. Dat. at Kidderminster, Tuesday after the Annunciation of the Blessed Virgin Mary, 10 Edward III. (1336). [*Egerton MSS*., 462.] Brown seal of Henry de Feckenham: three bars.

"In July 1381 John Malpas of Kyderminster gave to his son William one tenement formerly William Hickeson's, then held by William Hulpole—"which tenement is situated in *Covyntre Street*." Witnesses—Rich. Ov'don, Nicholas Polton, Bailiff. *(Prattinton MSS.)*

"Grant by Thomas Mal, Vicar of Kidderminster, and Henry de Penne chaplain, to William son of Thomas Kent of Kidderminster of lands granted to them by the above Thomas Kent within the Manor of Kidderminster. Witnesses William Hulpole, John Sugge, Bailiffs of Kidderminster, John Mal, William Hayle, Geoffrey Heryng, John Janyns, Constantine Baker, Alice ——. Dat. at Kidderminster Monday before S. Barnabas 11 Rd. II. (1388). Appended are two seals, one of them in red wax containing the arms of Thomas Mal, viz., a chevron between three mauls or wooden hammers. [*Eg. MSS.* 465.]

"Release by Thomas Hetheye son and heir of John Hetheye son of Lucy Hygne of Kydermynstre to William Malpas Chaplain of a tenement in *Church Street (in vico qui ad ecclesiam ducit)*. Witnesses: Sir Walter de Cokesey, John Pryntour, John Horewode, Bailiffs, Henry Mal & others. Dat. at Kidderminster Thursday after S. John *ante Port. Lat.* 1 Henry IV. (1400) [*Eg. MSS.* 470]. A red seal of Hethey is appended with arms—a chevron betwen three escallops.

"Grant by William Bleke of Haberley to Richard Becke of Pokelyston (Puxton) and Cristina his wife of a tenement called Gronclonde in Franche which he had from William Bernard of Haberley. Witnesses: John Hoke, William Brede, John Lorde, &c. Dat. at Franche, Thursday after S. Matthew's day 9 Henry V. (1421). The dark green seal of John Ponet is affixed. The device appears to be that of an Apostle with a staff in his hand. *Eg. MSS. No. 472.*"

From these deeds it may be noticed that much of the land was beginning to pass from the great lords into the possession of the traders and yeomen.

The practice of granting repairing leases for a long term of years was in use as early as 1440.

"This Indenture made between Robert Prior of Maiden Bradley and Zenanus Troghman of Wrybenhalle witnesseth : That the Prior and Convent have conceded to Zenanus one messuage and half a virgate of land in Trympley, which were John Rogers's together with a marsh *(Mera)* lying near Caldwell Mill which was formerly John Oldenhall's To be held to the end of 90 years, by paying annually 6s. 8d. and doing all other services due by ancient custom ; but they shall be relieved from the offices of Bailiff and Beadle ; and on condition that Zenanus and his assigns shall well and competently repair and keep up three houses. Dat. Sunday before Lady Day 18 Henry VI."

I have not been able to trace the destination of the old Court Rolls of the Manor. In them there would most likely be a mine of information. The *Wanley MS.* (p. 167) preserves one day's proceedings more than 400 years ago. The feudal system was still kept up in form, but was becoming more assimilated in its working to modern uses. The large tenant farmer has arisen with his 160 acres of land at Sutton, and most likely his own exclusive plough-team. Instead of his best horse or cow or iron-bound wagon for a heriot, he pays only the fixed sum of 20d. The rental of 2½d. an acre would not be thought exorbitant in these days!

"Kedermynstre. At a Great Court held there on The Hill (*super Montem*) on Wednesday next after the Feast of S. Michael the Archangel in the 4th year of King Edward the Fourth after the Conquest.

"Nicholas Wakemon came and surrendered into the Lord's hands 5 virgates of land with appurtenances in Sutton and one Parroke lately in the tenure of Thomas Rugge ; and after this came John Symons and Thomas Dukeford Cooper, and took the aforesaid 5 Virgates and a Parroke, which the Lord granted to the same John and Thomas to be held by them and their heirs for the term of 79 years. Rendering thence annually for each virgate 5s. 8d., and for the Parroke 9d. ; besides which they shall be free from the offices of Beadle (*Bedellus*, perhaps the 'Catchpoll') and Bailiff. And each of them shall give the Lord for a Fine 6s. 8d. and a Heriot after his death 20d.

"There was also granted to them and John Kay, licence to catch conies in the arable land there. And after this they did fealty to the Lord and were admitted tenants.

"In testimony whereof the seal of the Steward (*Seneschallus*) is appended."

Sir Humphrey Stafford, of Grafton Manor, near Bromsgrove,

owned lands in Kidderminster, and fought for Richard III. at Bosworth. He was afterwards attainted and executed and his lands granted to John Darell, John Pympe, and Sir Gilbert Talbot. In 1487 a pardon and restitution of possessions was granted by the Crown to Thomas Kynfare *alias* Taillour, Town Clerk of Kidderminster.

Burgesses of Kidderminster were occasionally appointed Collectors of the Royal Subsidies for the county, viz., 10 Ed. III., Hugh de Cokesey; 18 Ed. III., Robert Attwood; 25 Ed. III, Edmund Dunclent; 45 Ed. III., John Clare; 18 Rd. II., John Spicer; 2 Henry IV., Walter Clare; 2 Henry V., Richard Shareshull; and 8 Hy. VI., John Stodeley, goldsmith.

Where any misunderstanding had arisen concerning property, the matter was often settled as a "Final Concord" before the Judges. Some of these have been recorded. [*Lansdowne MS.*, 30c, fol. 174. *Impensis Dni Thomæ Phillipps, Bart.*, 1853.]

1 Edw. III. (1327). Walter de Cokesoye and Isabella his wife with Richard de Portes concerning a tenement in Leitleye.

Adam de la Lowe with Richard le Taylor of Kyderministre.

Richard of Stone and Cecilia his wife with Richard son of the said Richard.

Joan wife of ———— with Robert Pipard about tenements in Kidderminster and Stone.

1330. Robert de Ribbesford with Henry de Ribbesford concerning the manor of Ribbesford, lands in Roke and Lindon, and the advowson of the church aforesaid.

1334. Hugh Mustell and Isabella his wife with John son of Thomas le Boteler, chevalier, concerning one messuage, one shop, one carucate and 10 acres of land, 16 acres of meadow with appurtenances in Haberley, Kyderministre, and Pokelston.

William le Botelier and Sarra his wife with William de Okhampton and Joan his wife, about lands in Great Comberton.

1349. Nicholas le Peyntour of Kydderminstre with Richard de Bohhull and Isabella his wife, about tenements in Chadeleswyche and Winlyngwyche.

John de Beauchamp of la Holte and Isabella his wife with Richard Shope of Bewdley [*de Bello Loco*] and Agnes his wife, about lands in Children-hanley.

THE BOROUGH.

1350. William son of Hugh de Cokesey with Hugh de Cokesey and Dionisia, about lands in Cudbaldesheye, Purshall, and Upton.

1355. Hugh de Cokesey and Dionisia with Hugh their son, about lands in Aldermonstone.

8 Rd. II. (1385). John Beauchamp of Holte with Sir Walter Romesy, Kt., about the manor of Kyderminster.

1386. Sir Walter Romesey, Kt., with Sir John Beauchamp of Holte and Joan his wife, about the manor of Kyderminster.

1393. Thomas Kendale of Wyche with Thomas Santon of Kyderminster and Lucy his wife, about lands in Kyderminster.

Hy. IV. 1411. Walter Elyot Parson of the Church of Rybbesford with Richard Parlour and his wife Margery, about 3 messuages 3 virgates of land 20 acres of meadow and 200 acres of Common in Colyngwyck and Alveton.

Hy. V. 8. Thomas Henster with Robert Nelme, of Worcester, about 2 messuages, one carucate of land, 7 acres of meadow, and 11 marks of rent, in Leykhull (Lickhill), Nethermytton, and Kyderminster.

Hy. VI. 1. Richard Beauchamp Earl of Warwick with Thomas Longeley Bishop of Durham, John Throkemorton, and John Barton about the manors of . . . Ribbesford, Rook, Lyndon, 14 salt works, 37 bullaries, . . . and the advowson of the church of Ribbesford.

Hy. VIII. 13. Simon Rice with Gilbert Clare about tenements in Kidderminster.

16. Gilbert Clare with John Hore about the manor of Hethey with appurtenances, and tenements in Hethey and Kidderminster.

17. Simon Rice with Henry White about the manor of Over Mitton and tenements in Mitton, Over Mitton, and Nether Mitton.

23. Thomas Englefield with Richard Lorde about tenements in Kyderminster and Wragenhale.

26. John Pakyngton with John Hale, clerk, about tenements in the city of Worcester, Over Mytton, Kedermynster, and Oldyngton.

30. Thomas Baylly with Agnes Hyll about tenements in Nether Mytton and Lykehull.

34. Thomas Ratsey with Rd. Colley gent. about property in Heref., Salop, Devon, and Kidderminster.

Hy. VIII. 34. John Wannerton with John Coston about tenements and common pasture for 100 sheep and 40 animals in Wannerton.

38. Adam Lutley with John Pakynton about tenements in Over Mytton, Woldyngton, and Kederminstre.

Ed. VI. John Harward with Roger Wall about property in Waresley.

,, 4. John Hambury with Wm. Beste—Waresley.

Car. II. 1649. Rd. Baker with Milo Clent gent.
Robt. Haye with Rd. Hobday *alias* Lacy.
Wm. Browne with John Browne.
Wm. Yarranton with Walter Higley (Astley).
John Vincent with Thos. Vincent (Trimpley).
Simon Potter with John Browne.
Humphrey Burton gent. with W. Smyth gent. (Wribbenhall).

1650. Thos. Hunt with John Radford gent.
Rd. Sergeant clerk with W. Toy (Hagley).

1651. W. Bund gent. with Daniel Dobbyns arm.
Walter Wilkes with John Freeston and Wilkes.
John Freeston clerk with Thos. Dawkes and Freeston.

1652. Thomas Powys Esq. with Edmond Walker Esq. and Dobins.
Lawrence Pearsall with Jane Radford.
Richard Clarke with Wm. Bowyer and Hunt.
George Clarke with John Clare.
Nicholas Addenbrooke gent. with Thomas Wannerton (Churchill).
Wm. Grove with Edward Grove (Over Mitton).
Thomas Lewes with John Wade and Sawyer.
Ursula Tompkins *alias* Weaver with John Soley gent. (Horestone).
Henry Malpas with John Winford and Hayward Smyth.

1653. Wm. Browne with Joane Churchyard widow and Bennett.
Rd. Hanbury Esq. with Matthew Odhams.
Rd. Hanbury Esq. with Alice Longmore, widow (Horestone).
Hy. Wheler Esq. with John Stephyn Esq. and Willetts.
Wm. Browne with Adam Hough gent.

Car. II. 1653. Thos. Crane with Simon Uffemore.

Humphrey Wyldye with John Clare.

[Sir Thomas Phillipps has printed a list down to 13 Anne.]

The steady growth of individual liberty among the commonalty between 1334 and 1500 is well illustrated by the privilege they had acquired of making a testamentary disposal of their property. At the earlier period, when a customary tenant died, his best iron-bound wain, half his pigs, half the bacon, half of the cloth not assised, and all his horses (not the mares) became the property of the lord. The tenant had apparently no power of making a will, but his goods and tenant-right, after three public proclamations, were assigned to his next-of-kin, according to the custom of the manor. Sir Thomas Phillipps *(MSS.,* No. 21,064) has made a collection of Worcestershire wills, of which a few specimens will be of interest as throwing light on the domestic life of three or four centuries ago :—

"1509. In the name of God, Amen. I William Coton of the parish of Kyddeminster. *Imprimis* I leave my soul to God the Father Almighty, the Blessed Mary and all the Saints, and my body to ecclesiastical sepulture in the church of All Saints at Kyddeminster. I leave to the mother church of Worcester 4 pence ; to the high altar 4 pence ; to my wife three cows half of my rye and 2 brass pots. Also I leave to Roger my son all my sheep at Hurcote 5 oxen and all the crops growing upon my land, and 2 pots. Also to John Myll one cow, to Agnes Walker one cow. Also I leave to the chapel of the Blessed Mary in the churchyard of Kidderminster 6 shillings and 8 pence. Also I leave to Johanna my daughter half of my rye and 5 animals of three years old. Also I leave to John Bagger 2 sheep. Also I leave to Thomas Garet one sheep. The residue of all my goods, not disposed of, after payment of debts, I give and leave at the disposal of Roger my son and of Alice my wife, and I ordain and constitute them my executors to dispose of my goods as may seem to them best for the good of my soul. These being witnesses,

"Sir JOHN BARNETT, Chaplain, WALTER FLEMYNG,

WILLIAM BUKNYLL, and others."

The next will is that of Thomas Forest, who was probably the Bailiff to whom Lord Bergavenny addressed his letter in 1485 (see p. 38) :—

A HISTORY OF KIDDERMINSTER.

"1511. I, Thomas Forest of Chaddesley bequeath to the high altar of Stone 12d. I bequeath to our Ladye of Pyté in Kydderminster 12d. for the lights before her. I bequeath to our Ladye in Kydderminster next the Trynite 12d. Item to Jesus Awter in Kidderminster 12d. Item to our Ladye of Hartilbury 12d. Item to our Lady's service of Stone 20 shepe of thos that be in the keeping of Thomas Parkes, or the valew, And all my beefs which be with John Oldenall. Item I bequeath my londe att the Lye and my house in Stone to the Wardens of our Ladys Chapel of Stone for everlasting times, being for increase and founding of a priest's service."

"In the name of God Amen the 23rd day of Marche in the yere of our Lord God 1546. I William Hyheway of Kidderminster sike in body hole of mynd and of perfect Rememberance ferying deathe Shulde me approache make this my last will. First I bequethe my soul unto Almighty God our Lady Saynt Mary to all the holy company of heavyn, and my body to be buryed in the church yard of Kidderminster. Item unto the high alter of Kidderminster 12d. Item to the reparacons of Bewdley brydge 12d. to Agnes Beterton my daughter the house in Worcester Strete, the barne in the barne Strete, my wiffes seconde gowne, a payor of Shetes and a kercheffe. Itm to Alice Rise my daughter the house in Mylstrete a Red heyfur, a payer of shetes a kertell and a smocke. Item to Thomas Gilis the house that I dwell in with a bedde. Itm to Thomas Trupe my worste wheles and my tomberell my 2nd gowne and my best fether bed. Itm I bequethe to Margarett Warall my daughter all my right and interest of deltses closse which I hold by indenture, my black horse, 20 strike of malte, a payer of shetes, my best potte and panne. Itm I bequethe to the children of my brother John, Agnes, Alis, Margery, and Margaret, my daughters all my bees indifferently to be devyded amongst them. I bequethe to my coson William Willies one pece of new cloth conteyning 3 yds. Itm I bequethe to my brother John my best gowne my best wagne wheles and my wayne body. Itm I bequethe to Peter Abraham a shete."

'In the name of God Amen. In the year of our Lord 1546 and of the Reygne of Henry VIII of England France and Ireland Kyng defensor of the faythe and in erthe of England and Ireland hedd supreme the 38th year the 30th May. I Rychard Hill of Kyddmistre make my test, in this wyse followinge. I bequethe my soule to God and my body to be buryed in the church yard of all seynts in Kyddmistre. I bequethe to the hye Alter there 4d I bequethe to my son Wyllm 40s in money and my best gowne Itm I bequethe to Johane my daughter a kowe 16s 8d my best fether bed my best cover with all that belongeth to the bed. I bequethe to Elnor my daughter a kowe my best pott and the taking of the house that I dwell in duryng the yeres of my Indentur, but I wyll that her mother have the halfe of the house and the Londs duryinge her wydowhood and if she mary Elnor to have the hole. Itm I bequeth to Thomas my sonn my second gowne and 6s 8d Itm I bequethe to John Sherman my servant a bastard lambe with all belongethe thereto. Itm I will that Alyce my wife have all such thyns as were pmysed

to her at her maryage as hyr wryttynge will playnely showe. Itm I bequethe
to Elizabeth Hotton my sister my third gowne &c.
  " I make my executors
      " PETER ABRAHAM.   DAVID WACNA.   THOMAS DOLYTTYLL.
                       "£12 9 7¼."

Under Richard Duke of York and his son King Edward IV.
the neighbouring town of Bewdley had made rapid strides in
prosperity and population, chiefly owing to its position as the
highest *depôt* on the Severn whence the Bristol merchandise
could be conveyed to the midland and northern counties. Its
important bridge, its beneficent charter, its royal palace, its
Court of the Marches, its sanctuary, its abundance of timber,
its oak bark and tanneries, its salmon fisheries, its troops of
pack horses, its numerous trows—all these, combined with the
skill and enterprise of its inhabitants, had enabled it by the
beginning of the Tudor period to surpass its more ancient
neighbour both in numbers and wealth. A long rivalry sprang
up between these towns, separated from each other by only
two miles—a rivalry which only ceased within the last genera-
tion. The feud rose to such a pitch in 1494 that Arthur Prince
of Wales and his Council of the Marches were obliged to
intervene, and the following ordinances were made between the
inhabitants of the town of Bewdeley and the inhabitants of
the town of Kiddermyster. *(Blakeway MSS.)* :—

  " It is divised, ordayned, and determined, att the Cittie of Hereford by
the Counsaille of Prince Arthure the first begotten son of our said Sovereigne
Lord, for a finall concord, love, peace and amytie from hensforth to be had
bytwene all th' inh'itants and resiants of the Towne of Bewdeley on the one
part and all th' inh'itants and resiants of the Towne of Kiddermyster on th'
other ptie that they and every one of them shall obey observe fulfill and
kepe the Articles hereafter ensuing. In eschuyng all maner gruggs debats,
variances or discords, that now been, or that hereafter might happen to be
between them for any old or new matters—First &c. . . item &c. . . .
It is by the said Counsell ordeyned and determyned that if hereafter shall
happen anie new grugg or variaunce to be betweene the inh'itants of the said
townes, that then they, nor anie of them, take upon them to justify or avenge
their said quarrels, but alwaies from tyme to tyme when and as often as the
cause shall so require, come and resort unto the sayd Prynce and his Counsell, ther to show the causes of the same variaunces, and to abide, obei and
fulfill the direction and determinacioun at all seasons that shal be therein
taken by the said Prince and his Counsell.—In witness whereof and of all

the p'misses the said Prince hath hereunto putt his signett, the right reverend Father in God the Bishop of Ely, president of his Counsaill with other of the same Counsaill, have subscribed and put to their hands the daie and yeare before rehearsed.

"JO. ELY   R. POWES   R. CROFT
"ROBT. FROST   T. POYNTZ   NEWTON."

John Leland visited the town about 1539, and has left us this description of it :—

"Entringe into the Towne of *Kidderminster*, a Markett Towne in *Worcestershire* I passed over by a Faubourge, and soe over a Bridge of 2 or 3 Arches upon *Stower* River. The head of this River is about the pooles of the late Priory of *Halesowen* a 6 miles of.

"The fayre and chiefe Part of *Kidderminster* is on the left Ripe of *Stower* standinge on an hilly Piece of Ground. There is a pretty Crosse environed with 6 Pillars about and Arches of Stone, with the 7th Pillar in the middle to bear up the Fornix. It is in the Markett Place.

"The Church is very fair, and one . . . Coxye a Knight al richly buried there in the Quire. This Towne standeth most by cloathinge. In tymes past this Town belonged to the *Bisetts* ancient Gentlemen. After It came to the 3 Heires Generall of *Bisett*, whereof one being a *Lazer* builded an Hospitall at *Maiden Bradley* in *Wiltshire* to a Priory of Chanons. She gave her part here *in pios usus*, and the Parsonage of Kidderminster was impropriate to *Maiden Bradley*. The other 2 Partes came to the Lord *Abergavenny*, and in that family it yet remaineth.

"*Dowr* alias *Stour* Ryver—goethe to *Sturton* Castle—Thens to *Kidour-Mynstre*, a good Market Towne, and runnethe throughe the mydle of it, and at Rages, drownythe a Pece of it. In *Kidourminstre* is but one Churche, but it is large. The Personage was impropriate to the Chanons of *Mayden Bradley* in *Wiltshire*. A little benethe *Kidour* is a fayre manor place on *Stour* caulyd *Cundalewel*. It was the *Coxeyes*, and now It longethe to the *Wintors* men of fayre Lande."

In the same year (1539) in which Leland paid his visit to the town, the parish scribe was beginning to chronicle that most reliable source of all our local and family history for the past 350 years—the register of the old church. In this, with only a few short omissions, are recorded all the baptisms, marriages, and deaths which took place in the parish from that time to the present. Few places possess such a complete record, and if this precious heritage could be printed in its entirety the work would be most valuable. In the appendix will be found a list of all the family names which appear from 1539 to 1565, with the date when each name first occurs. The number of separate surnames is 283, and this coincides in a remarkable manner with Bishop Sandys' answer to the Privy Council (5 Eliz., A.D. 1563), wherein he stated that Kidderminster contained 260 families and Mytton Chapel 23. Of course, in some cases there would be more than one family of the same name, whereas others would be strangers, like John a Combe of Stratford, who came here to be married. From these figures, the only reliable ones for enumeration since A.D. 1086, it is computed that the population at this time was 1125. The average of burials from

1564 to 1585 amounts to	...	41
1598 to 1617 ,,	...	49
1642 to 1651 ,,	...	78
1674 to 1697 ,,	...	100
1721 to 1750 ,,	...	128
1751 to 1760 ,,	...	142
1771 to 1773 ,,	...	207
In 1793 ,,	...	251

In 1776 Bishop North reported Kidderminster as containing 1600 families. In 1793 the population was found to be 6199. For the figures from 1801 and upwards we shall be able hereafter to make use of the accurate census returns.

Up to 1752 there was no fixed formula for the registration, so from time to time many curious entries occur throwing light on the moral, social, and religious life of our forefathers, and of these some specimens are also to be given. The following callings were exercised in the town between 1540 and 1655:— Weaver, millner (miller), corveser (shoemaker), haberdasher, saddler, fuller, sawyer, wiredrawer, cutler, mercer, dyer, tailor, fletcher (arrow-maker), barber, surgeon, sherman, tanner, glover, capper, baker, millwright, jockey, butcher, singer, freemason, currier, mountebank, bellman, clothworker, "doctoure of Phissicke," apothecary, schoolmaster, vicar, deacon, minister, knight, esquire, soldier, "professed doctor," ragman, grinder, spooler, papermaker, &c. The inns mentioned are the Crown, Bull, Talbot, Angel, and Bell.

The frequent recurrence of the "sickness," with its terrible lists of victims, notably in 1604, 1637, 1727, 1728, 1729, shows the significance of the prayer, "In the time of any common Plague or Sickness," which we find in our Prayer Book.

In 1635, Feb. 16, John Savage, Sheriff of Worcester, states his accounts concerning ship money. The county was assessed at £4000, of which Worcester city was to pay £266, Evesham £84, Bewdley £70, Droitwich £70, Kidderminster £30, and the clergy £110 18s. 8d., the residue falling upon the county.

In the Exchequer Decree Book of Charles I., No. 12, fol. 230, is the record of an action brought by Sir Henry Nevill, kt., Lord Bergavenny, 31 Oct., 1631, against John Dawke, John Pearsall, and others, touching the right of toll and profits of fairs and markets in the town of Kidderminster, wherein Edward Broad, of Dunclent, testified that his Lordship's ancestors had enjoyed the said profits. Also that Sir Edward Blount, kt., to whom the manor had been let for the term of one or more lives, had given the toll corn to his servant, John Nash, who had quietly enjoyed the same above ten years, and that upon the death of Nash the defendants had gathered the toll by some agreement with Sir Edward Blount. The Bailiff and Burgesses pleaded only prescription, and confessed that they were no corporation. This confession seems to have been felt as a humiliating one, for very soon afterwards (Feb. 18, 163⅔) the Burgesses presented a petition to King Charles I. for a confirmation of their privileges and a new charter. *(Hist. MSS. Reports*, iii., 191.) The matter was referred to Noy, the Attorney-General, and upon his report he was ordered to prepare a grant of incorporation. On 163⅘, Jan. 30, the King ordered that the charter should pass as thus prepared by Noy. It was dated 4 August, 1636, and is enrolled in Patent Roll, Chas. I., pt. 2. This charter, as transcribed by Mr. de Gray Birch, fills 52 pages, and we can only give a brief outline of its chief provisions :—

"Charles by the Grace of God King of England &c.

"To all to whom the present letters shall come greeting. Whereas the Borough of Kidderminster is an ancient Borough and of great commerce for the working and manufacture of cloths and of other merchandize of divers kinds, and by reason thereof and by the confluence of many thither daily it is very populous, the upright men of which Borough indeed have for a long

THE BOROUGH. 73

time had, used and enjoyed divers Liberties, Franchises, immunities, exemptions, customs, pre-eminences and privileges by pretext alone of divers prescriptions uses and customs in the same Borough anciently used, as well in the time of our very dear late Father James of blessed memory, as in the times of our most illustrious progenitors lately Kings and Queens of this kingdom of England ; and whereas our beloved subjects now inhabitants of the Borough aforesaid have most humbly besought us . . . that we would create the upright men inhabitants therein into one body corporate and politic, and grant such liberties . . . as shall be most expedient for the public good and usefulness of the said Borough and country adjacent. . . . We therefore desiring the amendment and usefulness of the said Borough . . . and that that Borough for perpetual time to come may be a Borough of peace and quiet, and that deeds of justice and good rule therein be better kept and done . . . We do ordain that the same be and remain for perpetual time to come a free Borough *(liber Burgus)* of itself, and that the upright men and inhabitants shall for ever hereafter be one body corporate in deed fact and name by the name of the Bailiff and Burgesses of the Borough of Kidderminster . . . and able to possess lands, tenements, meadows, feedings, pastures, liberties, franchises, jurisdictions, also goods and chattels and all other things whatsoever . . . and to plead and be impleaded in courts of law . . . and have a common seal. . . . There shall be one Bailiff and 12 upright Burgesses called Capital Burgesses to form the Common Council of the same Borough . . . to have power of assembling themselves, and making from time to time such laws, statutes, rights, ordinances and constitutions as to them or the greater part of them shall seem to be good, wholesome, honest and necessary for the good rule and government of the Bailiff and Burgesses and of all and singular the officers, ministers, artificers, inhabitants and residents of the Borough, and to levy reasonable sums of money upon the inhabitants for the repair and maintenance of the bridges, streets, pavements, ways, paths and other passages. . . . Also to ordain pains, punishments and penalties, either by imprisonment of the body or by fines against offenders, and levy the same fines by distress or taking of beasts of burden, goods and chattels of every delinquent. . . . And we do nominate our beloved John Freeston to be the first and modern Bailiff of the Borough . . . and our beloved John Radford, Richard Potter, William Best, John Pearsall, Elias Artch, William Yates, Robert Greene, John Doolittle, Simon Potter, William Syner, Simon Doolittle and William Browne to be the first and modern Capital Burgesses to be continued in the same office during their natural lives, unless they be removed for badly behaving themselves. . . . Also they shall have the power of electing yearly upon every Monday after the feast of St. Michael one of the Capital Burgesses who shall be the Bailiff of the Borough for one whole year. . . . And if one of the Capital Burgesses dies or is removed then the surviving Capital Burgesses and Bailiff shall fill up the place, and he who is thus elected may have the same office during his natural life and good behaviour. . . . And further we do grant to the Bailiff and Burgesses that they may elect one discreet man who shall be called the Capital

J

Steward of the Borough, and we do appoint our beloved subject and Serjeant Ralph Clare of Cawdwell, Knight of the Order of the Bath, to be the first and modern Steward for the duration of his life. And they shall have one discreet and fitting man, learned in the laws of England, who shall be Under Steward of the Borough, and we have nominated our beloved John Wyld Esquire to be the first Under Steward. And all the Officers appointed by virtue of these presents shall be sworn, and we do give authority to our beloved Edward Sebright, Knight and Baronet, Francis Lacon, Knight, Walter Blunt and John Wyld or two or more of them of administering an oath to them upon God's Holy Gospels. . . . And we do grant to the Bailiff and Burgesses the right of appointing twenty-five men of the more honest and upright inhabitants residing within the Borough who shall be called Assistants of the Bailiff and Chief Burgesses in all affairs which concern the said Borough . . . and they may within a month of Easter appoint certain Burgesses to be Constables for one whole year. . . . And further for the better education and instruction of the children and youths within the Borough aforesaid in good arts, doctrine, virtue, and erudition, to be for ever educated and trained, of our more abundant special grace we have granted and ordained that from henceforth for ever there may be one Grammar School which shall be called the Free Grammar School of Charles King of England in Kidderminster . . . and that the aforesaid school may be of one Master and one Usher *(Subpedagogus* or *Hypodidascalus)* . . . and that the Ordinary of the Diocese of Worcester and all ordinaries and their successors hereafter, and the Bailiff and Burgesses for the time being shall be called Governors of the goods, possessions and revenues of the Grammar School of King Charles . . . and they shall be one body corporate and politic in deed fact and name . . . to have perpetual succession . . . and from henceforth for ever they may have a common Seal, and it shall be lawful for them to make anew that Seal at their pleasure . . . and the Governors shall be persons fit and in law capable to have and possess goods and chattels, manors, lands, tenements, meadows, feedings, pastures, revenues, rents, services, Rectories, tithes and other possessions for the sustaining of the said School . . . and to plead and be impleaded before our Justices . . . and they may elect and appoint one upright erudite and God fearing man to be the Master and one other discreet and fit man to be Under-Master of the same School. . . . And also we give and grant to any of our subjects free and lawful power and authority that they may give grant and bequeath manors, messuages, lands, tenements, woodland, tithes and rents to the Governors of the Grammar School of King Charles and their successors. . . . And further we grant that the Bailiff, and the preceding Bailiff for the past year, and the Under Steward of the Borough for the time being, shall henceforth for ever be the Justices of us our heirs and successors for keeping the peace within the Borough aforesaid, and for executing the Statutes made for Vagabonds, Artificers and Labourers, and for weights and measures. Provided that they shall not determine of any murder or felony or of any other matter touching loss of life or limbs within the Borough. . . . Saving however all rights and jurisdictions to

THE BOROUGH.

Henry Lord Abergavenny and to the aforesaid Ralph Clare and to all others the Lords of the Manor Town or Borough of Kidderminster and their heirs, and all other rights belonging to their courts leet and views of frankpledge. . . .

"And we do grant to the Bailiff and Burgesses all the manors, messuages, lands, tenements, fairs, holidays and markets, which anciently they held and enjoyed for corn, grain, cattle and animals, and all other things, together with tolls, tollages, customs, stallage, pickage, and all other emoluments belonging to the same fairs holidays and markets, privileges, and immunities which the Burgesses and Inhabitants of Kidderminster heretofore lawfully enjoyed . . . by reason of any Charters or Letters Patent heretofore granted by our ancestors; although they may have been not used or badly used; and although they may have been forfeited or lost. Being unwilling that the Bailiff Burgesses and Inhabitants should henceforth be molested, grieved, or in any manner attacked or disturbed by reason of the premises by us or any whomsoever the Justices, Sheriffs, Escheators, Coroners, Bailiffs or Ministers of us our heirs or Successors. Commanding by these presents the Treasurer, Chancellor and Barons of our Exchequer, the Justices, the Attorney and Solicitor General of us our heirs and successors . . . that they shall not cause any writ or summons of *Quo Warranto* or any writs or processes against the aforesaid Bailiff and Burgesses . . . before the completion of these presents. . . . In witness whereof these our Letters we have caused to be made Patent.

"Witness me myself at Banbury, on the fourth day of August in the twelfth year of our Reign.

"By writ of Privy Seal,
"WOLSELEY."

In accordance with this charter, on Dec. 16, 1640, the Bailiff and Capital Burgesses assembled at the "Court-house" and drew up by-laws and ordinances for the good government of the borough. If any one of the Twelve or Five and Twenty neglected, without sufficient excuse, to answer the Bailiff's summons to a consultation about the town matters he was to pay 5s. If any difference of opinion arose the *puisne* of the 25 was first to deliver his opinion, and then each one in ascending order of seniority, concluding with the Bailiff, after which a vote was to be taken without any disturbance or interruption. Before the next S. Thomas's-day each of the Twelve and Twenty-five was to provide himself with a comely and decent black suit, and a comely and decent Townsman's gown or black cloak to be worn upon Sundays and other festival days and all solemn meetings of the Corporation, under a penalty of 12d. for each day's neglect. On Sabbath days and festivals the Twelve and Twenty-five, in their said comely gowns, must attend the Bailiff from church under penalty of 5s.

The Bailiff and Justice were not at any time during their tenure of office to appear in the streets of the town without a comely and decent gown, cloak, or coat : forfeit 5s.

Fines were imposed upon all who refused to accept any offices to which they were chosen, viz.—Bailiff, £10 ; Capital Burgess, £5 ; the Twenty-five, £2 10s. Every burgess and inhabitant must help the Bailiff and Constables in case of affrays, and to this end must keep in his house or shop, conveniently and readily prepared, one staff, club, bill, or halbert, upon pain of 10s. for every month that it is deficient. Innkeepers must not allow any persons to use unlawful games in their houses, nor to sit tippling on Sundays or holidays or other time, by day or by night, excepting travellers only. Immediately after the beginning of the 2nd Lesson on Sunday at morning and evening prayers the Churchwardens and Constables must go out of church and make diligent search into all taverns and ale-houses. If they find there householders and men of worth they are to take special notice of them, and present them to the ordinary ; but if they be idle and vagrant persons, or of no worth and ability, they shall arrest them and bring them before the Bailiff to receive condign punishment. If any person remove soil, muck, or compost from his stables and leave it in the streets he must clear it away within six days or be fined 12d. a day. Every inhabitant must cause the street before his house to be made clean on Saturday afternoons before sunset, on pain of 12d. No one might exercise any trade, mystery, or occupation without special consent of the Bailiff and Burgesses, unless he were a Burgess or had served seven years' apprenticeship in the town : the penalty was 10s. for every market day. A fine of 20s. was incurred by anyone who entertained a stranger within his house longer than six days, unless he had licence beforehand from the Bailiff. Every Capital Burgess and innkeeper was required to set a lanthorn with a burning candle therein at his house door on every dark night from 6 p.m. to 9 p.m. from Nov. 1 to the

Feast of the Purification of the Blessed Virgin Saint Mary yearly : penalty 4d. each night.

On 11th April, 1655, it was further ordered that no inhabitants should suffer their swine to go abroad without a keeper, from St. Andrew's-day until one of the town fields was turned open : penalty 4d. each swine.

When the Great Rebellion broke out Lord Wharton's and Lord Brooke's regiments held Kidderminster for the Parliament, while Bewdley was garrisoned for the King under the command of Sir Thomas Lyttelton. In the *Paston Letters* (Report VII., p. 530) we meet with the following details :—

"1642 Oct. 19 *Sub nocte*, to Sir Wm. Paston kt. at Norwich. On Tuesday letters came from my Lord Wharton that he had made a soldier-like retreat from Kidderminster excusing his not fighting with Prince Rupert in regard of the inequallity of numbers ; but it is commonly and confidently reported by others that for haste and fear he left some waggons and 3 or 4 pieces of ordnance behind him. There came last night from Worcester 3,200 weight of plate."

This hasty retreat will perhaps account for an entry in the registers here :—" 1642 Oct. 14 buried one Thomas Kinge a pliament souldier that brake his necke fallinge downe the rocke towards Curstfield into the hollowway that leads to Beawdley." Prince Rupert's presence in Bewdley is shown in the Corporation records by a present made to him there of a hogshead of claret, costing £4 10s. In 1643 three Parliament " souldiers " were buried at Kidderminster. Another was slain at Caldwell on March the 11th, 1645, and on July 1 a woman was buried " wounded at the battle in Leicestershire." Sir Thomas Aston had an outpost at Trimpley, perhaps on the Wars-hill camp : one of his soldiers was slain Nov. 8, 1645 ; another died there in Jan., 1649. A few days after the fight at Trimpley two soldiers under Captain Dungham were killed in the town. In the following March Captain Charles Dungham and one of his soldiers were killed here on the same day. On April 19th, 1646, a soldier was buried here " slaine at the skirmish at Worcester."

In the *Hist. MSS. Reports* is a letter from Colonel Frazer, Stourbridge, June 6, 1644, offering to march between Worcester and Easum (Evesham) " where there is no other way for his

Matie to passe to Prince Rupert but through Worcester and soe to Shrewebery. No intelligence yet, but last night there appeared at Kittermaister at 12 of the clocke at night a partie of 120 horse wch threatened the inhabitants to ruine them if they sent any provisions to your Lordship's armie." On June 7th, 1644, an order was issued to all commanders, &c., in the service of the King and Parliament, to forbeare to plunder the cloth in the fulling mills in Kidderminster and Hartlebury belonging to Robert Willmott, treasurer to the committee for the county of Stafford.

After the battle of Worcester, Sept. 3, 1651, Charles II. is said to have galloped along Chester Lane, in Kidderminster, on his way to Boscobel. Many of his fugitive soldiers passed through the town. Richard Baxter says:—

"Kidderminster being but 11 miles from Worcester the flying army past some of them thro' the town and some by it. I was newly gone to bed when the noise of the flying horse acquainted us with the overthrow: and a piece of one of Cromwell's troops that guarded Bewdley Bridge, having tidings of it came into our streets, and stood in the open market place before my door, to surprise those that past by. And so when many hundreds of the flying army came together, when the 30 troopers cried Stand and fired at them, they either hasted away or cried quarter, not knowing in the dark what number it was that charged. And so, as many were taken there as so few men could lay hold on, and till midnight the bullets flying towards my door and windows, and the sorrowful fugitives hasting by for their lives, did tell me the calamitousness of war."

In 1665, March 6, coals were first brought to Kidderminster from Stourbridge by water. *(Parish Registers.)*

The Registers make mention of an earthquake here between 7 and 8 o'clock at night on Jan. 4, 167$\frac{8}{9}$.

In the 17th century there was a dearth of halfpence and farthings in the monetary circulation of the country, so many local tradesmen supplied the demand from dies of their own. In this county Worcester issued 48 varieties, Evesham 19, Kidderminster 17, Bewdley 11. From time to time these coins still turn up, and a list of them taken from Mr. Cotton's work may be of interest. Many of them have reference to the special trade of the town:—

THE BOROUGH. 79

1. O. AT . THE . RAVEN . IN=A raven.
   R. KIDDERMVNSTER . 1652=R. M. B.
2. O. THOMAS . BALAMEY . IN=The Weavers' Arms T. M. B.
   R. KIDDERMINSTER . 1667=HIS HALF PENY.
   The Weavers' Arms are : On a chevron between three leopards' faces, as many roses.
3. O. FRANCES . CARTER=A pair of shears.
   R. IN . KITTERMINSTER=F. M. C.
4. O. EDWARD . CHAMBERLIN=HIS HALF PENY.
   R. IN KIDDERMINSTER=E. A. C.
5. O. EDWARD CHAMBERLIN=A man making candles.
   R. OF . KEDERMINSTER=E. A. C.
6. O. WILLIAM . MOVNTFORD=A tankard. W. M.
   R. IN. KIDDERMINSTER . 1666=HIS HALF PENY.
7. O. LAWRENCE . PEARSALL=Arms: St. George's Cross, in the first quarter a lion's head erased.
   R. IN . KIDDERMINSTER=HIS HALF PENY.
8. O. SIMON . PITT . 1670=HIS FARTHING.
   R. IN . KIDERMINSTER=S. E. P.
9. O. WILL PRITTY MERCER=A pair of scales.
   R. IN KITTERM STER 57=W. P.
10. O. RICH . RADFORD . HIS . HF . PENY=The Weavers' Arms.
    R. OF . KIDDERMINSTER . 1666=The Merchant Tailors' Arms.
    The Merchant Tailors' Arms are : A tent between two robes, on a chief a lion passant gardant.
11. O. EDMVND & WILLIAM . READE=The Weavers' Arms.
    R. IN . KEDERMINSTER . 1666=THEIR HALF PENY.
12. O. IOHN . ROWDEN . IN=A nag's head.
    R. KIDDERMINSTER . 1656=I. A. R.
13. O. NEVIL . SIMMONS . BOOKSELR=IN KIDDER MINSTER.
    R. EDWARD . BVTLER . MERCER . 1663=THEIRE HALF PENY.
14. O. THO : SADLER . HIS HALF . PENY=The Tallow Chandlers' Arms.
    R. IN . KIDDERMINSTER . 1664=T. A. S.
    The Tallow Chandlers' Arms are Per fess and per pale, three doves, each holding an olive branch.
15. O. WALTER . THATCHER=A shuttle.
    R. IN . KIDDERMINSTER HIS HALF PENY . 1670.

In 1745 a band of volunteers was enrolled here to oppose the invasion of the "Young Pretender." Tradition says that they had set out on the march for Derby, and were a mile or two from the town when a woman in a plaid suddenly appeared at a bend in the road, and mistaking her for one of Prince Charlie's advanced guard, the volunteers were so alarmed that they hastily turned back and came home again!

In 1753 the population of the town had increased so much that Lord Foley laid out fresh streets and built 200 new houses. At this time the map was prepared by John Doharty, showing the new streets as planned.

John Howard, the famous Bedfordshire philanthropist, paid a visit to Kidderminster gaol. There were two rooms, called dungeons, about 10ft. by 6ft., under the market house, down a flight of six steps. There was neither court, water, nor sewer. The town-crier was the keeper, with an allowance of a shilling a month for attendance, and a shilling a month for straw for the prisoners' beds!

In 12 Geo. III. (1772), cap. 66, an Act was passed for the more easy and speedy recovery of small debts within the borough and foreign of *Kidderminster* :—

"Whereas in the Borough and Foreign of Kidderminster there is carried on a large and extensive Manufactory, which employs several thousand People, many of whom contract Small Debts, which in the whole amount yearly to a great Sum of Money; and although such Debtors are well able to pay their respective Debts, yet they often refuse to do so, presuming on the Discouragements their Creditors lie under from the great Expence they are unavoidably put unto, and the Delays they meet with in suing for the same . . . be it enacted that the Bailiff, Recorder, High Steward, Lord of the Manor, Justice, Aldermen, and Common Council for the Time being and the Persons herein-after named, residing or having Estates within the Parish of Kidderminster aforesaid, are hereby declared and appointed Commissioners to hear and determine all such Causes and Matters of Debt:

Rev. Robert Job Charlton LL.D	John Folliott	William Wallis
Abraham Turner	William Williams	Joseph Callow
James Johnstone M.D.	Thomas Newnham	Daniel Best
Adam Hough	William Wheeler	Richard Colley
Rev. John Martin	Rev. Job Orton	John Butler
Francis Clare	Joseph Harper	Gregory Watkins
	Rev. Benjamin Fawcett	Francis Best

VIEW OF KIDDERMINSTER, 1780
(From The Copse.)

VIEW OF KIDDERMINSTER, 1782.

(From an Old Print)

THE BOROUGH.

John Watson	John Spencer	Matthew Thomas
Pochin Lister	Benjamin Cottrell	Jeffrey Jolly
John Jefferyes	Benjamin Lea	Thomas Fry
Joseph Austin	Samuel Lea	William Banks
Joseph Lea	John Ingram	Francis Hornblower
Matthew Jefferyes	Francis Lea	John Broom, jun.
Timothy Dobson	Rev. Thomas Wiggan	Joseph Broom
Josiah Lea	William Watson	Samuel Crane
William Lea	Ralph Powell	Edward Griffiths
John Cowper	Henry Darby	John Griffiths
William Best	John Hinton	John Richardson
William Roberts	James Hilman	John Stringer
Edward Crane	Samuel Harris	Thomas Richardson
Christopher Hunt	Stephen Miles	Joseph Orton
Samuel Crane	Samuel Stokes	Thomas Jones
Serjeant Crane	John Davies	Serjeant Hornblower
John Crane	John Cartwright	Benjamin Hanbury
William Yate	Stephen Miles, jun.	William Hornblower
Thomas Crane	John Cole	Richard Colley, jun.
William Doelittle	Thomas Wright	Alexander Patrick
Nicholas Pearsall	Henry Chellingworth	Jacob Esthope
George Boraston	Joseph Hancocks	John Yearsley
Benjamin Pearce	Joseph Baker	Samuel Talbot
Nicholas Pearsall, jun.	Thomas Jones	Thomas Beck
John Brecknell	Henry Bird	Edward Bellamy
John Spencer (Hurcott)	John Newcomb	Samuel Hill
Timothy Brookes	John Read	Nicholas Penn
Thomas Woodward	Joseph Child	John Steynor, jun.
John Mole	William Taylor	Henry Penn
Matthew Wilson	Joseph Baker, jun.	Richard Barford
John White	Josiah Patrick.	Samuel Southall
Andrew Cooper	George Hallen	Samuel Evans
John Cooper	Abraham Thomas	John Pearsall, jun.
Thomas Cooper	John Pearsall	Henry Matthews
Joseph White	John Acton	John Wallis
Joseph Patrick	Henry Perrins	James Wynde

"Three or more are authorised to meet once in every fortnight by the name and stile of the Court of Requests for the Borough and Foreign of Kidderminster. Thomas Jacob White Gentleman is appointed Clerk to the Court and John Steynor jun. Beadle. Persons may sue for Debts under 40s. Nothing in this Act shall prejudice the Jurisdiction of an Ancient Court Baron held by the Lord of the Manor of the Borough of Kidderminster and his Predecessors, Time immemorial, within the said Borough."

The patriotic spirit of the Burgesses was displayed in 1798 by the enrolment of a strong band of Volunteers under Captain

Boycott: they were disbanded in 1825. The Volunteer movement was again taken up here in 1859, and there are now 280 men in the ranks, under the command of Col. W. H. Talbot, Lieut.-Col. R. T. Watson, Majors J. Morton and J. R. Goodwin, Capt. J. Watson, and Lieuts. Dixon, Mossop, Thursfield, Batten, and E. Talbot.

In 1812 wheat was 18s. and 20s. a bushel. £500 was subscribed in the town to buy potatoes for the poor.

In 1813 an Act was passed for paving, cleansing, lighting, and watching the town. In 1818 gas was introduced. In 1821, after Queen Caroline's acquittal, 3000 weavers subscribed 1s. each, and presented her with a carpet 10 yards square. In 1825 a public meeting was held to pass a vote of confidence in Wakeman and Turner's Bank. A new charter was granted to the town by George IV. in 1827. In 1828 there were serious riots, and damage to the amount of £3000 was done before the 14th Dragoons appeared on the scene. The windows of Messrs. Cooper, Simcox Lea, Best, Brinton, Hallen, and Talbot, and of the Town Hall and Black Horse, were broken. In 1832 the Reform Bill re-allotted a Member of Parliament to the town.

The *Kidderminster Messenger* was started on July 8, 1836, by Mr. Arthur Brough. The title was afterwards changed to *Ten Towns Messenger*. The paper was discontinued 30 June, 1849, and revived as the *Sun* in 1876. It advocates the Conservative side in politics, and is now owned by Mr. Joseph Mears. The *Shuttle* was started as the Radical organ in 1870, with Mr. E. Parry as editor and proprietor. It gives special prominence to all matters connected with the carpet trade. The *Kidderminster Times* is neutral in politics, and is only partly printed in the town.

By the Municipal Corporations Act, passed in 1835, the title of Bailiff was changed to Mayor, and the Council was to be elected by the popular voice. There are 18 Councillors, who hold office for three years each. The Councillors elect six Aldermen, who sit for six years. Previous to 1887 there were two wards—North and South. There are now six wards, each of which chooses one Councillor yearly.

THE BOROUGH.

The old Town Hall, which had been used for municipal purposes for some centuries, stood at the bottom of High Street, and the site is now occupied by a cab stand. The spacious and convenient new Hall was opened 19th Jan., 1877. It stands on the site of the old vicarage house, and was designed by Mr. J. T. Meredith. The older borough archives are carefully preserved in a glass case in the "Mayor's parlour." On the staircase are portraits of William Butler Best, William Boycott, and Thomas Tempest-Radford. The silver-gilt "loving cup" is a very handsome specimen of Elizabethan work, standing with cover nearly 2 feet high. The chief ornamentation consists of arabesques of dolphins and shells in repoussée work. The H.M. is 1592, and the maker's monogram A.B. The inscription runs :—" Given formerly p Thomas Jennens of Kitterminster and inlarged p his Granchild Thomas Jenens of the Citty of London Grocer A° Dni. 1623." The arms are : *A chevron between 3 gryphons' heads erased ; on a chief a lion passant.* The original donor, Thomas Jennings, was probably churchwarden in 1553. In 1542 he married Agnes Benbowe. The grandson, Thomas Jennings, married Elizabeth Edgeley, of Park Attwood, in 1602. They are both mentioned as benefactors on the boards in the chantry. The Mayor's chain and badge of office was presented to the borough in 1875, in the mayoralty of Daniel Wagstaff Goodwin. The names of the donors—former mayors of the town—are engraved on the links. A large shield in the centre bears the arms and motto of the borough, and there are also various emblems representing "Art" and "Industry." The massive silver gilt mace was presented by Mr. G. Holdsworth in the "Jubilee Year of Queen Victoria, 1887." The design is based upon that of the cup before-mentioned. The vase portion has in enamel a raised shield with the arms and motto of Kidderminster.

The Corn Exchange and Music Hall were opened 4th Jan., 1855. The Corporation Waterworks were erected in 1872. The cemetery of 16 acres was opened June 1, 1878.

To do justice to the remarkable expansion of the town in the present century would require volumes, and such a task is beyond the scope of the present work. Two views of the town taken from the same spot ("The Copse") in 1780 and 1890 will show how the meadows by Stour-side have been covered with factories, and how the town has pushed its way outward and covered the surrounding hills. Lists of the Members of Parliament, census returns, and a few local statistics may be of interest, and with these we must conclude this long chapter.

ELECTIONS OF MEMBERS OF PARLIAMENT.

(Electors: 1832—390; 1868—2465; 1874—3365; 1889—4184.)

1832—Dec.
Godson Rd. (L.C.) 172
Phillips Geo. R. (L.) 159

1835—Jan.
Phillips Geo. R. (L.) 197
Godson R. (L.C.) 121

1837—Aug.
Godson R. (L.C.) 195
Bagshaw John (L.) 157

1841—July
Godson R. (L.C.) 212
Ricardo Samson (L.) 200

1847
Godson R. (L.C.)

1849
Best John (P.) 217
Gisborne T. (L.) 200

1852
Lowe Robert (L.) 246
Best John (C.) 152

1857
Lowe Rt. Hon. R. (L.) 234
Boycott W. (C.) 146

1859—April
Bristow Alf. R. (L.) 216
Huddleston John W. (C.) .. 207

1862
White Hon. Luke (L.) 229
Talbot John G. (C.) 219

1865
Grant Albert (C.) 285
White Hon. L. (L.) 270

1868—Nov.
Lea Thomas (L.) 1272
Makins W. T. (C.) 821

1874—Feb.
*Grant A. (C.) 1509
Lea Thos. (L.) 1398

1874—July
Fraser Sir W. A. (C.) 1651
Lea G. H. (L.) 1318

1880—March 31
†Brinton John (L.) 1795
Grant A. (C.) 1472

1880—May 7
Brinton John (L.)

1885
Brinton John (L.) 2172
Godson Aug. F. (C.) 2024

1886
Godson A. F. (C.) 2081
Blunt W. S. (G.L.) 1796

* Void.   † Accepted the Chiltern Hundreds.

POPULATION.

Date.	Houses.	Borough.	Foreign.	Total.
1793	—	6,199	1519	7,718
1801	1295	6,110	1926	8,036
1811	1606	8,038	1987	10,025
1821	—	10,709	2043	12,752
1831	2768	14,981	2932	17,913
1841	—	17,500	—	—
1851	—	20,852	—	—
1861	—	15,399	—	—
1871	—	20,814	—	—
1881	4468	22,299	5376	27,675

Stourport and Lower Mitton are not included in the above figures. The progress of Stourport and the foreign may be seen from the following table:—

	Houses.	Population.		Houses.	Population.
1831 .. Stourport..	545	2952	1831 .. Foreign ..	591	2932
1881 .. ,,	684	3358	1881 .. ,,	1022	5376

The Church.

" HEARE should I begin," says Habingdon, " in thys faire churche but with the founder thereof, who appearethe in the middest of the highe and stately East window of the Quyre consistinge of seaven panes, in a long robe uppon his knees offeringe in his hand the portrature of the churche to God: neyther are we ignorant of hys name beeinge Johannes Niger de Kidderminster." We have already twice met with the name of *Niger* (pp. 21, 22), the Latin form of Black or Blake, but the owners of the name were then in a condition of villenage. The architecture of the present chancel of the church (Middle Pointed) corresponds with the date of the consecration of the greater altar by Walter de Maydeston, Bishop of Worcester *(Reg.*, f. 29), 5th June, 1315. For his fee the Bishop received four marks in the pure currency. Within a few days of his visit here the Bishop consecrated the altar of Hadsor, and the churches and great altars at Kineton and Kinwarton. It is suggestive that the Rector of Kidderminster from 1305 to 1312 was Robert Niger or le Blake, and that the chancel—the gift of John Niger—was consecrated in 1315. Possibly the work was done by a relative as a memorial of the Rector. There were also peculiar circumstances in the appointment of Robert le Blake to the Rectory, leading to the conclusion that he may have been a man of wealth ; for when the monks presented him he was a layman, and after taking minor orders at Bredon on Dec. 19th, he was instituted Feb. 12, whilst still an acolyte. At the Trinity ordination, 1306, he was advanced to the sub-diaconate with 68 others, and amongst them were three more--two of them at least of noble families—who had been holding rectories whilst only in minor orders, viz., Sir Roger Corbet, of Chaddesley Corbet, William de Dalby, of Atherstone, and Richard de Stafford, of Bela Broughton. The Diocesan Register shows that Robert le Blake was further ordained Deacon in Worcester Cathedral; and Priest at Hartlebury on the Sunday after the Feast of S. Lucy, 1306.

But there must have been a church here long before this. About 1170 we find Robert of Hurcott in possession of the Rectory; and in 1256 Richard, *Rural Dean* of Kidderminster, held his court at Broome, and gave a verdict in the suit between the Prior of Hales Owen and the Chaplain of Frankley. Moreover, the church must have been a large and important one, for in 1303 William, Bishop of Worcester, held his Whitsuntide ordination in Kidderminster parish church, and ordained 29 sub-deacons, 68 deacons, and 46 priests. Some of the sub-deacons were "villeins," who, by the Constitutions of Clarendon, could not take orders without their lord's consent, so we find appended to their names *de precepto domini*. (*Reg. Geynes*, f. 38a.)

There is nothing to guide us as to the date of the present nave and tower except the architecture. The fine old massive tower, 85 feet high, is a good specimen of the Third Pointed style, and was at first detached, but now occupies the western bay of the south aisle. The nave and aisles are rather late Third Pointed, measuring 84 feet by 62 feet, having six bays divided by channeled octagonal piers with stilted bases. On the north side are eleven square-headed clerestory windows of two lights; and on the south are eight windows, the tower taking the place of the three others. In 1464 Bishop Carpenter granted forty days' indulgence to those who contributed to the building of the parish church of *S. James*, near *(juxta)* Kidderminster. This date would suit the architecture but not the dedication of the present church—unless, indeed, there was a re-dedication at the time of the erection of the nave. For only six years later we have an entry preserved in the P.R.O. (*Pardon Roll*, 8 and 9 Ed. IV., 677, membrane 9) of a pardon granted to "John Lawcher of Kedermester clerk *alias* Sir John Lagher of Kedyrmynster clerk, *alias* Sir John Lagher perpetual chaplain of the Chapel of the Blessed Mary of Kedermynster within the churchyard of the parish church of *All Saints* of Kedyrmester &c. Feb. 5th, at Westminster." The various wills (see pp. 67, 68) refer to the church of All Saints, and it is thus designated in Doharty's map of 1753. In quite modern times the chantry of S. Mary appears to have superseded the ancient and proper dedication of the parish church.

In 1850 a south aisle was added to the chancel of good Middle Pointed character, and divided from it by an arcade of three arches with clustered piers. In 1874 an organ chamber was erected on the north side of the chancel, and the side galleries were removed. In Baxter's time there were five galleries, reduced to three in 1787; but by way of compensation the church was beautified (?) by a flat plaster ceiling, which gave way in 1850 to a panelled one. In 1887 a cloister was attached to the south side of the chancel in memory of the late Earl of Dudley, whose restoration of the chancel is thus recorded: — "In gloriam et laudem DEI honoratissimus Gulielmus Baro Ward totum hunc Chorum Instrumentumque ejus reparavit refecit et ornavit anno Incarnationis Dni MDCCCXLVII. Tua sunt omnia et quæ de manu tua accepimus dedimus Tibi."

Previous to 1850 the place of the east window was occupied by a copy of Raphael's cartoon of the Stoning of S. Stephen, which had been presented by Dr. Butt. The new east window is of six lights, and this, together with the other chancel windows, and the large Third Pointed west window, is filled with stained glass by O'Connor. The westernmost window of the north side of the nave, representing "Faith, Hope, and Charity," was given in 1889 by Mr. T. S. Bucknall in memory of his father and mother. The east window of the chancel aisle was presented by those who had been ordained "Deacons" of the church.

In 1880, June 6th, a new reredos was unveiled, from the design of Mr. Hopkins. It extends the whole length of the east window, and is executed in alabaster. The central subject

ALL SAINTS' CHURCH, KIDDERMINSTER. 1890.
(View of Tower from the South-East.)

ALL SAINTS' CHURCH, KIDDERMINSTER, 1890
(North Side.)

THE CHURCH.

is the Lord's Supper in alto-relievo, and in compartments on either side are figures of Moses and Elijah. In the chancel are three sedilia and an aumbry. A beautiful stone pulpit, having niches with figures of our Lord and SS. Peter, Paul, and John the Baptist, replaces a wooden Jacobean one, presented to the church in 1621 by Mrs. Alice Dawkes, and now preserved at the "New Meeting." The octagonal font is modern : on its sides are sacred symbols—Christ the Good Shepherd, Christ blessing little children, the Ark, the Dove, and the Lily. Looking eastward the view is very impressive, showing an uninterrupted space of 147 feet. The external length of the building, including vestry and chantry, is 215 feet.

The value of the benefice in 1288 was £20 13s. 4d.; in 1334, £25 1s. 8d.; in 1536, £30 15s. 7½d.; and in 1890, £1034 (gross) and £322 (nett). In 1774 an Act of Enclosure was passed whereby the Vicar was allowed 150 acres on Kidderminster Common in lieu of the small tithes east of Stour.

THE BELLS.

There is a melodious peal of eight bells, and on these, with four additional bells presented by the Freemasons in 1882, various tunes are played every three hours. The diameter of the tenor bell is 4ft. 5in., and its weight 1 ton 9cwt. 3qrs. 14lbs. The inscriptions on the bells are as follows :—

Treble.
The : Gift : of the Rt : Hon : Ld : Foley : A : R : 1751 :

2.
When : you : us : Ring : we'll sweetly sing A : R : 1754 :

3.
Fear God Honour the King : A : R : 1754.

4.
Peace : and : Good : neighbourhood : A R : 1754

5.
Prosperity : to this : Parish : and : the : Trade : thereof
A : R 1754

L

6.
We : were : all : cast : at Gloucester : by : Ab : Rudhall : 1754 :

7.
Non : Clamor : sed : amor : Cantat : in : urbe : Dei :

The Rev. Legh Claughton
           Designate Bishop of Rochester

Henry Toye Woodward ⎫
James Minific   ⎬ Churchwardens
Charles Bannister   ⎪ April 20 : 1867
John G. Boraston   ⎭

Tenor.
I : to : the : Church : the : living : call : and : to : the : grave : do : summon : all :

C : and : G : Mears : founders : London ;
    The Revd Legh Claughton Vicar.

Herbert : Willis : Moses : ⎫
William ; Knowles :   ⎬ Churchwardens
Joseph : Page :   ⎪ 1857
William Richd Morton ⎭

Sanctus Bell.
: Come away : make no delay : 1780

NEW BELLS.
1.
I : Taylor : and : Co : Founders : Loughborough : 1882
Redeem : the : time ; that : flies as : we : chime
                             T L Claughton Vicar

Samuel Stretton   ⎫
Harry Taylor   ⎬
Chas Bannister   ⎪ Churchwardens
Michael Tomkinson ⎪
Jas Chambers   ⎭

2.
In : Terra Pax :

3.
Gloria : in : Excelsis : Deo

THE PLATE.

The plate, as described by Archdeacon Lea, consists of three cups, three patens, a flagon, and an alms dish. The cups are of modern mediæval pattern, with the h.m. of 1849. Each of them has the following inscription in a band on the exterior:—"Calicem salutis accipiam et nome Dni. invocabo." Of the patens, two are salver patens. One of them is inscribed, "Given by Thomas Jennens of the City of London Grocer anno 1623." This paten has an interest of its own, as it must have been one of the sacred vessels of the church during Baxter's ministry. The third paten is a small one, and bears the h.m. of 1860. The flagon and alms dish are also of modern date. Round the alms dish is the inscription:—"All things come of Thee, and of Thine own have we given unto Thee." There is also a perforated spoon with the h.m. of 1796.

The following benefactions are recorded on the board in the chantry:—

"Thomas Jennings gave a Cup to be used in the Communion Service and to be carried before honest people of this town when married."

"Thomas Jennings his Grandson gave a cover and plate to the Cup."

The paten only is now left at the church. The cup and cover appear to have been lent to the Corporation. (See p. 83.)

THE MONUMENTS, &c.

The monuments of the Cokeseys, Philips, and Blounts have been described in the "Baronage." Other memorials of the dead who rest in or near the church are these:—

On a brass on north wall of chancel: William Butler Best Esq. d. Feb. 1, 1865 aged 73. He was first Mayor of the Borough.

Thomas Ingram the last surviving son of John Ingram Esq. of Ticknell near Bewdley d. 1 May 1817 aged 75.

Jacob Turner of Park Hall Esq. d. Jan. 6, 1820 aged 65.

William Lea late of Areley House Esq. For many years an active magistrate of this county b. Jan. 14, 1781 d. July 12, 1840. He married Eliza Frances Turner dr. of the late Jacob Turner of Park Hall Esq. by whom he had 8 children, who together with his widow survive to lament his loss. As Chairman of the Bench in this his native town he was laborious impartial and affable. He was of a cultivated mind and deeply read in the Sciences. Remarkable for the extent and accuracy of his knowledge, benevolent charitable, upright, and of gentle manners. As husband, father, brother, friend, beloved and respected. He died in peace Relying on his Redeemer's merits in hope of a better resurrection.

A brass tablet on the south wall of chancel aisle records the names of several members of one family :—

   Joseph Lea d. 1780. Susannah his wife d. 1781.
    Stephen Lea 1788. William Lea 1801.
  Josiah Lea 1805. Elizabeth wife of Wm. Lea 1830.
  Joseph Lea 1821. Ann wife of John Lea 1833.
   William Lea 1840. Sarah Lea 1844.
  Susanna w. of John Corrie 1851. Hannah Lea 1852.
   John Lee 1858.

On marble tablets on north wall : John Soley of Sandbourn d. Feb. 14, 1775. Elizabeth Soley d. Aug. 18, 1761 dr. of Chancellor Lloyd and granddr. of Bishop Lloyd. [Arms of Soley imp. Lloyd.]

Elizabeth wife of John Soley son of above d. Oct. 29, 1784.

Elizabeth d. of John Soley widow of Rev. Joseph Brooksbank d. Feb. 27, 1786.

John Soley of Sandbourne House d. Sept. 25, 1836 aged 69.

Joanna his wife dr. of late Sam. Skey Esq. of Spring Grove d. March 24, 1843 aged 85. [The arms of Soley imp. Skey.]

Joseph Butler draper d. 18 Dec. 1752.

John Taylor sergeant in the 4th or Queen's Own Regiment of Dragoons d. at Elvas in Portugal Nov. 14, 1809 aged 27.

Robert and Elizabeth Cooper : This Remembrance is humbly made by their 2nd son Robert in the 81st year of his age. A.D. 1731.

On an alabaster monument on south wall of chancel aisle these arms : Arg. on a fess between 2 chevrons gu. 3 mullets of the field. " M.S. Henrici Toye Bridgman, gen. qui honesta stirpe oriundus præclaram indolem feliciter expolivit, nec minus aliis vixit quam sibi : legis peritiam summa probitate, pari modestia, singulari pacis studio, ceteris demum bonis artibus ornavit ; prudens, integer, pius, suis charus, amicis jucundus, omnibus semper benevolus facilisque, post vitæ spatium cum laude merita peractum senio confectus morbo simul correptus (eheu) paralytico placide . . . agebat animam : Vir, si quis alius, desiderabilis obiit die 7 Novemb. ann. Di. 1713."

On an oval monument of white marble : " In memory of the Rev. John Martin M.A. late rector of St. Helen's and Oddingley, head master of the Free Grammar School, and near 50 years curate of this parish—much esteemed as a friend, a scholar, and a clergyman. He died 7 December, in the 73rd year of his age, 1775."

THE CHURCH.

Some other monuments, now destroyed, are recorded in Nash :—

Simon Wood d. 7 May 1725 aged 59; Ellen Wood his wife 9 Jan. 1721 aged 67.

John Farr d. Dec. 24, 1694 aged 46; Frances his wife d. Dec. 27, 1694 aged 46.

William Toye, gent. d. 28 Jan. 1728 aged 40. [Arms *Toye*, imp. ten roundels; on a chief a lion passant.]

Mrs. Frances Toye, ob. 26 Apr. 1706 ætat. 63.

Henricus Toye, gen. ob. 7 Nov. ætat. 78.

H.S.E. Johannes Reynolds gen. 7 Sept. 1710 ætat. 51. *Hic defessi quiescunt*. [Arms, 3 cocks, imp. a leg between two spears.]

Mary wife of Joseph Cox gen. d. 13 April 1727 aged 52.

Joseph Cox: he was bred an attorney, and practised near 40 years in this borough. A man so dexterous in business, and withal so faithful to his clients, that the late Lord Chancellor Talbot in a public manner from the bench declared him to be, both for ability and integrity, an honour to his profession. Born 28 Feb. 1677 d. March 1737.

Mrs. Hester Jefferys d. Jan. 8, 1722 aged 66.

Mrs. Elizabeth Spilsbury, wife of Mr. James Spilsbury d. Ap. 27, 1710. [Arms: a bend engrailed cotized a mullet in sinister chief.]

Capel Hanbury Esq. d. 14 Jan. 1704 in his 79th year. [On a bend a star.]

Kal. Maii 1676 febre obiit Simon Degge filius unicus ex conjugatis Sim. Degge Equ. et consiliario insigni, et Alicia uxore verè Christiana.

William son of Thomas Cox, late Rector of Market Orton, Rutland, d. 4th May 1715 aged 51.

Hic situs est sub spe resurrectionis Adamus Hough generosus; ob. 26 Apr. 1681 ætat. 78.

Elizabeth wife of Adam Hough gent. who died 20 June 1731 aged 54; and Adam the son of Adam Hough and Elizabeth his wife, d. 9th Feb. 1731 aged 18.

Edvardus fil Joannis et Eliz. Cotton, ob. 18 Sept., 1688.

William Brittol 14 March 1711 aged 79. Sarah his wife 25 May, 1703.

Mr. Thomas Crane of Haberley, d. Nov. 1, 1728 aged 48.

Thomas s. of Edward Burton minister of Shrawley d. Nov. 20, 1689 aged 2.

John Penn late of Trimpley, d. 31 March 1729 aged 25.

Dorothy wife of William Waldren minister d. Aug. 26, 1662.

H.S.E. Reverendus Joannes Best; Scholæ Kederministeriensis per 30 plus annos archididascalus, ad seros usque posteros, mortuus licet, vivendi recte magister futurus; vir antiquæ fidei, et pietatis simplicis; mores ne ipsa unquam incusavit calumpnia: Doctrina sibi soli semper visa est parvula: Charitatis vix plures audivere famam quam senserunt fructum; hanc autem singularem sibi laudem potuit vendicare, nisi in eo omnia essent singularia, quod spretis mollioris vitæ otio, utilioris questu, difficilem docendi provinciam quam juvenis nactus est non deseruit senex; obiit 7 die Augusti A.D. 1729, ætatis suæ 59.

John his eldest son was buried in St. Edward's chapel in the University of Cambridge Apr. 13, 1726 aged 18 years.

In the churchyard: "Here lie the remains of Mr. William Greaves, citizen and weaver of London, whose generous endeavours for the benefit of the trade of this place procured him esteem while living, and his death sincerely lamented. . . . He died 28 July 1725, aged 52. His mother Mrs. Elizabeth Greaves Sept. 17, 1729 aged 89."

Mr. John Spilsbury, an eminent dissenting minister d. Jan. 30, 1727, aged 60. Mr. Matthew Bradshaw his son-in-law and successor d. 4 Nov. 1742 aged 42.

Tradition says that the grandfather of the great Lord Somers was buried near the cross in the churchyard.

THE CHANTRIES.

There were formerly three chantries connected with the mother church of Kidderminster. Towards the end of the thirteenth century the cult of the Virgin Mary received a great impetus, and "Lady Chapels" were founded extensively in England. In 1305 we have the first presentation of a chantry priest to the chapel of the Blessed Mary of Kidderminster *(Reg. Geynes.)*, which appears to have been built in the churchyard *(infra cimiterium)*, a few yards to the east of the church. The present building was restored or built by Simon Rise in the early part of the sixteenth century, and after the suppression and confiscation of the chantries in 1549, it was used as a Grammar School. In 1848, when the new Grammar School was built at Woodfield, the chantry was improved by Lord Ward, and given back to the Church for parochial uses. On the north wall is a rude inscription :—" Here lieth Simon Brotherton Belman Buried June ye 17th 1628." On the same

THE CHURCH.

wall may still be seen shot holes made by the bullets of the Parliamentary army.

The chantry priests, according to *Nash*, were as follows :—

PATRONS.	PRIESTS.
Sir John Byset, Lord of Kidderminster, with the Community of the whole Borough	Robert de Ryppel, 2 Id. July 1305
	William Bacoun, 4 March 1347
Hugh de Cokesey	John Symondes de Grafton, 22 Nov. 1349 John de Feckenham, 13 Oct. 1350
Dionsia de Cokesey	Philip Belenger, 14 Dec. 1358 Henry de Penne, 1 April 1365
Maculinus Delamare	John Hankys, 5 Jan. 1391 John Pottare, 10 Jan. 1395
	William Malpas, 12 May 1400
Sir Wm. de Beauchamp	Brian Ricardes, July 1403
Joane Beauchamp, Lady Bergavenny	William Snagge, 15 April 1420 John Westbury, 23 Aug. 1422 Robert Scrivener, 4 May 1424
Anna, Lady Bergavenny (wife of the "Kingmaker")	William Hill, Sept. 1435
The Bishop (jur. dev.)	Thomas Gilbert, 3 June 1446
Lady Joyce Beauchamp, sister and heir of Sir Hugh Cokesey.	John Lawher, 5 April 1468
	Thomas Strynger, 21 April 1469
Joyce Beauchamp, widow	William Wakeman, 29 March 1473
Sir John Grevil	John Notynham, 30 Dec. 1479
Sir John Mortymer, Thomas Jenyns, Bailiff, William Colsell, and other more worthy parishioners of the Church of Kydermyster	Nicholas Wright, 27 June 1499
Sir Edward Grevil, cousin and heir of Sir John Grevil, son and heir of Joyce Beauchamp.	Roger Charouse, 26 May 1515
King Henry VIII.	William Tomyns, 6 June 1542

The chantry of the Assumption of the Blessed Virgin Mary in the chapel of Trimpley, within the parish of Kidderminster, was founded by Sir John Atwood in 1370. The ancient family of Atwood, de Bosco, or Boys was seated at Wolverley as early as Henry III. In 22 Edw. I. (1294) Peter Sebright granted to John de Bosco one parcel of land in Kidderminster. In the time of Edw. I. or Edw. II. Edmund de Luttelton (ancestor of Lord Cobham) married Lucia daughter of John de Bois,

(Collins' *Peerage*, vii., 420.) Robert de Bosco had the wardship and marriage of John de Beauchamp, son and heir of Richard de Beauchamp, late Lord de la Holte (died 1327), and in right thereof presented to the church of Holt Jan. 27, 1329.

John Boys had the Bishop's licence to celebrate divine service in his oratory or private chapel at Wode Acton, Wolvardle, and Trympeleye for a year, Jan. 19, 1357. The same Sir John built the chapel of Trimpley, and founded the chantry, and gave one messuage and one virgate of land, 4 acres of meadow, and 4 acres of wood in Trimpley, and one messuage and one virgate of land, with rent and reversions, at La Lee, in the manor of Wolverley, Friday after S. Mark, 44 Edw. III. (1370). By another charter, dated Wolverley, Sunday after feast of S. Ambrose, 46 Edw. III. (1372), he gave 40s. of silver yearly rent out of land in Rusholte (Rushock), which John de London then held, to William de Pedmore, chaplain of the chapel of the Blessed Mary of Trimpley, and his successors, who shall celebrate divine offices therein for ever. If the chaplain exercise traffic, tavern keeping *(tabernas)*, or frequent any plays *(ludibria)* or unlawful shows *(illicita spectacula)* for three months, another must be presented in his room. He must reside in the house in the churchyard, and shall have a clerk to assist at mass at his own charge. The books, vestments, ornaments, &c., are to be found by Sir John and his successors, who shall keep the chapel and house in repair.

Sir John Atwode was buried at Wolverley 15 Rd. II. (1392), and John Beauchamp, son of Sir John Beauchamp, of Holt, was found to be next heir.

The incumbents of the chantry were these :—

Patrons.	Priests.
Sir John Atwode	William Pedmore, 10 Feb. 1381
John Atwode..	William Pranke, 3 Aug. 1450
Sir Walter Skull	{ William Lincroft, 18 Dec. 1456 { Richard Barbour, 31 March 1467
John Atwode..	James Pyry, 20 April 1501
The King, by reason of the minority of Francis Inglefield.	William Churchley, 12 July 1543

The rentals and other particulars of these chantries, as recorded in 1549, will be given later on. The chantry house was occupied by the late incumbent in 1549, but before Habingdon's time it was "levelled with the soylle." Its situation is indicated by the following record:- "On Saturday after the feast of S. George the Martyr 16 Hen. VII. John Gyldon of Kyngeslowe parish of Worfield conveyed to Richard Eugeley of Trimpley and Julia his wife, Thomas Pope and David Maddocks, half a yard-land, lying near to the Chapel of the Blessed Mary of Trimpley, called *Gyldons* with the grove below." The "Gyldons" still appears on the parish ratebook.

The chantry of S. Katharine was founded by Lady Joyce Beauchamp *(née* Cokesey) in 1469, and occupied the easternmost bay of the south aisle. The tomb of the foundress is built into the wall under an arch within pillars of stone of very elegant design. The work was sadly mutilated during the Puritanic *régime*, and the heads of the saints and angels have nearly all been knocked off. Roger Chance was incumbent in 1549.

The chantry of S. Katharine, with rents in Habberley and Trimpley, was granted to Robert Thomas, Merchaunt Taylor, and Andrew Salter, Esq., for £1142 5s. 3½d. on 10 March, 4 Edw. VI. *(Patent Roll,* part 4.)

Thomas Reve and John Herdson, 15 May, 4 Edw. VI., for £1572 4s. 5½d. get charity lands, including tenement and mill belonging to the chantry in Kidderminster. *(Patent Roll,* 4 Edw. VI., part 7.)

Cecilia Pickerell, widow, obtains 25 August, 4 Eliz., lands called our Lady's lands and All Hallows lands, in tenure of the churchwardens, being given to superstitious uses. *(Pat. Roll,* 4 Eliz., pt. 3.) The same Cecilia obtains 6 February, 5 Eliz., the grant of a close in Kidderminster in the tenure of William Ferne, and a blade mill in the tenure of Thomas Lamb; also chapel lands. *(Pat. Roll,* 5 Eliz., pt. 5.)

William Grice, Esq., and Anthony Forster, on 18 September, 6 Eliz., obtain grant of a half-virgate of land called the Deanes, and two closes of land on either side of a lane near the two

Yates, in the tenure of Thomas Agborough, and a cottage. (*Pat. Roll*, 6 Eliz., pt. 4.)

There was afterwards some dispute about this property, for among the Corporation deeds is a re-lease by Roger Maunsell, of Pedmore, to Edward Blounte, of Kidderminster, of one half-virgate, called Le Deanes, two closes on either side of a certain lane near to the two "Les Yates," &c., a meadow called Trinity Moore, that whole mill called a blade mill, &c. "And I will warrant the above premisses to Edward Blount against certain Bartholomew Buckesbie, John Walker, William Grice, Anthony Foster, Cecilia Pickerell, and any one of them. Feb. 11, 1576."

Inventory of church goods, 6 Edw. VI. (Public Record Office: *Exch: Q. R.* $\frac{2}{10}$) :—

This Inventory Indented of all the plate Belles and ornaments belonging to the same made and presented to the kyngs Maties Commysoners the ixth day of August Anno Edwardi Sexti sexto by Willyam Spyttell curatt Willyam fferne and Thomas Bocher Thomas Jennyns and Robert Clerk Churchwardens

In primis hangynge in the Steple iiij Belles

Item on Sannct Belle

Item ij chalyces of Selver with Patens

Item on peyre of great Candelstyckes wth ij peyre of lytle candelstyckes all of brasse

Item on lampe of brasse

Item xij Copes of sundry colours some of velvett and some of Sattin

Item vi peyre of Vestments with theyr suets lackynge iij amyasses of lyck as the Copes be

,, ix towells

,, iij Crasses of Coporas

,, ij Censers of Coporas

,, on holy water pott of brasse

Item theyre ys a Chappell belongynge to the said churche called mytton
In which theyr is on challis of Silver with a paten

Item on payre of Vestments of sylver beyinge old

Item on Cope motley colors not sylke

Item ij Belles

J. Russell   William Spytull
Wm. Sheldon   Curatt
George Watt

THE CHURCH.

Mem. There is a parcell of land in Kethermynster aforesaid which is employed to the mayntenance of one ye irly obyte within the sayd paryshe churche of Kethermynster valewed by yere at iiijs

To the poore owt of the said obyte xx*d*

[In P.R.O. *(Patent Roll,* 12 Jas. I., part 2) is a grant made 9th Feb., 1612, to George Low and another of a parcel of land in the tenure of the churchwardens given for an obit in Kidderminster. Also *(Pat. Roll,* 14 Chas. I., pt. 7) Sir Edw. Sawyer, kt., obtained a meadow situated at Netherton, in Kidderminster parish, given for an obit in the Church of Hartlebury.]

 2 Edw. VI. (P.R.O. Calendar of Certificates of Chantries 25. 29—; 60. 19—; 61. 15)

 The Paryshe of Kyderminster wherein be the number of DII hundred houselyng people

 Chauntry B.V.M. Wyllyam Tommyns Incumbent of the age of three score and twelve years learned and of honest convsation

 Yerely value viilib xviiis iid

 Plate—none. Goodes—none. Prechers—none. Scole—none

 Poore iilib Clere viilib xviis viiid

 Mem. the said Sir William Tommyns is Vycare of the paryshe of Kethermynster and his Vicarege or benefice is valued to be of yerely worth xxxlib

 Chauntry of St. Kateryn. Roger Channce Incumbent of the age of fourscore yeres competently learnyd and of honest conversacon

 Yerely value viiilib viis vid Wherof in repryses xxviiis iid ; clere vilib xixs ixd

 Plate—none. Goodes psed at iiis ivd. Prechers—none. School—none. Poore iilib

 The Chauntry of our lady within the Chappell of Trympley beyng two myles dystant from the sayd paryshe churche—Willyam Churchley Incumbent of the age of fortie and foure yeres learned and of honest conversacon

 Yerely value xlib xvid wherof in repryses viiis iid Clere ixlib viiis iid

 Plate—one challis gilte in the custody of Sr Robert Acton Knyght weighing vii *unz*.

 Goodes prised at xs Prechers—none. Scole—none. Poore iilib

A HISTORY OF KIDDERMINSTER.

Rental of all lands lately held by the Chantry of the Blessed Virgin Mary.
(*Aug. Off. Misc. Books*, vol. 374.)

Margaret Wylde, lands &c	12d.	Humphrey Mydlopp	6s.	2d.
Dominus Blunt	20d.	Michael Hetylson	8s.	0d.
Thomas Costin	4d.	Thomas Butler	5s.	0d.
William Jennyns	4d.	John Tomyns	8s.	0d.
Gilbert Clare	12s. 10d.	Eleanor Garnett	10s.	0d.
Thomas Dolyttle	4d.	John Mundye	3s.	0d.
Thomas Gyll	6d.	Alice Smith	1s.	8d.
Henry Dawke	6d.	John Tyllyatt	11s.	8d.
Anthony Wood	20d.	John Burnynson	9s.	0d.
Richard Brotherton	2s. 2d.	Humphrey Mydlop	..	10d.
Robert Wynter	15s.	Thomas Agborough	7s.	2d.
John Cergen	20d.	John Thurston	3s.	0d.
John Standishe	£1 13s. 4d.	William Tomyns	2s.	0d.
William Wakeman	6s. 8d.	Sum	£7 14	6
John Complayn	20d.			

Rentals of Trimpley Chantry.

	£	s.	d.
From Anthony Wood in Rushock Parish	2	0	0
Gilbert Clare		1	0
James Apen	2	0	0
Ramyston pasture: John Whyston	2	6	8
R. Longmore		10	4
Est hamsley: R. Pytt		10	0
Great lentall: William Fearn		12	0
Little lentall: R. Bocher		10	0
The Leeys, Wolverley: John Byrd	1	3	4
The Chantry House, in the occupation of the late Incumbent		8	0
Sum	£10	1	4

Payments:—

	s.	d.
To Henry, Lord Abergavenny for rent from Ramyston	1	11
John Earl of Warwick for rent	10	0
Dean and Chapter of Worcester	5	5

Rentals of S. Katharine's Chantry.

	s.	d.
Robyns Ground in Haberley by Thomas Pope	5	0
John Juke		4
Thomas Blonte for Blonte Meadow		4
Edward Gryffyn, Habberley	5	0
Humphrey Channce ,,	5	0
Thomas Cooke ,,	3	0
John Hurtyll ,,	8	3
Richard Bocher ,,	3	2

Near the Bridge, Richard Ibery	..	..	..	2	1	4
Ye Lake, John Serg ant..	..	:	..	..	4	0
Ye Lake, William Ferne ..	..	..	..	..	1	8
Hale Street, Edward Townclarke	..	..	..	5	0
Wyldlyes, Trimpley : Rd Fewsterell	..	..	..	6	8
„ „ Humphery Channce	..	..	3	4
Leonard Egeley					6	0

Payments :—

					£	s.	d.
To Henry Lord Abergavenny	..	..	..	..	1	2	8
Sir Richard Lygon..	..	..	..	..	..	4	0
Thomas Grey, Armiger	..	..	..	..	..	1	6
John Earl of Warwick	..	..	..	one pound of pepper

There was a Chauntrye of our Ladye in Kethermyster the particulars whereof we delivered to the Erle of Warwick.

Also Trimpley to the Erle of Warwick.

Irrotulantur.

THE "PROCESS" OF THE CHURCH OF KYDERMINISTRE.

(As Narrated by the Monks of Maiden Bradley.)

"The Lord Manser Biset, founder of the Convent of Leprous Women of Bradley, conferred the church of Kyderministre on the Convent of Bradley after the death of Robert de Hurecote the parson then living :—

"Know all men present and to come, that I Manasser Biset, Dapifer of Henry King of the English have granted in perpetual alms to the Lepers of Bradley the Churches on my Manors after the decease of their Parsons, to wit, the Church of Kokebourne by the assent of Henry Bishop of Winchester after the death of Crispin ; and the Church of Kyderministre after the death of Robert de Hurecote by the assent of Roger Bishop of Worcester. Wherefore," &c.

Next follows the full text of charters, confirming this gift, by (1) Henry Biset, son and heir of Manser, (2) King Henry II., and (3) Roger Bishop of Worcester (1164—1180). The monks were impatient of the delay in getting possession, so in the episcopate of Henry de Soilli (1193—1196) they persuaded Robert to resign on a pension of 100s. They then presented Master Adam to the *perpetual Vicarage*, and required him to pay the 100s. to Robert, the former Rector, and 100s. to *themselves*. The Dean of Kydeministre inducted them into possession of the temporalities of the church, and has left us this memorial of the fact :—

"To all the sons of Holy Mother Church to whom this present writing shall come, Calixtus Dean of Kydermini-tre, Health in the Lord. Know all of you, that at the Mandate of Mauger the Bishop (1200—1214) I have admitted the Leprous Sisters of Bradley, by Andrew their Procurator, into corporal possession of the parsonage of the church of Kyderministre. And that this may be known at all present and future times, I have appended my seal. Witnesses: Richard Chaplain of Kydeministre, Robert Chaplain of Wlferdesleia (Wolverley), Laurence Chaplain of Chedestre, Walter Chaplain of Stanes (Stone), Philip Chaplain of Mytton, Robert Deacon of Chedesleia, Robert de Chedeston, Roger Deacon of Kyderministre, Thomas, Sacristan of Kyderministre, Hamon Clerk, Hugh Spiringe, and many others."

" By and bye, when the said Adam the Vicar went away, the Prior Brethren and Sisters of Bradley presented a certain Master Robert to the vacant Vicarage ; and John Biset, son and heir of the said Henry Biset, lord of the manor of Kyderministre, presented a certain other person. But when this dispute had continued beyond six months, Lord William de Bleys (1218—1237), then Bishop of Worcester, as if by lapse, presented the church to Master Thomas of Upton ; and by the title of a perpetual benefit, he ordered the *Rector* to pay the convent 20 marks yearly." Archbishop Stephen Langton, the famous champion of the English Church and liberties, issued a charter confirming this benefit of 20 marks.

" Afterwards the said John Biset, who unjustly disputed the right of patronage of the church, ceased from strife, and remitted in writing his claim to the Convent of Bradley. But, nevertheless, when the above-mentioned Rector, Thomas of Upton, died, the same John Biset presented a certain Roger de Essex to the church of Kydermestre, and in spite of the Prior's objection, he was admitted and instituted to it. However, Walter [Cantilupe] Bishop of Worcester assigned to the Lepers certain tithes in the parish by his charter, given at Kemsey in 1241." In place of the annual rent of 20 marks, he assigned the Convent all the tithes of corn and hay on the western side of the parish between Severn and Stour, excepting the tithes of the vill of Mytton, and the tithes from lands held in fee by the Burgesses of Kidderminster. If any new land was taken into cultivation the tithes were to go to the mother church. John Biset, Roger de Essex, and the Prior and Chapter of Worcester severally confirmed this arrangement.

"But when the Lord John Biset was dead, the Lady Alicia Biset, his wife, was dowered with the whole manor of Kidderminster, together with the advowson of the church; and she, after the death of Roger de Essex, presented Master John de la Mare to the whole portion which his predecessor had held, and the Bishop admitted him. And for a long time the Prior Brethren and Sisters went to law with him both in England and in the Roman Court, before various Judges, as is shown by several writings in the treasury of the Convent. At length the litigation was settled by the mediation of friends, and concord was made in the presence of E. Dean of Wells and Osmund Canon of the Blessed Mary of Warwick, the Auditors appointed by the Apostolic See, May 12, 1266. [The proceedings touching the said lawsuit, together with a Bull of the Lord Pope Urban IV., with letters and commissions of H. Bishop of Ostia and Wells, and other instruments and sealed letters, are in the treasury.]"

"Afterwards, when Alicia Biset was dead, the manor and advowson descended to three co-heiresses of the Lord John Biset, namely, to John de Rivers *(Ripariis)*, son and heir of Margery, the eldest daughter of John Biset, and Margery's two younger sisters, Ela and Isabella, who renounced all their right in the advowson of the church to their nephew, John de Rivers, for an annual rent of 2 marks; and he confirmed the advowson to the convent in perpetual alms."

On the death of John de la Mare, Master William de la Lade was presented; and in a full Chapter of the Deanery of Kidderminster, held at Elmele-Lovet on Wednesday next after the Octave of S. Michael, A.D. 1276, attended by the Rectors, Vicars, and Chaplains of that Deanery, it was found that the said William was legitimate, of free condition, of good report, and of honest conversation. After an incumbency of four years William died, and John de Ubeton was inducted into corporal possession of the church by Robert de Leth, his proxy, at Kidderminster, March 9, 1280.

In 1305 John de Ubeton vacated the living on his appointment to the church of Berewyke, in the diocese of Salisbury, and his successor was Robert le Blake, whose character was approved in a Chapter held in the chapel of Belne Broicton (Belbroughton).

The next Rector was John de Carsleghe, 1312, in whose time the present chancel was built, and the greater altar of the church consecrated.

"During the lifetime of Master John the Rector, Henry de Frome, Prior, diligently examined all the records of the above-mentioned lawsuit, and after deeply meditating as to how the ancient advowson, so negligently and unjustly lost, could be recovered, he sent his fellow-Canon, William de Chiwton, to the Roman Court with a petition in the form which follows:—

"To the most holy Father our Lord the Pope, the Prior brethren and sisters of the Convent of leprous women of Maydene Bradeley of the order of S. Augustine make their supplication. By their simplicity and ignorance in presenting divers secular persons to the church of Kydermenstre for the space of 40 years and more they have lost the appropriation which at one time had been justly made to them, and they entreat that their ancient right may be restored to them by the authority of the Lord Pope. For on account of the number of guests flocking to their House, because it is situated near the King's Highway close to the Forest of Selewode, and by reason of the frequent dearths, and the grievous murrain of their cattle, and the various exactions and unfair procurations with which they are burdened, they have been reduced to such great poverty that they cannot support the bréthren serving God there, and the sisters miserably languishing under the disease of leprosy."

By means of the above petition the said William, the Prior's nuncio, obtained one Bull "de Bonis," and another "Of the Intrusion of the Rector," which are as follows:—

"BULL 'DE BONIS.'

"Benedict Bishop [Benedict XII 1331] Servant of the servants of God to the Venerable Brother the Bishop of Worcester health and Apostolic benediction. It has come to our hearing that our beloved Sons the Prior and

THE CHURCH.

Convent of Maydene Bradeley and their predecessors have granted tithes, rents, lands, vineyards, possessions, houses, cottages, meadows, pastures, granges, woods, mills, rights, jurisdictions and certain other property to the heavy damage of the said Priory * * * And because it is of importance that we should provide a suitable remedy for this, we command your Fraternity to recover for the Priory all their alienated property, notwithstanding all letters, instruments, oaths, renunciations, and penalties: by compelling all gainsayers with ecclesiastical censure, the right of appeal being withheld. And if any witnesses shall withdraw themselves by favour, hatred or fear, you shall compel them by a like censure to bear testimony to the truth Given at Avignon April 5th, in the first year of our Pontificate."

"BULL 'DE INTRUSIONE RECTORIS.'

"Benedict Bishop, Servant of the servants of God, to the Venerable Brother the Bishop of Worcester, health, grace, and apostolic benediction. Our beloved Sons, Henry the Rector, commonly called Prior, and the brethren of the Convent of leprous women of Maydene Bradeley have complained to us, that although the Church of Kydermenstre has been canonically united to the Convent, and they long and quietly held the same: nevertheless John de Carsleghe priest of the diocese of Worcester by his rashness has intruded himself into the said Church, and seized upon it, and still occupies it, to the prejudice and injury of the said Prior and brethren. Therefore we order your Fraternity by apostolic writings, to summon the parties and to hear the cause, appeal being removed, and make a suitable decision, causing what you decree to be firmly observed under penalty of ecclesiastical censure. Given at Avignon April 1, in the first year of our Pontificate."

This visit of William de Chiwton to Avignon 556 years ago led to a serious alienation of the property of the church here which has never been recovered, and it gives us a glimpse of the encroachment of the Bishop of Rome in the internal affairs of England. In the fourteenth century nearly all the Bishops of Worcester owed their position to Roman influence, and of course supported his pretensions. Edward III. was only 21 years of age when William de Chiwton procured the Bulls in favour of the Monastery; but as the King's power became consolidated he refused to be a slave to the Court of Rome, and it was rendered penal to procure any presentations to benefices from Rome, and every person who carried any appeal to the Pope was outlawed. In 1393 the statute of *Præmunire* was passed, severely punishing any one who at Rome or elsewhere procured processes, bulls, &c.

As soon as Simon Montacute received the Pope's Bulls, he proceeded to act upon them by converting the Rectory of Kidderminster into a Vicarage. After "sufficient, diligent, frequent, and solemn deliberation" with the Prior and Chapter of Worcester Cathedral, he issued a commission to William de Logwardyne, Rector of Hartlebury, and the Dean of Kidderminster to make an inquisition into the value of the living, as well by the clergy as by twelve laymen of the parish of Kidderminster, "worthy of trust and sworn." The jury thus summoned have left us the following interesting particulars :—

"They say that the House of the Rector of Kydermenstre at Hurkote, with the demesne lands, fish ponds, and dove cot, is worth per annum 40s.

The Rents of the said Rector with the labour of the Natives (villeins) of Hurkote are worth 58s. 3d.

The Rent of Pepper and Cummin . . 12d.

Hay from the demesne of the said Rectory 30s.

The Heather is not sold, but may be taken for Hous-bote.

The Mill of Horkote .   20s.

Pleas and Perquisites . . . 18d.

The Tithe of Rye *(Siligo)* of the said Church 30 quarters value 100s. at 40d. a quarter.

The Tithe of Barley—20 quarters, value 60s. at 3s. a quarter.

The Tithe of Beans—half a quarter, value 2od.

The Tithe of Oats—12 quarters, value 20s., at 20d. a quarter.

The Tithe of Hay is worth in common years 26s. 8d.

The Tithe of Wool—£4.

  ,, ,, Lambs—13s. 4d.
  ,, ,, Calves—12d.
  ,, ,, Cheese—12d.
  ,, ,, Apples—2s.
  ,, ,, Flax—13s. 4d.
  ,, ,, Onions—13s. 4d.
  ,, ,, Garlic—2s.
  ,, ,, Pigeons—3s. 4d.
  ,, ,, Little Pigs—10s.
  ,, ,, Hawks—3s.
  ,, ,, Game—2s.
  ,, from the sale of Wood, nothing, because it is included in the Pleas.

THE CHURCH.

The Obventions of Wax per annum 30s.
Oblations of the Altar   ,,   £4.
Proceeds of the Lenten Roll ,,   66s. 8d.
From Milk, Peter's Pence, and the Tithe of Curtilages nothing, because they appear on the Lenten Roll.
Live Mortuaries   .   20s.
Dead Mortuaries . . .   6s. 8d.
Dovecots near the Churchyard 13s. 4d.
Tithes of the Fisheries at the Stakings, 2s.
Tithes of Honey, 3s. 4d.
Eggs at Easter, 3s. 4d.
Herbage in the Churchyard 12d.
Wheat at Easter, one strike, 5d.
Tithes of the Mill of Kydermenstre, 2 quarters, 8s.
Of Tol-corn 2 quarters, 6s.
Of "capital" malt, half-a-strike, 3½d.
Of "cursal" malt, 4 quarters, value 10s. 8d.
Tithes of the Mill of Sandulbourne (Sandbourne) for certain, 2s.
Tithes of the Mill of Mytton half a quarter of Wheat, value 18d., and 6d at the Feast of the Lord's Nativity.
Tithes of the Mill of Caldewell for certain 12d.
Rents of the Altar, coming from Affemor (Offmore), 5s.
From Tithes of Pannage, 12d.

The Sum of the true Value of the Fruits and Profits of the Church of Kydermenstre £38 6s. 1d.

Obventions and Profits of the Chapel of Mytton in the same Parish.

Tithes of Corn *(Frumentum)* in common years, 2 qrs., value 8s.
Tithe of Rye *(Siligo)*, 5 qrs., 16s. 8d.
Tithe of Barley, 3 qrs., 9s.
   ,,   of Beans, Peas, and Vetches, 21d.
   ,,   ,, Oats, 6 qrs., 9s.
The Altarage there, with the live and dead Heriots, which are ordained for the service of the Chaplain, 53s. 4d.

The Sum of the true Value of the Chapel of Mytton £4 18s. 9d.
The Sum Total of both Church and Chapel £43 4s. 10½d.

But the necessary Expenses of the Church and Chapel aforesaid, and of the Rectory of Kydermenstre consist in the following payments :—

The Stipend of the Parochial Chaplain, who receives per annum 66s. 8d.
The Stipend of the Secular Chaplain, 50s.
The Stipend of the Deacon, 20s.
The Archdeacon's Procurations, 7s. 5½d.
Peter's Pence, 3s. 4d.
Sevagium (?), 2s.
Wax for the Chancel Lights, 5s.
Oil for the Chancel Lamps, 20d.
Incense, 3d.
For Straw for the Church, three times a year, 12d.
For Repairs of the Chancel, 3s. 4d.
For finding one Peroferum, if it is wanted } 53s. 4d.
For the Stipend of the Chaplain celebrating at Mytton }
Also for Autumnal Expenses in collecting the corn and hay at Horkote 50s.
For collecting Fruits at Mytton, 6s. 8d.
For providing Corn for the Eucharists, and Blessed Bread on Easter Day, 2s. 10d.
For Wine for the whole year, including Easter Day, 20d.

The Sum of all the things required, £13 15s. 2½d.

Also the Tenth to be paid for the same Church on its taxation of 31 marks, supposing it to run continuously, amounts to £2 1s. 4d.

The Sum Total of the Ordinary and Extraordinary Burdens £15 16s. 6½d.

And the additional annual Burdens which the Prior and Convent of Maydene-Bradeleghe have taken upon themselves, after they shall have obtained peaceful possession of the said Church, are these :—

An annual Pension of one mark to the Lord Bishop of Worcester and his successors for ever.

Also another annual Pension of one mark to the Chapter of Worcester Cathedral.

Also the large and small tithes coming from the Woods of Trympeleye and Eymor, which have been granted to the said Chapter, in recompense for the emoluments which they might have received during the vacancies of the church, if this appropriation had not been made, 20s.

Sum Total of old and fresh Burdens £18 3s. 2½d.

And thus the Church, with Mytton Chapel, when the said burdens are deducted, is worth in common years £25 1s. 8d.

THE CHURCH.

The Obventions and Tithes which the Religious were accustomed to receive before the Appropriation, from a time previous to which memory does not exist, are these:—

Tithe of Corn, 16 qrs. 64s.
Tithe of Rye, 40 qrs., £6 13s. 4d.
,, ,, Barley, 12 qrs., 36s.
,, ,, Beans, Peas, and Vetches, 1 qr., 3s. 4d.
,, ,, Oats, 40 qrs., 66s. 8d.
,, ,, Hay 19s.

Two Cart-loads of Hay from the Meadow called Eymores-meadow, 4s. 4d.
One Cart-load of Hay in Stonhammes-meadow, 2s. 2d.
Two Cart-loads from the Meadow called Pokeles-mor 4s. 2d.
One Horseload from Suttones-meadow 4d.

Total £16 13s. 4d.; from which is to be subtracted the Expenses of carting the said tithes 56s. 8d.

And thus their portion is worth, nett £13 6s. 8d.

May the Most High preserve you for long ages for the Government and support of His church.

Given and done at Kydermenstre Feb. 10th A.D. 1335."

On receiving this report Simon Montacute, Bishop of Worcester, drew up a lengthy "Ordinance of the Vicarage," of which the following is an outline:—

"To all the Sons of Holy Mother Church &c. greeting.

"We Simon, Bishop determine in this wise. The Vicar shall have for his dwelling house one suitable Manse near to the south side of the Church in which the Parish Priest *(Parochialis Presbiter)* was accustomed to reside, together with the Dovecot close to the churchyard, and the grass growing in the churchyard. Also 12 acres of arable land belonging to the church viz. Bondecroft (3 acres), the Helde lying towards Comberton (2 acres), Colvercroft adjoining the churchyard (2 acres), Dodeleghes-croft near Whytmers (3 acres), and one croft near Uppe-medue (2 acres). The Vicar shall also have the tithe of hay coming from the three hamlets of Agberewe, Comberton, and Heathy; also the tithes of milk, cheese, chickens, calves, little pigs, falcons, pigeons, bees, wax, honey, apples, flax, hemp, onions, garlic, of gardens and curtilages with whatsoever seed they are sown, of feedings and pastures; also of woods *(boscorum)*, of fallen timber, of pannage, game *(vivarii)*, fisheries, ponds, eggs; also of the mills now within the parish viz. Kydermenstre, Sandelbourne, Mutton, and Caldewell and of those which shall be hereafter erected, the mills of the Rector only excepted. He shall have all mortuaries, dead animals, and tricennials, and all oblations whatsoever within the parish; moreover the whole altarage of the Chapel of Mytton with the living and dead heriots, the tithes of lambs, wool, and all other smaller tithes of the same chapel; and the Lenten offerings which have from ancient times been inscribed on the Lenton Roll, and all the smaller tithes of the whole parish.

"SAVING TO THE CONVENT all the tithes of lambs, wool, and hay except those already mentioned, and the living mortuaries, as also all smaller tithes whatsoever coming from the manor of Oldington, and from the Court of the Rectory of the church, when it shall have come into their hands by reason of this appropriation: also the tithes from woods *(silvis)* and trees; and the smaller tithes from the parks of Trymple and Eymor, which we have lately conceded to our church of Worcester.

"The Vicar shall have the rent of 5s. due to the altar of the church proceeding from Affemore (Offmoor) and the Easter wheat. He shall officiate by himself or suitable ministers in the Church of Kyderminstre and the Chapel of Mytton. He shall provide the Archdeacon's procurations, Peter's Pence, the Synodal rents, and all other taxes except the one mark due to us, and the one mark to be paid to the Prior and Chapter annually: which payment, and the charge of littering the church with straw at the usual times, we wish to pertain for ever to the Religious. But the Vicars shall provide the lights in the chancel, the bread, wine, and incense, books and ornaments at their own expense. The reparation or rebuilding of the Chancel shall pertain to the Convent.

"For their better memory and observance we have caused these our present letters to be written in triplicate and confirmed by our own seal and that of the Brethren and Sisters of Maiden Bradley: one to be kept in the treasury of our church at Worcester, one to be in the custody of the Religious, and the third to remain with the said Vicar and his successors for ever.

"Given at Bredon 2 Ides April A.D. 1336."

"But as time went on the Venerable Lord Symon Bishop of Worcester abovementioned was translated to the See of Ely, and the religious man Lord Wolstan Prior of Worcester by the grace of God was raised to the Bishopric. Master John de Carsleghe Rector of Kidderminster died, and after his death the Prior and Convent immediately were solemnly inducted into corporal possession of the church by the Venerable Official of the Archdeacon of Worcester, as is more fully seen by his certificate." The certificate is dated at Kidderminster on Thursday the Feast of S. Margaret the Virgin, A.D. 1340.

"As soon as the Prior and Convent were thus inducted, they forthwith presented Sir John de la Doune to the perpetual Vicarage in the portions assigned by the aforesaid Ordinance:

and he immediately after dinner, after the induction of the Prior and Convent, was inducted to the presentation of this kind.

"When these things had been done and graciously completed, the said Sir John de la Donne, like an ungrateful man *(quasi homo ingratus)* after peaceful possession of his said Vicarage, when only a short time had elapsed, raised a quarrel about the insufficiency of his Vicarage to support the burdens laid upon it. And this he did by the advice of the clergy, the bishop, and his other friends, and especially of his parishioners, who perchance desired easy rents *(pingues redditus)* for their own advantage, especially because the Vicar resided personally among them. So at length the Prior and Convent, as if compelled by necessity and for the sake of peace, were obliged to consent to a new ordinance of the said vicarage."

The bitter feeling then so widely prevalent between the parish clergy and the monks is expressed in an old carving now on the pulpit of Ribbesford church, but at one time forming part of the rood screen. A fox habited as a monk is preaching to a congregation of geese : some of the silly birds have already been captured, and are sticking out from the cowl at his back.

Wolstan Bransford (1339—1350) was one of two Bishops of Worcester (out of 14) who were elected in the fourteenth century without papal interference ; and it is evident from the monkish historian's confession that his sympathies were with the parish clergy against the encroachments of the Convent. Under his auspices the following more favourable appropriation was obtained :—

"The Vicar and his successors for ever should have the whole manor of Horkote where the Rectors formerly were accustomed to reside, with its buildings, lands, heriots, and everything pertaining to the said manor ; also all the fruits, profits, oblations, and tithes great and small which Master John de Carsleye the last Rector had held.

"EXCEPTING the tithes of sheaves and hay proceeding from the lands and meadows between Stour and Severn ; and the tithes coming from the Convent's demesnes of Ohlynton and Borelassch ; and the tithes from all land newly brought into cultivation between Stour and Severn and containing less than one acre which are commonly called Burgaieries; and all tithes from the Parks of Trympele and Eymour already conceded to the Prior and Chapter of Worcester.

"But the Vicar and his successors must every year pay to the Convent 20 marks of silver of good and legal money in their manor of Oldynton, and one mark to the Bishop and one mark to the Prior of Worcester. The Vicars shall likewise pay the tenths and procurations of the Cardinals and Legates and Nuncios of the Apostolic See, and all other taxes and burdens on the Church, together with repairs of the Chancel up to 40*d.* per annum. But if the reparation or rebuilding of the Chancel happens to exceed 40*d.* it is the duty of the Convent to pay it.

"And if at any time the Vicar shall be in arrears with his payments (which God forbid!) the Monks may sequestrate his goods wherever found in the diocese of Worcester; and they may re-enter his manor of Horkote and distrain on all goods and cattle found therein, and may drive them off and shut them up in their manor of Oldyntone until all arrears, damages, and expenses have been fully satisfied.

"And immediately after institution the Vicars shall swear corporally upon the Holy Gospels of God that they will pay the 20 marks and other dues faithfully every year at the place and times appointed.

"Sealed in the Chapter of Maiden Bradley 11th Dec. 1340.

"John de la Doune agreed at Hertlebury 14th Dec. 1340.

"The Bishop affixed his seal at Hertlebury 18 Dec. 1340."

The narrative, which has hitherto carried us on without a break from Henry II. to Edward III., a period of nearly 200 years, here ends abruptly; and for the next two centuries, ending with the final repudiation of the Pope's authority over the English Church, we have only scraps of information derived for the most part from the Diocesan Registry. With the growth of wealth and luxury in the monastic orders, the Scriptorium appears to have been neglected, and all our later information from the chartulary refers only to rents and leases. Much, however, might be written on the condition of the country 555 years ago, as revealed by the exhaustive valuation then made of the income of the Rectory. We notice the extensive cultivation of flax, an article absolutely necessary before the introduction of cotton. The only vegetables grown were onions and garlic. All the apples in the parish were valued at only 20*s.* per annum, while pears are not even mentioned. Sugar was unknown: honey was its substitute. Wool was the most valuable commodity of the realm, and supplied the main portion of the King's revenue. There is some difference of opinion as to the correct rendering of *siligo*, or (as it is written in the original of William Coton's Will, page 67) *sigolum*. Hale gives it as "very white wheat, winter wheat"; but Du Cange considers it synonymous with the French *seigle*, rye, and this latter view is strengthened by the return of 18 qrs. of wheat *(frumentum)*, at 4s. a quarter, in addition to 75 qrs. of rye *(siligo)*, at 3s. 4d. a quarter. It was cheaper than wheat. By multiplying the tithes by 10 we get a rough agricultural return of the average produce of the parish, viz., wheat 180 qrs., rye 750 qrs., barley 350 qrs., beans, peas and vetches 20 qrs., and oats 580 qrs. Some portions of the district are still known as the ryelands.

In 1399, May 12th, Richard II. claimed the presentation of the church, and ordered Tideman Bishop of Worcester to institute John Brugge or Bridges. This was one of the last legal (?) acts of the tyrannical King, settled just before he started for Ireland; and one of the first acts of his successful rival, Henry IV., was to restore the patronage to Maiden Bradley, 23rd Nov., 1399. Bishop Tideman appropriated the Vicarage again on 14th April, 1401. Another ordinance of the Vicarage was made by Richard Clifford, Bishop of Worcester, 13th April, 1403. The Vicar was to provide "bread and wine for the communion of the Parishioners, processional candles, incense, the lights necessary for the morning masses and other canonical hours to be celebrated daily in the choir, and one lamp burning before the great altar in the church of Kydermynstre."

LIST OF VICARS.

Appended will be found a list of 44 Vicars of Kidderminster in a continuous succession for more than 700 years. Of a few of them we get some further details:—

JOHN WITHERS was M.A. and Proctor of Oxford University 1491, and was made Doctor of Canon Law by papal bulls. On 3 July, 1513, he supplicated to be incorporated as

D.Can.L. of Magdalen. In *Modern Wilts*, pp. 103-106, is an exemplification of proceedings between the Prior of Maiden Bradley and John Wythers, Vicar of Kidderminster, concerning an annual rent of 5 marks issuing out of the church of Kidderminster, with a judgment for the Prior and Convent, Mich., 21 Henry VII. His name is not recorded in *Nash*.

RICHARD JENYNS disp. at Oxford 13 Dec., 1515.

WILLIAM PYKENHAM, PIKNAM, or PYGNAM, Oxford B.C.L., sup. for B.Can.L. 15 Nov., 1508; for D.Can.L. 27 June, 1509; 15th June, 1510, disp. 30 May, 1511, 5 Nov. 1516. *(Oxford Hist. Soc.)*

JOHN HARLEY, sup. for B.A. July, 1536, adm. 5 July, det. 1537, disp. Mar., June, Dec., lic. for M.A. 4 June, 1540, inc. July, of Magdalen. He was born at Newport Pagnel, and was elected Fellow of Magdalen about 1537. He was Rector of Upton-on-Severn, Vicar of Kidderminster (1550—1553), and Prebendary of Worcester. Wood says that he was tutor in the Duke of Northumberland's family, and a preacher at Oxford against the Romanists in the reign of Edward VI. Leland praises him for his virtues and learning, especially in classical authors, for his fine vein of poetry, &c. On May 26, 1553, he was consecrated sixty-seventh Bishop of Hereford at Croydon. Queen Mary deposed him from his See on account of his being married, and he died in obscurity about 1557.

ALEXANDER CREKE was chaplain to the Duke of Northumberland (father-in-law of Lady Jane Grey), at whose request he was presented to the Vicarage by Sir William Cecil. *(Domestic State Papers, vol. xv.)*

THOMAS WILLOUGHBY or WYLLOBY, sup. for B.A. Jan., 153⅜, adm. 30 Apr., disp. Feb., 153⅜, because he is going to take holy orders, det. in Lent, sup. for M.A. 17 Feb., 153⅜, lic. 3 May, 1539, inc. and disp. 7 July. (Oxford.)

RALPH SMITH, sup. for B.A. 12 June, 1567, lic. for M.A. 24 March, 157¼. (Oxford.)

THE CHURCH.

JOHN ODELL, sup. B.A. 5 Nov., 1584, lic. M.A. 1596. (Oxford.) The burial ground adjoining Mytton chapel was consecrated during his incumbency, Nov. 13, 1625.

GEORGE DANCE was appointed in 1627 by Sir Edward Blount, whose choice was far from being a happy one. Baxter in one place speaks of him as "a weak and ignorant man, who preached only once a quarter," and also as a "frequenter of ale houses;" but to Bishop Morley he admitted that he was a "man of unblameable life and conversation, though not of such parts as would fit him for the care of so great a congregation." He resided in the Vicarage-house, on the site now occupied by the Town Hall. The Sir Rowland Hill statue, Messrs. Brinton's works, the Bank buildings, &c., stand on ground once forming part of the Vicar's garden. The " Swan " has taken the place of the old Tithe Barn. During the vigilant administration of Archbishop Laud, a "terrey" of the church property was made, which is of interest when compared with the earlier " ordinances " of 1335 and 1340 :—

"An Inventory or Terrey of the Gleebe Lands, Howseinges Tyethes, and Priviledges belonginge to the Vicaridge of Kidr

"To all true Christian People to whom this present Inventory or Terrey Indented shall come to be seene, reade or understoode George Dance Clerke Vicar of Kidderminster sendeth greeting in Our Lord God everlastinge, That Whereas the Right Reverend Father in God William by God's Providence Lord Archbishopp of Canterbury, Primate and Metropolitan of all England at his Metropolitan Visitation holden within the Dyocese of Worcester Anno Dni 1635 and in the Eleventhe Yeare of the Reigne of our Sov^n Lord Charles by the Grace of God of England Scotland Fraunce and Ireland Kinge Defender of the Faith gave forth unto his Clergy of that Dyocese certayne Articles or Interrogatoryes amongst wch. one was for the giveing in an Inventorye or Terrey of all such lands of any sorte as they or any of them together with theire Churchwardens and Persons of Credytt coulde fynde to be Lande Areable, Leasowes, Meadowes or Pastures, Commons or other Commoditys &c. and the same in Parchment fayerly written should deliver unto the Principle Register of the Byshopp of Worcester under their Handes subscribed.

"Know Ye that I the said George Dance together with Humfrey Pagett James Heminge Thomas Hurtle William Garmson Churchwardens Elias Artche and John Pearshall High Baylyffs of the Towne of Kidderminster have taken veyue and survey of all the sayd lands &c. as the same heretofore hath bin had and used reputed and taken beyond the memory of man and soe continued unto the Day of the date hereof. Inprimis the Mansion Howse of the Vicaridge contayninge eight Bayes or thereabouts, one Howse over agst the sayd Vicaridge used for a Barne and Stable contayninge syx Bayes. And of Gleeb Landes as followeth viz. the Churchyard, one Acre and a halfe or thereabouts, the Whytmarsh called Dudlesse Grounds being fyve Closses twelve acres or thereabouts, the Pasture called Culvercroft contayninge twoe Acres or thereabouts, the Bryckfield the Barne Closse, the little Meadowe between the Barne and the Brick field containing 7½ acres, the longe Meadowe adjoininge to the Bryck feild syde 2 acres, one Akre of Arrable land beinge in Leaswall feild, one Garden belonging to the Vickaridge and a little spare Ground on the back syde of the Vickaridge Howse.

"There is alsoe a Chappell at a Towneshipp called Nether Mitton in the sayd parish wch doth belonge to the sayd Parish Church of Kidr with Glebe Land belonginge to the same which is annexed to the aforesayd Vickaridge wch. hereafter followeth viz. the Chapell Church Yard containeing one Akre, the Chapell Hill containinge 12 acres of Arrable Land, in the Church fild a peece of eareable land conteininge 4 acres in the same field, at Newland Gate one acre, in the Wall field at the Middle hedge three parcels of ear- rable Land contayninge 4 acres, in old follow one peece of earrable land 2 acres, one Meadowe called Priest's Meadow contayninge 2 acres with a Tenement to the same contayninge one Bay and half two parcels in the Cow Pasture called the Leigh containing 3 acres, one parcell of Meddow in the upper end of the Lampytt next to the Hedge, ½ acre. In Tythes and Tenths as followeth of all manner of Corne and Grayne from the Ryver of Stower unto Dearne Foarde, Allsoe the Tythe Hay of Mytton wth. all other Tythes here underwritten throughout the psh of Kidr. All the Tythes of Woods (except the Woods of Mayden Bradley and Eymore Parke) and of fyshe, of wool, lambs, pyggs, geese, pidgeons, eggs, fruits, hempe, flax, onions, garlick, honey, hoppes, mills, for Servants Wages and Craftsmens Hands, allsoe Herbage and Joycements, for the Milke of a Cowe a Penny; for every Calfe sould the tenth penny, for every calfe reared a half peny, for the fall of a colt a penny, a Garden Penny, for every Sheep sould between Michaelmas and the Annunciation of the B. V. Mary a halfe peny, and from thence till Sheare tyme a penny, of every Parishioner a Communicant, communicate at Easter 2d., the dutyes of Weddings, Buryinges, and Purifyings as are accus- tomed, and Mortuaries, all which Premisses are now in the possession of the sayd George Dance Vicar or of his Assignes. There are alsoe certayn other Groundes mentioned in a Terrey dated 1588 as belonginge to the Vicaridge of Kidr viz. the Meadow called Pyntolatchett Meadowe 2 acres, one parcel of earrable land called the Healde lyinge above the Worcester Crosse con- taininge 2½ acres, one little meadow between the Vicaridge Howse and Stower and enclosed with the Vicaridge Brooke contayninge ½ acre, which 3 parcells are now and have byn in the handes of other men from before the tyme of the said George Dance his Institution. In Witness whereof &c. Dated 14th day of January 11 Charles Anno Dni 1635"

THE CHURCH.

After 13 years' ministry the Vicar offered to allow £60 per annum to a Curate, to be chosen by 14 of his parishioners, and on 5 April, 1641, the famous Richard Baxter was legally appointed. During the Civil Wars in 1646 Dance was deprived of his benefice, but was allowed to live in the Vicarage, with a pension of £40 a year. At the Restoration he sent in a petition (*Rep.*, vii., p. 121), 23 July, 1660, setting forth that about 14 years since he had been sequestered out of his Vicarage for his allegiance to his late Majesty, and praying that he might have the benefit of the order for detaining the tithes in the hands of the churchwardens and overseers. He was soon reinstated, and held the living till his death in 1677.

RICHARD BAXTER was for 14 years *quasi* Vicar of Kidderminster, and his name and fame will ever be associated with the town. His biography is national rather than local, and has been so fully illustrated by his own Narrative, and by Calamy, Orme, Sylvester, Long, Bates, Fawcett, Davies, Dean Boyle, &c., that only an outline need be given here. He was born at Eaton Constantine, in Shropshire, 12 Nov., 1615, and was educated first at Wroxeter School, and afterwards by the Rev. Richard Wickstead, Chaplain to the Council of the Marches at Ludlow Castle. His education was of a somewhat desultory character, and he did not study at any university. His chief delight was in logic and metaphysics and controversial divinity. In 1633 he was introduced to Sir Henry Herbert, of Ribbesford, Master of the Revels, with whom he lived about a month at Whitehall; but a Court life was not to his taste, and he returned to Shropshire. About 1638 Mr. Thomas Foley, of Kidderminster and Stourbridge, built and endowed a new Grammar School at Dudley, and offered the Head Mastership to Baxter, who was then ordained at Worcester by Bishop Thornborough, and preached his first sermon in the upper church at Dudley. A year afterwards he removed to Bridgnorth as Curate to the Rev. William Madstard, who had been Incumbent of St. Anne's, Bewdley. On 5 April, 1641, he was appointed Curate of Kidderminster church, "and thus," says he, "I was brought by the gracious providence of God to that place which had the chiefest of my labours, and yielded me the greatest fruits of comfort." About the end of 1642 a Parliamentary order was issued to deface images of the Trinity and pull down the crosses in the churchyards. The townsmen were indignant at this iconoclasm, and Baxter deemed it prudent to retire for a time, during which he acted as Chaplain to the Parliamentary army. In 1647 he lived in retirement, chiefly at the house of Sir Thomas Rouse, of Rouse-Lench (and the Hall, Kidderminster), where he had a serious illness. Here he commenced his greatest book, *The Saints' Everlasting Rest*, which he finished and published while at Kidderminster in 1650. He lived in the old house in High Street, of which the lower part has been modernised, but the upper part (and especially the attics) has been left untouched. About 60 of his 168 published works were issued during his residence in Kidderminster, including *The Call to the Unconverted*, *The Reformed Pastor*, and *The Saints' Rest*. The latter work was dedicated to his " Dearly Beloved Friends, the Inhabitants of the Borough and Foreign of Kidderminster," Jan. 15, 1649. The second edition was published in 1651, and a copy of it was presented by the author to the High Bailiff of the town, and has ever since been most carefully preserved among the Corporation archives. The inscription on the fly leaf, in Baxter's own handwriting, is as follows :—" This Booke being Devoted, as to the service of the Church of Christ in generall, so more especially to the Church at Kederminster; the Author desireth that this Coppy may be still in the custodye of the high Bayliffe, and intreateth them carefully to Read and Practice it, and beseecheth the Lord to blesse it, to their true Reformation, Consolation, and Salvation.—Rich. Baxter." Many of his works were " Printed for Nevil Simmons, bookseller in Kederminster," whose " halfpenny" was issued in 1663 (page 79, No. 13), and who afterwards settled in London and continued to print for Baxter. In the chancel of the parish church is an old oak chair with inscription carved on the back, " Rev. Rd. Baxter born nr. Shrewsbury in 1615 and died at London in 1691. Chaplain to King Charles II. Rev. T. Doolittle M.A., Sr H. Ashurst Bt., Kidderminster A. 1650 D." Baxter speaks of " Mr. Thomas Doolittle, born in Kidderminster, a good schollar, a godly man, of an upright life and moderate Principles, and a very profitable serious Preacher." To Sir Henry Ashurst, Bart., Sylvester dedicated his *Reliquiæ Baxterianæ*, 1696. He also stood by Baxter in the day of his trial and distress, paid the fees for his six counsel, and when the trial before Judge Jefferies was over, led Baxter through the crowd, and conveyed him away in his coach. He was also Baxter's executor, and it is possible the chair may originally have belonged to him. *(Bradley.)* The pulpit of the parish church in use in Baxter's time is preserved at the New Meeting. There is an oil portrait of him in the vestry of the church, and another, dated 1691, in the vestry of the Old Meeting. The paten used in Baxter's time is still at the church, and it seems probable that the Jennings cup at the Town-hall was used by him at the Holy Communion. There is apparently nothing in the Parish Registers in his own handwriting, and most of the marriages, &c., were taken by his assistants, Thomas Baldwin and Joseph Read. There is one solitary exception :-- " 1659 Aug. 15th. Thomas Woodward and Mary Richards were joined in marriage by Mr Richard Baxtar minister." In holiness of life, intense earnestness, devotion to duty, obedience to conscience, untiring diligence, and loyalty to his Master, Richard Baxter has few equals. " Once started as an author, he literally poured out book after book—great folios, thick quartos, crammed duodecimos, pamphlets, tractates, sheets, half-sheets, and broadsides." *(Nat. Biog.)* His works would make nearly 40,000 closely-printed pages! His theological opinions, however, were unique, and he has left behind him no distinct class of followers. " He opposed Calvinism ; he opposed Arminianism ; he would not allow himself to be considered an Episcopalian in the ordinary sense of the word ; he denied that he was a Presbyterian ; and scorned to be thought an Independent." *(Orme.)* With John Tombes, the leader of the Baptists, he had a famous dispute in Bewdley church, before a crowded congregation, lasting from 9 o'clock in the morning till 5 o'clock at night. In his pastoral work in the town he was eminently successful. He preached once every Sunday and once every Thursday. On Thursdays he held an evening meeting of his parishioners, when one of them was called upon to repeat the sermon, and another to pray. In the early part of his ministry he catechised in church, but afterwards two days in each week were devoted to private catechising, he and his assistant taking fourteen families between them. " On the Lord's day there was no disorder to be seen in the streets ; but you might hear a hundred families singing psalms and repeating sermons as you passed through them. . . . Yet many ignorant and ungodly persons there were still among us ; but most of them were in the *parish* and not in the town. And whereas one part of the parish was impropriate and paid tithes to laymen, and the other part maintained the church, a brook dividing them, it fell out that almost all that side of the parish which paid tithes to the church were godly honest people, and did it willingly without contestation, and most of the bad people of the parish lived on the other side. . . . Three or four of my neighbours managed the tithes for me, of whom I never took account ; and if any one refused to pay his tithes, if he was poor, I ordered them to forgive it him. After that I was constrained to let the tithes be gathered as by my title, to save the gatherers from law suits. But if the parties were able, I ordered them to seek it by the magistrate, with the damage, and give both my part and the damages to the poor ; for I resolved to have none of it myself that was recovered by law, and yet I could not tolerate the sacrilege and fraud of covetous men. When they knew that this was the rule I went by, none of them that were able would do the poor so great a kindness as to deny the payment of their tithes. . . . It much furthered my success that I staid still in this one place near two years before the wars, and above 14 years after ; for he that removeth oft from place to place, may sow good seed in many places, but is not likely to see much fruit in any, unless some other skilful hand shall follow him to water it." At the Restoration Baxter was offered the Bishopric of Hereford, which he refused. He asked only to remain at Kidderminster ; but Dance was still legally Vicar, and could not be removed except by his own consent. The King and Lord Clarendon both favoured Baxter's wish, but his impatience of all ecclesiastical authority led Bishop Morley to refuse to grant him even a licence to the Curacy. In his parting address to his flock he advised them " to keep to the public assemblies, and make use of such help as might be had in public, together

RICHARD BAXTER OF KIDDERMINSTER
(From an Old Print)

with their private prayers." To this he made three exceptions: when the preacher "set himself to make a holy life seem odious," or "preached heresy," or "was utterly insufficient." After leaving Kidderminster he went to London, and preached under licence of Bishop Sheldon. He refused to comply with the Act of Uniformity in 1662, and retired to Acton, in Middlesex, where he wrote many books. In the same year he married Margaret Charlton, daughter of a Shropshire magistrate, who was residing with her mother in Kidderminster. His excellent wife, much younger than himself, died in 1681, and he then wrote a touching "Breviate" of her life. The intolerant spirit of the time twice led to his imprisonment. On the latter occasion he was tried for sedition, before Judge Jefferies, who grossly insulted him, as described so graphically by Macaulay. He went to his rest Dec. 8th, 1691, and was buried in Christ Church, London. A beautiful statue by Brock, placed in the Bull Ring, was unveiled by Mrs. Philpott 28th July, 1875, when addresses were delivered by Dean Stanley and the Rev. Dr. Stoughton. [A full account of "Baxter in Kidderminster" was contributed by the Rev. E. Bradley to the *Leisure Hour*, August, 1872.]

RICHARD WHITE was instituted 18 Oct., 1677. "A census of the parish taken at this time returned 1587 Churchmen, 8 Papists, and 14 Nonconformists—which looks as if the inhabitants had taken Baxter's parting advice and contented themselves with the ministry of the Church." Mr. White was the author of "The Reward of Christian Patience, as it was discovered in a Sermon preached at the Funeral of Mr. Thomas Baldwin, a Nonconformist Minister of Kidderminster, 1693."

GEORGE BUTT was son of Dr. Carey Butt, physician, of Lichfield, and was born 26 Dec., 1741. He was educated at Stafford Grammar School, then on the foundation at Westminster 1756, and thence elected to Christchurch, Oxford, where he graduated B.A. in 1765, M.A. in 1768, and B.D. and D.D. Oct., 1793. He was ordained to the Curacy of Leigh, Staffs., in 1765, which he resigned for the post of private tutor to the son of Sir E. Winnington. In 1771 he was presented to the Rectory of Stanford and Vicarage of Clifton, and in 1773 married Martha Sherwood, daughter of a London silk merchant. In 1778 he was presented to the Vicarage of Newchurch, Isle of Wight, which he afterwards exchanged for Notgrove Rectory, Gloucestershire. In 1783 he was appointed Chaplain-in-Ordinary to the King. In 1787, on the application of Dr. Markham, his old master at Westminster, he was appointed by Lord Foley to the Vicarage of Kidderminster, which he held along with his other cures. He took up his residence in the town, but in 1794 returned to Stanford, and used to ride into Kidderminster to take the services. On 30 June, 1795, he was struck with palsy, and died on 30 Sept. following at Stanford, where he was buried. He left a son, John Martin Butt, who took orders, and became the author of some theological works, and two daughters, both well-known authoresses, Mrs. Cameron and Mrs. Sherwood. Dr. Butt published *Isaiah Verified*, 1784; several Sermons on special occasions; in 1791, *Sermons*, in 2 vols.; in 1793, *Poems*, in 2 vols., dedicated to the Hon. George Annesley, afterwards Lord Valentia, one of his former pupils.

ARTHUR ONSLOW was born 30 Aug., 1746. He was son of Lieut.-General Richard Onslow, and nephew of the Right Hon. Arthur Onslow, for thirty years Speaker of the House of Commons. He went from Eton to Exeter College, Oxford, from which he was elected a Fellow of All Souls. In 1770 he was ordained Deacon, and in 1772 married Frances Phipps. In 1774 he was presented to the living of St. James', Garlick Hithe, and next year was appointed Chaplain to the House of Commons. In 1779 he was made Canon of Christchurch, and in 1782 he was nominated to the Curacy of Maidenhead. In 1785 he was collated to the Archdeaconry of Berks. In 1795 Mr. Onslow succeeded Dr. St. John as Dean of Worcester, and in the same year was instituted to the Vicarages of Kidderminster and Wolverley. He resigned Kidderminster in 1801 to his eldest son, Archdeacon R. F. Onslow. When he was instituted to the Vicarage of Lindridge in 1811, he also resigned Wolverley. He died at Lindridge 15 Oct., 1817, and was buried in the crypt of Worcester Cathedral. He left three sons, Richard, Arthur, and Phipps; and three daughters, one of whom was married to the Rev. E. Winnington Ingram.

THOMAS LEGH CLAUGHTON gained the "Latin Verse," "Latin Essay," and "Newdigate" prizes at Oxford, where he graduated B.A. (First Class Lit. Hum.) in 1831. He was Fellow of Trinity College and Public Examiner (1835-6). In 1841 he was presented to the Vicarage of Kidderminster by Lord Ward. The population of the borough at his coming amounted to 17,000, with only two clergymen and two churches. There were no daily services, and no services on Saints' days. One "railful" of communicants was considered a large number. To ask "Who was the meekest man?" was considered sufficient preparation for confirmation. High pews, galleries, and whitewash disfigured the fine old church. Scarcely a response was heard except the clerk's, and sprigs of holly were stuck in each seat for Christmas decoration. Church membership was scarcely understood, and there was but little intercourse between different classes. There were occasional "Charity Sermons," but the privilege of Christian almsgiving was little realized by Churchmen. It is not cause for wonder that many of the earnest men and leading families of the town were Dissenters. Whatever we may think of the "Oxford movement" doctrinally, we cannot shut our eyes to its influence in raising a truer conception of reverence and solemnity in the worship of God, and in arousing the feeling of individual and corporate responsibility and of self-denial for humanity. Under Mr. Claughton's able administration a new era was begun in the Church life of the parish. Baxter's influence 200 years before had had great results, but he had to deal with a population of which all the adults could be gathered into the parish church at one time. The population had now been allowed to grow far beyond the church accommodation, and most vigorous exertions were required to grapple effectively with the spiritual destitution. For twenty-eight years the work was unweariedly and successfully carried on; and when the life of Dr. Claughton is written, his labours in Kidderminster will form not the least valuable part of it. As with Dr. Hook at Leeds, his active parochial work drew to his side a band of earnest helpers, who longed to learn the spirit and power which animated it. Among the Curates of the parish may be mentioned some well-known names:—A. Blomfield (Bishop of Colchester), W. Walsham

How (Bishop of Wakefield), Hon. A. G. Douglas (Bishop of Aberdeen and Orkney), W. R. Churton (Senior Fellow of King's College, Cambridge), G. D. Boyle (Dean of Salisbury), Hon. George Herbert (Dean of Hereford), Hon. H. Douglas (Vicar of St. Paul's, Worcester), A. E. Seymour (Archdeacon of Barnstaple), H. J. Fortescue (Vicar of St. George's, Leicester), C. Warner (Vicar of Clun), B. Gibbons (Vicar of Stourport), A. C. Thynne, W. W. Douglas, A. L. Peel, T. L. Inge, W. F. Wilberforce, J. S. Chesshire, &c. In 1867 Dr. Claughton was consecrated Bishop of Rochester, and when in 1877 the new See of St. Albans was formed, he became its first Bishop. He married the Hon. Julia daughter of William tenth Baron Ward, and has several children, one of whom is Duchess of Argyle.

GEORGE DAVID BOYLE was of Exeter College, Oxford, B.A. 1851. He was ordained to the Curacy of Kidderminster in 1853, and remained four years. After three years' Curacy of Hagley, he was appointed (1861) to the Perpetual Curacy of St. Michael's, Handsworth. In 1867 he came back to Kidderminster as Vicar, and for 13 years carried on most efficiently the work inaugurated by his predecessor. As an expert in educational matters he rendered great service to the town in his capacity of Chairman of the School Board during the first years of its existence. Mr. Boyle was also an examiner in several branches of H.M. Civil Service. In 1880 he was promoted to the Deanery of Salisbury. He is the author of *Sermons ; Confession according to the Rule of the Church of England ; Lessons from a Churchyard ; The Trusts of the Ministry* ; *My Aids to the Divine Life ;* and *Richard Baxter, a Sketch.*

THOMAS LEGH CLAUGHTON was son of the Bishop of St. Albans, and nephew of the Earl of Dudley. He graduated at Oxford in 1871, and was ordained in 1874 to the Curacy of Ashbourne. From 1876 to 1880 he was Vicar of St. Mary, Kingswinford, which he left on his appointment as Vicar of Kidderminster. In 1886 he was made Canon of Worcester, and in the following year he resigned Kidderminster and accepted the poorer parish of St. Andrew, Worcester.

SIDNEY PHILLIPS, the forty-fourth Vicar whose name is recorded, is of Brasenose College, Oxford, and was ordained in

THE RIGHT REV. THOMAS LEGH CLAUGHTON, D.D.,
FIRST BISHOP OF ST. ALBANS
VICAR OF KIDDERMINSTER 1841-1867

THE CHURCH.

1864 in Kidderminster church. He was for three years Curate of Newland, and afterwards held in succession the benefices of Castle Hedingham, Essex, Monmouth (1875-79), and Nuneham Courtney, Oxon. In 1887 he succeeded Canon Claughton at Kidderminster.

PATRONS.	RECTORS.	Date of Induction between
Manser Biset	Robert	1164—1180
Prior and Convent of Maiden Bradley (jur. dev.)	Adam	1200—1203
Bishop William de Blois (jur. dev.)	Thomas de Upton	1218—1237
John Biset	Roger de Essex	1241
Lady Alicia Biset	John de la Mare	1265
Convent of Maiden Bradley.	William de la Lade	1276
" "	John de Ubeton	1280
" "	Robert le Blake	1305
" "	John de Carseleghe	1312
	VICARS.	
" "	John de la Doune	1340
" "	Thomas Payne	1362
" "	John Porter	....
King Richard II.	John Brugge	1399
Convent of Maiden Bradley.	Thomas Malle	1402
" "	William Sutton	....
" "	William Baker	1420
" "	William Mountford	1431
" "	Edward Caldecote	1463
" "	John Newman, LL.B.	1485
" "	John Wythers, D.Can.L.	[1506]
" "	Richard Jenyns (Prior)	1515
" "	William Pykenham, D.Can.L.	1520
" "	William Tomyns	1535
Michael Betonson	John Harley, B.D.	1550
King Edward VI.	Alexander Creke	1553
Thomas Blount	Thomas Willoughby, M.A.	1561
"	Ralph Smith, M.A.	1587
"	John Columbine	1589
"	John Odell, M.A.	1625
Sir Edward Blount	George Dance	1627
A Committee of 14	Richard Baxter	1640—1660
Thomas Foley	Richard White, B.D.	1677
"	William Jordan	[1682]
"	John Howard, M.A.	1701
Thomas Lord Foley	William le Hunt, B.D.	1729

Patrons.	Rectors.	Date of Induction between
Thomas Lord Foley	Robert Job Charlton, LL.D.	1746
,,	Thomas Wickens, M.A.	1776
Lord Foley	George Butt, D.D.	1787
,,	Arthur Onslow, D.D.	1795
,,	Richard Francis Onslow, M.A.	1801
,,	James Farley Turner, M.A.	1836
Lord Ward	Thomas Legh Claughton, D.D.	1841
Earl of Dudley	George David Boyle, M.A.	1867
,,	Thomas Legh Claughton, M.A.	1880
,,	Sidney Phillips, M.A.	1887

THE DAUGHTER CHURCHES.

The original parish of Kidderminster contained no less than 19,800 acres, or about 31 square miles. Four Vicars of district churches now relieve the Vicar of Kidderminster of a large part of his responsibility. As long ago as A.D. 1200 the chapel of St. Michael at Mytton had been founded to supply the spiritual wants of a district four miles from the parish church. (Pp. 102, 107.) From Bacon's *Liber Regis*, it would appear that in 1535 this chapel had fallen into the hands of the Monastery of Hales Owen. In 1563 Mitton chapelry contained 23 families. In 1625 (Nov. 13) the ground lying round the chapel was consecrated for burials by John Thornborough, Bishop of Worcester. Mr. John Odell, Vicar of Kidderminster, John Yarranton and John Wilkes, chapelwardens of Mitton, and John and Humphrey Grove, gentlemen there, were the petitioners. *(Nash,* ii., p. 59.) What the original chapel was like we have no record: the present building (1791) is supremely ugly, and is very characteristic of the entire deadness to the sense of beauty which prevailed in the eighteenth century. The foundations of a new church—which, when finished, will be one of the finest in the county—were laid on Sept. 8, 1881. Only the porch and south aisle are finished as yet, but they serve to show the beauty of Mr. J. O. Scott's design.

THE CHURCH.

In 1844 (June 19) the hamlet of Lower Mitton was made a chapelry district; by Lord Blandford's Act in 1866 the Perpetual Curate became Vicar. The earliest register is 1693, and the value of the living is about £600, with residence.

There are some monuments in the church :—

Here rest the remains of Rebecka Lugg widow of Arthur Lugg Esq. daughter of John Foley Esq. and grand daughter of Thomas Lord Folliott, who dying without issue (Oct. ye 1st, 1745) Devised her Manors of Mitton, Lickhill, &c. to John Folliott (Lieutenant General of ye King's forces, Governor of Ross Castle and Colonel of the Royal Regiment of Ireland) her nearest relation of the name Folliott Who dying Feby 26, 1762 also without issue devised the same together with the rest of his estate in England and Ireland to his first cosen and sole executor John Folliott Governor, Representative in Parliament of the town of Kinsale Who agreeable to his kinsman's instruction and his own inclination hath caused this monument to be erected to perpetuate the memory of an excellent person, in every circumstance respectable, equal to the most accomplished an I worthy

On ye west side of this chancell doore lyeth interred the body of the Honourable Anne Soley wife of John Soley of Lickhill Esq. who was ye eldest daughter of ye Right Honourable Thomas Lord Folliott and departed this life the 28 April 1696 aged 40 years.

Also near to the S. side of the Chancell lyeth interred ye body of Humphrey Soley second son of ye said John Soley and Elisa his wife who died 27 Feb. 1700 aged 5 months.

In memory of Joseph Craven of Park House Streeten-in-Craven Leeds who died 30 March 1867 aged 61 years. He was for many years a Deputy Lieutenant of the County of York. Also Lord of the Manor of Lickhill and Lower Mytton.

Also of John William Craven who died at Uphall near Edinburgh 12 Oct. 1871 aged 33 years and was interred at Dalmahoy Scotland.

Sacred to the memory of Richard Jukes Esq who was born May xx MDCCLXVIII and died May xxix MDCCCXXXIV. He was eminently distinguished as a medical practitioner for superior sagacity in detecting disease, generous devotion to the cause of humanity, and disinterested benevolence. These elevated qualities attracted general admiration and esteem, and secured to him a brilliant career of professional usefulness. As a friend he was singularly warm and confiding, and inspired in those who knew him sentiments of regard and veneration

Also of Lucy widow of the above died Jan. 17, 1846 aged 74

The chappell was repaired and beautified by the inhabitants of Lickhill and Lower Mitton and this Loft was built by Pynson Wilmot Gent he being Chappell warden for the year 1707.

To the memory of Richard Heath Esq. late of Stourport Who died 9th of Sept 1850 aged 57 This tablet is by his friends and fellow townsmen affectionately and gratefully inscribed. With that true liberality and kind forethought for the poor which characterized his life, he at his death bequeathed £1000 to the Church-wardens and Overseers of Lower Mitton and their successors, directing that the interest should be equally divided between the schools connected with this church and the most deserving poor of this parish.

The hamlet of Upper Mitton (formerly in Hartlebury) has recently been attached to Lower Mitton; and All Saints Church and Schools have been erected there at the sole cost of Mr. Alfred Baldwin, of Wilden House. St. Gabriel's Mission Church is in Stourport.

In very early times a curious subterranean vault, cut out of the rock at Blackstone, and still in existence, was occupied as a hermitage. The recluse had a lovely view of the Severn. The chapel was about 30 feet by 14 feet, and there were several other rooms. A view and ground plan of it are engraved in Stukeley's *Iter. Cur.*, i., 13, and reproduced in *Nash* (ii., 48). The hermit is supposed to have received alms from the trows which passed up and down the river.

The old chapel of the Assumption of the Blessed Virgin Mary, with its chantry, founded at Trimpley in 1370, has already been mentioned (p. 96).

WRIBBENHALL.

After the long interval of 330 years the next chapel of "Christchurch in Wribbenhall" was built by subscription (1701). It was erected on a piece of garden ground held on lease by John Cheltenham under Lord Abergavenny. The Register of Baptisms and Marriages begins 8 April, 1723, but the chapel and burial-ground were not consecrated till 1841. In 1844 a district was assigned to the church, and in 1856, under 19 and 20 Vict., c. 104, Wribbenhall was constituted a separate parish. The old church was quite devoid of architectural beauty; so in 1879 the new church of All Saints was built on a site given some years previously by the late Walter Chamberlain Heming, Esq., of Spring Grove, to whose memory the

St. George's Church, Kidderminster, 1890

(North Side.)

beautiful east window (by Heaton, Butler, and Bayne) was erected. Mrs. Hemming contributed largely to the building fund. The church is of red sandstone, in the Early Decorated style, and contains sittings for 450 people.

There are beautiful windows in memory of Mr. J. W. T. Lea, of Netherton (Burlison and Grylls), Mr. Slade Baker, of Sandbourne (Heaton, Butler, and Bayne), and Miss Baugh (Hardman). There is also a monumental brass in memory of Colonel Philip Wodehouse, of the 15th Hussars, one of the heroes of Waterloo.

The old church has been pulled down, the burial-ground enclosed, and a stone cross erected on the spot where the altar once stood.

SOME INCUMBENTS OF WRIBBENHALL.

1720	Walter Jones.	....	—— Filewood.
1722	John Hassall.	....	George Warton, B.D.
1739	—— Bingham.	1836	William Hallen, B.A.
1742	Daniel Collins.	1850	Charles Warner, M.A.
1749	—— Boraston, M.A.	1864	Augustus William Gurney, M.A.
....	Thomas Wigan, D.D.		
....	Joseph Taylor	1878	James Lamb Chesshire, M.A.
....	William Miles, M.A.		
....	John Foley, M.A.		

ST. GEORGE

During the deadly warfare with Napoleon the struggle for existence had taken up all the energy of the nation, and had left little leisure for internal reforms. With the advent of settled peace came however into prominence the sad spiritual destitution which had been allowed to overtake our great cities and towns. As a thank-offering for England's safety, Parliament voted a million of money—the only money ever given to the Church by the State—to build new churches in populous places. To this grant we are partly indebted for the building of the church of St. George, containing 2000 sittings, of which 1200 are free. The site and burial-ground were provided by the parishioners, who also subscribed £2000 towards the building. The first stone was laid by the Vicar of Kidderminster, the Ven. Archdeacon R. F. Onslow, and the consecration took place 13 Sept., 1824. It has since become a Vicarage, with a population in 1881 of 8554, and yearly income of £500. When " Broomfield " was purchased for the Vicarage of Kidderminster in 1888, the old parsonage house (near The Copse) was sold to the Vicar of St. George's. In 1832 a musical festival was held in the church for the benefit of the National Schools. The total receipts were £1242—nett £450.

The reredos of alabaster represents the Ascension in alto-relievo in the centre, with medallions on each side symbolical of the Four Evangelists. It was erected (1874) in memory of " Charles John MacQueen Mottram 31 years a Minister of Christ in this town." The handsome silver-gilt alms dish was " presented by a former Curate " (Rev. B. Gibbons) 1854.

A beautiful window, representing the " Good Shepherd " and the " Light of the World," is dedicated in memory of Charles Harvey (born 25 May, 1812, died 5 April, 1889), " a true Son of the Church of England, who loved the place where God's honour dwelleth."

On marble tablets :—

In memory of Charlotte Mary Key dr. of Sir Kingsmill Grove Key Bart. and sister of the Rev. John Kingsmill C. Key M.A. She was for 3 years a Sunday School Teacher and earnest Church Worker in this parish, and was suddenly called away from earth on the day before she intended to set sail to work with her brother in the Central African Mission at Zanzibar Oct. 26th 1881.

Jane Hooman the beloved wife of James Hooman of Franche d. 11 Nov. 1825 aged 40 years.

Edmund Yates Peel son of Robert John Peel of Burton upon Trent Esq. d. at Waresley 20 Feb. 1826 aged 7 months.

INCUMBENTS OF ST. GEORGE'S.

1824 William Villiers, M.A.
1842 John Downall, M.A., Magdalen Hall, Oxford.
1848 T. Baker Morrell, M.A., Balliol Coll., Oxford.
1852 Chas. James Macqueen Mottram, B.A., Magdalen Hall, Oxford.
1872 Frederic Rawlins Evans, M.A., Exeter Coll., Oxford.
1876 Stephen Browne Bathe, M.A., Balliol Coll., Oxford.
1887 Theobold William Church, M.A., Keble Coll., Oxford.

THE CHURCH.

The mission church of St. Andrew in this parish was built in 1889 at the sole cost of the Rev. Clement Newcomb, one of the Curates.

ST. JOHN THE BAPTIST

The parish of St. John, though the youngest daughter of the Mother Church, is inferior to none in activity for the spiritual and temporal welfare of the people. One of Dr. Claughton's first plans for adapting Church work to modern times was the division of the old town parish into three districts, independent of each other, but all looking to the Vicar of Kidderminster as their patron. All Saints was in the centre, and St. George's on the east, so the new church of St. John was planted at the west end of the town. It is built of blue brick with Bath stone dressings, in imitation of the Norman style, but with a lofty spire. There are sittings for about 1100 persons, 800 being free. The cost of such a large building was only £4000, and it is hardly to be expected that it could be of very solid structure. In fact, it is not weather proof; but during its fifty years' existence it has welded together the parishioners, and brought about a unity of feeling which is now showing itself in an active attempt to make their spiritual home more worthy of the honour of God and more suited to the wants of the people. The arms of Bishop Pepys (who consecrated the church June 24, 1843) and Lord Ward are in the east window. Another window commemorates the chief benefactor : " Bless ye the memory of the late John Woodward Esquire by whose pious aid this church was in part built and the adjoining schools founded. He died April 7, 1838 ætat. LIX."

The reredos surrounding the apse is of alabaster in diaper work, with recesses enclosed by semi-circular arches. The central sculpture represents The Last Supper : other recesses form sedilia, aumbry, and piscina. " In honour of Almighty God and of the passion of His dear Son, and in pious memory of Edward and Ann Elizabeth Morton, this Reredos is dedicated by their loving children. A.D. MDCCCLXXX."

The north window of the apse was given by the Rev. Melsup Hill in memory of his wife. The window in the south transept commemorates Mr. Joseph Kiteley, who died 5 August, 1880.

Two mission chapels have been built in this parish—(1) St. Stephen's (1887), for the benefit of the very poor dwelling in the courts of Mill Street; and (2) The Holy Innocents (1888), for the more distant residents of Sutton Common and Foley Park. The population in 1881 was 7462, and the value of the benefice £400 with residence.

INCUMBENTS OF ST. JOHN'S.

1843 Richard Pritchard, B.D.
1844 Melsup Hill, M.A., Jesus Coll., Cambridge.
1857 George Robinson Kewley, M.A., Fellow of Univ. Coll., Durham.
1882 John Frederick Kershaw, M.A., Trinity Coll., Cambridge.

When the districts of the four daughter churches have been deducted, there still remains a population of 11,000, occupying an area of 8000 acres, or nearly 13 square miles, who look up to All Saints as their parish church. The hamlet of Trimpley, deprived of its chapel about 300 years previously, was again provided with its own House of God in 1844. The chapel is dedicated to the Holy Trinity, is built in the Norman style, and will accommodate 120 worshippers. There is a graveyard attached.

St. Barnabas, Franche, consecrated in 1871, was erected in memory of the late Rev. H. J. Fortescue by his daughters, on a site given by Mr. Joseph Chellingworth. There is a day school attached to the church, for which Mr. M. Tomkinson provided a teacher's residence as a "Jubilee" gift in 1887.

St. James's Church (1872), near the Horse Fair, was the generous gift of the Rev. H. J. Fortescue (Curate of Kidderminster 1867-1876, and now Vicar of St. George's, Leicester). It is a centre of vigorous work in a crowded district.

CHURCH OF St. JOHN THE BAPTIST,
KIDDERMINSTER (A.D. 1890).

THE CHURCH.

The Church of England Working Men have lately started a mission in a room on Larkhill.

In 1800 there was *one* working clergyman (a Curate) resident in Kidderminster: there are now thirteen. The Church service is celebrated in no less than fourteen buildings within the area of the old parish.

CHAPTER VI.

The Nonconformists.

HE "Old Meeting" is, as its name denotes, the oldest Nonconformist congregation in the town, and has lately replaced the plain barn-like building of 1824 by a handsome edifice in the Decorated Gothic style ; and has changed its name to "Baxter Church." This is considered to be the most handsome building possessed by the Independents in the county. It is 74 feet long by 48 feet wide, and affords accommodation for 1000 people. At the north end is an apse, with organ chamber on the left side. The spire, 140 feet high, forms a striking feature in the centre of the town. The windows are of cathedral-tinted glass, that on the north being of five lights, with symbols of " Charity," " The Beatitudes," " The Holy Trinity," &c. Mr. F. W. Tarring designed the building, which was erected by Mr. R. Thompson at a total cost of £8400. The first stones were laid 30 Sept., 1884, by Mr. T. Lea, M.P., and Mr. T. Banks ; and the opening ceremony took place 8 Sept., 1885, when the sermon was preached by the Rev. E. R. Conder, D.D., of Leeds.

The original trust deed bears date 11 Aug., 1694 : it states " that a dwelling house, with the garden and backside thereunto belonging, situate in the Bull Ring Street near the Town Bridge had been purchased of John Radford jun^r by Sam. Bowyer, Sam. Read, Wm. Smith and Thos. Doolittle of Kidderminster, and a meeting-house erected thereon for the worship and service of God."

The total cost of this first building was £383. Tradition

states that the Rev. Thos. Baldwin, sometime one of Baxter's assistants, had previously held services in a room in Mill Street ; but the first minister of the meeting-house was John Spilsbury, son of the Rev. John Spilsbury, M.A., Fellow of Magdalen College, Oxford, and nephew of Dr. Hall, Bishop of Bristol. In the diaries of Joseph Williams and Mrs. Housman there are many references to the earnest way in which he discharged his spiritual duties. He died 31 Jan., 1727, aged 60, and was buried in All Saints' churchyard. He was succeeded by his son-in-law, Matthew Bradshaw (1726—1742). After a vacancy of two years, Benjamin Fawcett, M.A., a pupil of Dr. Doddridge, was appointed : his success was great, and in 1753 a larger meeting-house was built on the old site at a cost of £1200. Mr. Fawcett died 18 Oct., 1780. He published an abridgment of some of Baxter's works, and was the author of twenty-four publications, including sermons, of which a list is given in his funeral sermon, preached by the Rev. Thos. Taylor, a native of Kidderminster, and prefixed to the last edition of his work, *The Grand Enquiry*. His *Sermon on the Murder of Francis Best* is in the town library. Mr. Best, of Caldwell Mill, was robbed and murdered 8 June, 1771, while walking along the footpath through the fields to Bewdley market. The murderer, John Child, of Wribbenhall, was hanged at Worcester.

Towards the end of Mr. Fawcett's ministry a strong minority of his congregation had accepted the Unitarian views which were then spreading so rapidly among Nonconformists, and which almost shattered the Presbyterians as an independent body in England. Thomas Wright Hill, a native of Kidderminster, and father of Sir Rowland Hill, tells us in his *Remains* (page 30), " My parents were of a very strict sect of Dissenters. The congregation [Old Meeting] with which we worshipped had the Presbyterian discipline, and was very much mixed as to doctrinal opinions. A considerable number, among whom were my mother and her nearest relations, were Calvinists ; a considerable number, of whom my father was one, were Arminians. My father too, and some of the Arminians, were likewise Arians." The next minister was John Barrett (1782

1798); but forty-six members refused to sign the invitation on account of their Arian beliefs, and decided to secede. They asked to be allowed to hold their services in the meeting-house during the intervals of public worship, and were requested in return " to resign up one of the parsonage houses for which they were in trust, agreeably to the intentions of the trust reposed in them by the congregation, at whose expense the said houses had been built." This they refused to do, and were therefore denied " the use of the Meeting House by the major part of the Trustees." They accordingly began to hold their services, 24 Feb., 1782, in a vacant warehouse, till the "New Meeting" Unitarian Chapel was opened 18 Oct., 1782. The ministers of the "Old Meeting" who succeeded were Alexander Steill, 1798; Thomas Helmore, 1810; Joseph John Freeman, 1820; Robert Ross, M.D., 1827; Thomas Greenfield, 1840; Albert Creak, M.A., 1850; Thomas Greenfield, 1853; J. Marsden, B.A., 1860; George Hunsworth, M.A., 1872; Benjamin Bryant Williams, 1881; Francis Henry Blanchford, 1886.

The Society of Friends had at one time a meeting-house in Kidderminster. In 1659 Robert Widder, " for speaking the words of truth to Baxter in the steeple-house at Kidderminster was imprisoned there, as also was William Pitt of Worcester who accompanied him; and Nicholas Blackmore, William Pitt and John Waite passing from Worcester to Kidderminster were set in the stocks there, under pretence of their having broken the Sabbath by travelling on that day." The Quakers would stand in the Market-place, and under Baxter's window year after year crying to the people, " Take heed of your priests; they deceive your souls," and if they saw any one wear lace or neat clothing they cried out to him, " These are the fruits of thy ministry!" *(Noake: Worcester Sects, page 216.)*

The secession of the Unitarians from the " Old Meeting," and the building of the " New Meeting " in 1782, has already been noticed. The chapel, situated in Church Street, received

THE NONCONFORMISTS.

a new stone " Perpendicular " front, &c., in 1883, at a cost of £2600, and will accommodate 700 persons. There are stained windows—" The Sower," in memory of Mr. William Talbot (by Pearce), and " Jesus as Teacher, Friend, and Risen Lord " (by Hardman), in memory of Miss Annie Stooke. Also the following tablets :—

To the memory of Nicholas Pearsall Founder of the adjacent Schools d. 2 July 1798 aged 71. Ann relict of the above and the last survivor of the family of Fincher of Shell in this county d. 5 May 1800 aged 82 years.

George Willey born 14 March 1791, d. 4 Aug. 1873.

Rev. Richard Fry 25 years Minister born 5 Nov. 1759 d. 12 March 1842.

In loving memory of my grandparents Henry Talbot who died 23 Oct. 1873 aged 70 and Caroline his widow who died 15 Jan. 1889 aged 87. Erected by C.E.W.

In memory of George Talbot J.P. born 14 March 1792 d. 4 Sept. 1868, and of Charles Talbot b. 26 Aug. 1804 d. 25 March 1841. In whose memory this Chapel was repewed and improved July 1870.

The ministers have been—R. Gentleman, 1782 ; — Severn, 1796 ; J. Lane, 1806 ; J. B. Smith, 1810 ; J. Ward, 1813 ; Richard Fry, 1813 ; John Taylor, 1836 ; Matthew Gibson, 1842 ; Edward Parry, 1855 ; Abraham Lunn, 1869 ; W. H. Fish, 1875 ; W. E. Mellone, 1876 ; W. Carey Walters, B.A., 1879 ; James Hall, 1888 ; Priestley Evans, 1890.

On 30 July, 1766, a petition was presented at the Quarter Sessions by John Pearsall, John Hill, and Josiah Butler, under the denomination of " Gospel Believers," certifying a tenement in the Park Butts as a place of divine worship.

John Wesley first visited Kidderminster in 1771, when it was included in the Gloucestershire circuit. " The brother that goes on circuit from *Worcester* goes on Wednesday to *Stourport*, Mr. *Cowell's* ; Thursday, to *Bewdley*, Mr. *James Lewis*, near the church, shoemaker ; Friday to Kidderminster, Mr. *James Bell*, shopkeeper, Mill Street ; Saturday evening, preach here also and Sunday morning."

K

Wesley preached May 16, 1780, at Kidderminster, where he sometimes spent an hour with "that good man Mr. Fawcett." On March 22, 1782, he came again from Worcester through roads almost impassable with snow. On March 23, 1787, he was at Stourport, "a small, new built village," where he speaks of Mr. Heath, "a middle-aged clergyman and his wife and two daughters, whose tempers and manners, so winning soft, so amiably mild, will do him honour wherever they come."

Again, 20 March, 1788, Wesley went to Stourport, "where," he says, "twenty years ago there was but one house; now there are two or three streets; and as the trade swiftly increases it will probably grow into a considerable town. A few years since, Mr. *Cowell* largely contributed to the building of a preaching-house here, in which both Calvinists and Arminians might preach; but when it was finished the Arminian preachers were totally excluded. Rather than go to law Mr. *Cowell* built another house, both larger and more convenient. I preached there at noon to a large congregation, but to a much larger in the evening. Several clergymen were present, and were as attentive as any of the people. Probably there will be a deep work of God at this place. On the 22nd breakfasted at Mr. *Lister's* in *Kidderminster*, with a few very serious and pious friends."

He was at Stourport for the last time on the 18th March, 1790, and found it "twice as large as two years ago." He died in March, 1791, at the age of nearly 88.

The Kidderminster Wesleyan Chapel in Mill-street was erected in 1803, and enlarged in 1821 : it will seat 600 persons.

The Baptist community of Kidderminster is an offshoot from that founded at Bewdley in 1646 by the famous John Tombes, B.D., the great opponent of Richard Baxter. In 1800 the Countess of Huntingdon's chapel in Mill Street was sold to the Wesleyans, but a few of its members kept together under the leadership of Thomas Price, and met for worship in the private house of Catherine Best. In 1807 four of their number were baptised in the meeting-house at Bewdley by Mr. George Brooks; these constituted "the church," and in 1809 John Kimberline's house in The Square (between the Grammar School and New Chapel Street) was licensed for worship. In 1813 a chapel was built in Union Street, of which George Griffin, cooper, of Bewdley, was appointed pastor. He was succeeded by T. R. Allom 1817, William Downes 1821, Henry Smith 1826, J. G. Stephens 1836, John Mills 1841, William Wright 1856, John Henry Jones 1857. In 1862 the present pastor, Rev. Thomas Fisk, commenced his ministry, which has been so successful that in 1867 a new chapel with seats for 600 persons was built at a cost of £3000, on a site formerly belonging to Sir Ralph Clare in Church Street.

The Roman Catholic mission in Kidderminster was commenced in 1831 by the Rev. Charles James O'Connor in a building in Chapel Street, formerly belonging to the Methodists, and now forming part of St. John's Infant Schools. In 1834 a new chapel, with accommodation for 240 persons, was erected at Leswell. Mr. O'Connor was succeeded by Peter Holland 1836, Ambrose Courtenay 1853, Alban Craddock 1859, Michael Power 1869, James McCave, D.D., 1870, Alfred Hall 1883, and Charles Ambrose Wheatley 1885. Father Courtenay obtained two years' absence, during which he travelled over the world collecting funds for the new church of St. Ambrose, which was built in 1858, together with school and residence. It is of brick, in the Early English and Decorated styles, and consists of nave, chancel, aisles, and Lady chapel. There are 400 sittings. It cost nearly £4000. The east window was erected by Dr. McCave, and has figures of SS. Ambrose, Helen, Augustine, and Thomas of Canterbury. In the Lady chapel is a window by Hardman in memory of Mrs. Shepherd.

The Countess of Huntingdon's plan of 3 March, 1790, formed Worcester, Evesham, and Kidderminster into the twelfth district. In 1800 their chapel was sold to the Wesleyans, and a few became Baptists. The rest held together, and, being strengthened by a secession from the Old Meeting in 1818 under Mr. Helmore, were able to build " The Countess of Huntingdon's Free Church " in Dudley Street, at a cost of £1100.

The Primitive Methodist Chapel, built in 1824, has 250 sittings. "Catholic Apostolic" services were held in Oxford Street; and the Christadelphians meet in the Co-operative Hall, Worcester Street. The Salvation Army have " barracks" near the Horse Fair.

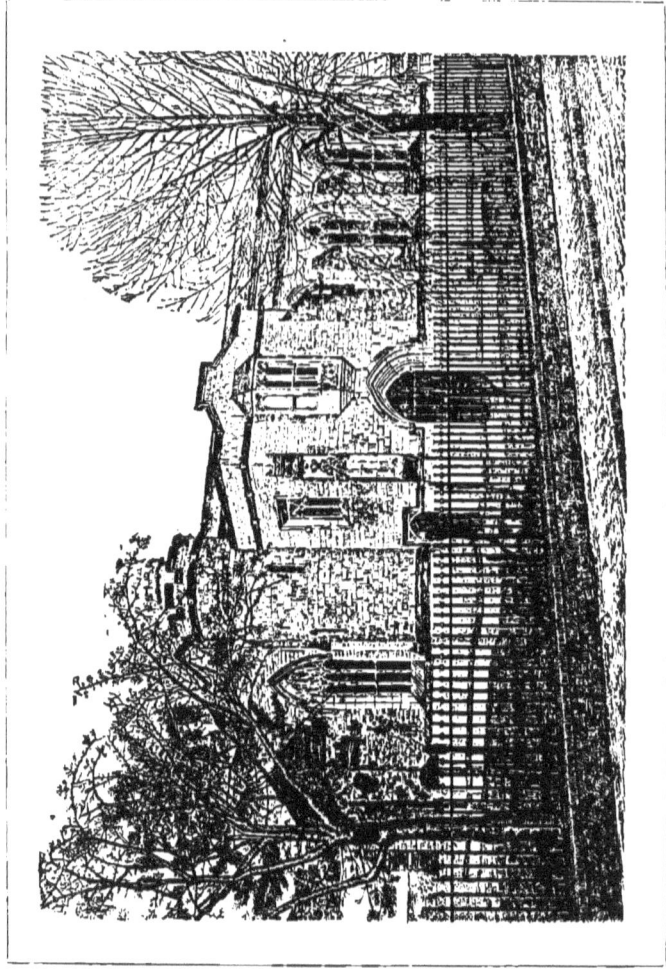

GRAMMAR SCHOOL OF 'KING CHARLES I.' KIDDERMINSTER.

CHAPTER VII.

The Schools.

THE Grammar School is by far the oldest educational institution in the town, but its origin is involved in obscurity. The earliest deed is a feoffment made by Henry Benton, High Bailiff of Kidderminster, and others, conveying lands to the school, and bearing date 12 Oct., 20 Elizabeth (1578). Sir Edward Blount was another benefactor 8 Jan., 1609. From time immemorial the chantry was used for the school, and possibly some of the chantry lands may have been given as an endowment. The common seal still in use is dated 1619, and was affixed to municipal deeds before the present borough arms were adopted. In 1636 King Charles I. granted a charter, in which he ordered the school to be called by his name, and bestowed upon it various privileges. The Corporation were made Governors, but administered its affairs so badly that they were superseded by a body of Feoffees specially appointed for the purpose. The earliest minute book commences 6 Feb., 1704, with a list of 28 Feoffees. By a new scheme drawn up by the Endowed School Commission in 1873, the management is vested in 12 Governors, viz. : The Chairman of the Magistrates *(ex-officio)*, four elected by the Town Council, three elected by the School Board, and four Co-optative. In 1785 masters' houses were built on the *west* side of Church Street close to the churchyard. In 1807 these houses were pulled down and converted into gardens, and the new houses (still standing) were erected on the opposite side of the street. In 1847 the Greenhill Farm of 51 acres, belonging to the school, was exchanged for Woodfield House and estate, with the new school built thereon. Some ill-feeling was created in the town by fears that the town boys would be neglected for the sake of the boarders, and litigation ensued. During its 300 years' existence the school has had a chequered career—the numbers having fallen occasionally as low as six—but it has sent out many scholars who have done good work in Church and State, and the present number of boys is about 80. The building has playing fields, gymnasium, and fives-courts attached. An annual medal has been endowed by John Brinton, Esq., M.P.; and challenge cups for the "*Victor Ludorum*" and "Senior Fives" have been given by A. F. Godson, Esq., M.P., and M. Tomkinson, Esq. Scholarships are annually awarded after competition to the best boys from the Elementary schools; and the great want of the school now is a scholarship which would enable clever boys of narrow means to continue their studies at some place of still higher education. The income for 1889 was:—From rents, £379 8s. 11d.; from dividends and interest, £293 11s.; and from fees, £338 13s. 8d.: total, £1011 13s. 7d. The following is a list of Headmasters compiled from the minute books and other sources:—

   [1650] John Pitt.
   [1667] Simon Potter.
   1699 Rev. John Best, M.A.
   1729 Rev. Thomas Cooke.
   1753 Rev. James Cooke.
   1757 Rev. John Martin, M.A.
   1776 Rev. Henry Matthews, B.A.
   1780 Rev. William Miles, M.A.
   1795 Rev. Thomas Morgan, M.A.
   1843 Rev. William Cockin, M.A.
   1852 Rev. George John Sheppard, D.C.L.
   1869 Rev. Lionel Bankes Penley, B.A. (Second Master).
   1873 Frederic Hookham, M.A.
   1885 Rev. John Richard Burton, B.A., F.G.S.

The Parish Church Schools may be proud of their origin, the founder being William Lloyd, Bishop of Worcester, one of the famous "Seven Bishops" of English history. At his visitation in 1702 he urged the formation of schools in the diocese, and promised to add a tenth part to the subscriptions. The Vicar, John Howard, was generously helped by the Society for Promoting Christian Knowledge, and soon 50 children were being taught and partly clothed. Sir Henry Ashurst and Edward Harley, Esq., as executors of Richard Baxter, contributed £20 from money left by him for charitable purposes. Other benefactors were Madam Rebekah Hussey, Lady Langham, Lady Bellamont, James Bruges, Mr. Ligon, the College at Worcester, Henry Hoare, John Hanbury, John Soley, Harry Gray, Sir Thos. Lyttelton, Lord Thanet, Sir John Thornicroft, Bowater Vernon, &c. In 1739 James Gilbert left £50, which was laid out in the purchase of the site of some of the present school premises. William Brecknell, in 1787, conveyed property exchanged in 1816 for the Crabtree Close, which in 1820 was sold as a site for St. George's Church. William Lea, of Stone House, in 1817, gave land on which a new school-room was built. In 1831 the two schools were educating 140 boys and 161 girls on the Madras system.

Simon Potter, Master of the Grammar School, conveyed land in 1667 to Nevill Simmons and others for a school for the children of godly poor parents to be taught to read the Bible and say the Assembly's catechism. Elizabeth Bowyer, in 1701, left property for the same purpose, and from these two bequests the Old Meeting Schools in Orchard Street were founded.

Samuel White, in 1772, left £150, the interest to be applied in teaching six Church children and six Dissenters.

Nicholas Pearsall, in 1795, "being desirous of promoting the welfare of his fellow-creatures, and persuaded that their welfare both in this world and another depended, under Almighty God, on their being taught to practice virtue and abstain from vice, resolved to establish a school to teach youth this important truth in the first place, and secondly so much of the arts and sciences as might enable them to fill up with advantage their respective stations in life." This foundation, known as "Pearsall's Grammar School," has since been merged in the "New Meeting" Schools.

The School Board of nine members was established April, 1871, and has had the following Chairmen:—

1871 The Rev. G. D. Boyle, M.A.	1886 Edward Parry, Esq.
1880 John Brinton, Esq., M.P.	1889 The Rev. S. Phillips, M.A.

Mr. W. M. Roden, solicitor, is Clerk to the Board.

A HISTORY OF KIDDERMINSTER.

ELEMENTARY SCHOOL ACCOMMODATION, 1890.

VOLUNTARY SCHOOLS.

Date of Foundation	Name of School.	Accommodation.					Cost of Buildings.
		Boys.	Girls.	Infants.	Mixed.	Total.	
1704	All Saints' (Churchfields)	340	300	—	—	640	Unknown.
1873	All Saints' (Broad street)	—	—	297	—	297	£1000
1874	St. Barnabas (Franche)	—	—	—	140	140	£1250*
1827	St. George's (Offmore Road	265	250	180	—	695	Unknown.
1850	St. George's (Worcester Cross)	120	—	100	—	220	£1200
1835	St. John's (Chapel Street)	—	—	300	—	300	Unknown.
1850	St. John's (St. John Street)	310	—	—	—	310	Unknown.
1855) 1885)	St. John's (Brook Street)	—	357	—	—	357	£1650
1795	New Meeting (Church Street)	180	180	—	—	360	Unknown.
1858	St. Ambrose (Leswell)	100	100	100	—	300	Unknown.
1853	Trimpley (Holy Trinity)	—	—	—	36	36	Unknown.
1842	Stourport	278	246	245	—	769	Unknown.
1882	Stourport (St. John's)	—	—	175	—	175	Unknown.
1850	Wribbenhall (National)	—	—	62	140	202	Unknown.
1881	Wribbenhall (British)	—	—	—	335	335	£1800
	Total	1593	1433	1459	651	5136	

* Including £300 for house, given by M. Tomkinson, Esq.

THE SCHOOLS.

SCHOOL BOARD.

Date of Erection	Name of School	Accommodation.					Cost of Buildings.
		Boys.	Girls.	Infants.	Mixed.	Total.	
1873	Coventry Street	304	215	233	—	752	£5367
1877	Hume Street	—	—	121	151	272	£1710
1883	Lea Street	129	129	131	—	389	£4282
1883	Mill Lane	153	156	156	—	465	£4484
	Total..	586	500	641	151	1878	

The School of Art was originally held in "Commercial Buildings;" but in 1879 Mr. D. W. Goodwin gave the site for the new building in Exchange Street. It is in the Early Renaissance style, and Mr. J. M. Gething was the architect. It contains a hall 62 feet by 39 feet for 120 students, master's and modelling rooms, antique room and painting room, &c. Under the able management of Mr. W. Tucker, this institution has proved most valuable to the town.

The School of Science was completed in 1887, at a cost of £4000. It forms the central portion of an intended triple institute of Literature, Science, and Art. Only the reading-rooms and library are now wanting to complete the full scheme, which is likely soon to be carried to a successful issue. The Public Libraries Act has been in operation for some years, and it is expected that advantage will be taken of recent legislation to place the schools, library, and museum under the fostering care of the Corporation. The School of Science contains classrooms for physics and languages, lecture rooms, chemical laboratories, dye house, cooking range, and reference library. In the rear is a museum 52 feet by 41 feet, with a gallery all round it, having excellent light for pictures. Some paintings, drawings, fossils, minerals, coins, and curiosities have already been presented by local donors; and these are supplemented by a collection from South Kensington, changed from time to time. Mr. W. Ray, F.C.S., is the first Headmaster. The Earl of Dudley is President, and G. W. Grosvenor, Esq., B.A., D.L., is Chairman, of both schools. In 1887 two "Jubilee Scholarships" were founded for the most proficient student each year in "Art" and in "Science." Mr. Cooper, of Kidderminster, in 1888, bequeathed £284 to each school as the nucleus of an endowment.

CHAPTER VIII.

The Charities.

IT is a delicate task to speak of generous deeds in the lifetime of the doers; so that although there are now living among us many men who have shown a public spirit equal to that of the benefactors of past generations, the details must be left to future times. By the help of the Charity Commissioners' Report we record the names and mention the gifts of

SOME BENEFACTORS.

EDMUND BRODE, of Dunclent (1597). Rent-charge of 6s. 8d. for poor.

SIR EDWARD BLOUNT (1630). Six almshouses.

THOMAS BUTCHER (1643). £2 12s. annually for bread.

WILLIAM SEABRIGHT (1620). £3. 0s. 8d. annually for bread.

THOMAS COOK, of Bewdley (1693). £2 12s. annually for bread.

JOHN OLDNALL. £2 annually for bread.

JOSEPH READ, of Atterley. £1 annually for bread.

EDWARD CRANE, of Hurcott (1820). £100 for bread.

DR. JOHN HALL, Bishop of Bristol (1718). £700 for Bibles.

By an inquisition taken 20th April, 1641, it was found that Thomas Lewes, of Kidderminster, held two barns and little closes in Barn Street, 4 acres of arable land lying in one of the common or leete fields, called the Church Field (1½ acre near the churchyard, one acre near Whorwood Shipton, half an acre

THE CHARITIES.

near Low Hill Style, and half an acre called Whitemarsh), which lands then were, and time out of mind had been, commonly called by the name of WHITNELL'S ALMS. Other property belonged to the same charity in Ellarne Field, Cole Field (near the two gates), &c. [The name "Whytnyll" occurs in the Registers as early as 1545.] The High Bailiff was to collect the rents, and pay the money to the churchwardens and overseers of the town or foreign for distribution among the poor. With Whitnell's alms, which now produces nearly £200 per annum, are incorporated gifts left by other donors, viz.:—

  JOHN GOWER, of Stone (1641), £1 yearly for poor; EDWARD MILLS (1615), £2 yearly for poor; ELIZABETH MILLS (1626), £2 yearly for poor; THOMAS DAWKES (1611), £1 yearly for poor; EDWARD DAWKES (1632), £1 yearly for poor; ALICE DAWKES (1615), 13s. 4d. yearly for poor; WILLIAM BUCKNELL, £5; THOMAS BURTON, £5; RANDELL GRIFFIN, 20s.; HENRY BENTON, £6 13s. 4d.; JOYCE RADFORD, £4; HUGH ATWILL, £1 6s. 8d.; WILLIAM MOSELEY, £13 6s. 8d.; WILLIAM CHILD, £10; NICHOLAS FREESTONE, £10.

SIR RALPH CLARE (1670). Six almshouses, and £30 to be lent to poor tradesmen.

HENRY HIGGINS (1684). Four almshouses, and £12 for poor children's shoes and stockings.

ABRAHAM PLIMLEY (1664). £3 yearly to one honest person.

RICHARD BARKER (1665). £200 for apprentices or poor.

ELIZABETH BOWYER (1701). £3 yearly to one poor person.

REV. JOSEPH READ, of Oldswinsford (1709). £5 yearly for a poor widow or education of a poor boy.

EDWARD BUTLER (1710). 40s. yearly for six poor persons.

DR. JOHN HALL, Bishop of Bristol (1708). £5 yearly to five poor men; £5 yearly to teach five poor children in the Christian religion; £5 yearly for clothes for aged and infirm; and residue in books to instruct poor persons in the Christian religion.

JOHN SPARRY (1717). £2 5s. yearly for one poor honest man.

THOMAS DOOLITTLE (1723). Interest of £50 to one poor person.

MRS. MARY GLYNN, widow of William Greaves (1734). £200 to be invested in land for repair of William Greaves' vault in churchyard, and residue for ten poor ancient and decayed women of the Church of England.

JOHN WALDRON. £1 yearly to poor.

—— WHITING. Ten farthing loaves weekly.

MRS. BRIDGEMAN. £50 for bread.

JOHN WRIGHT (1771). £25 for ten widows.

JOHN BRECKNELL (1776) by his will reciting that there had for time immemorial existed in the Church Street a certain society for the promotion of friendly intercourse among the inhabitants of the street, bequeathed £150 to John Watson, Nicholas Penn, and William Lea in trust to provide and give to every child or unmarried person, or an inhabitant of the Church Street aforesaid, one two-penny plumbcake upon the eve of every Midsummer day ; and further to provide pipes and tobacco and ale, &c., for the entertainment of the male inhabitants which should then assemble ; the residue to be given to the poor of the street.

HUMPHREY BURLTON (1645). 40s. yearly for poor of the foreign.

EDWARD BURLTON, of Shrawley (1694) gave to the Foreign the tenement and nook of land at Netherton on which Humphrey Burlton had previously charged the 40s.

There were other charities which are supposed to be lost.

With the changed circumstances of the times and the improved administration of the Poor-laws, the old dole system of charities often does more harm than good, and the beneficent spirit of later years has run in new channels.

In 1821 the Dispensary was founded near the churchyard : tens of thousands were benefited by it ; and it led to the erection in 1870 of a spacious and handsome Infirmary at the top of Mill Street, costing £10,000, of which the memorial stone was laid by the Countess of Dudley. In 1886 the fever wing

THE CHARITIES.

was transformed into a Children's Hospital, the cost being defrayed by Thomas Lea, Esq., M.P. The average yearly number of in-patients is 420, and of out-patients 1500. The President for 1890 is S. Stretton, Esq. The honorary surgeons are E. H. Addenbrooke, Esq., W. H. Moore, Esq., Dr. Preston, and J. L. Stretton, Esq.

A thriving town has generally to pay a penalty for its success in the rapid seizure of all its open spaces for building purposes ; and soon monotonous rows of houses shut out every vestige of nature, forcing the little children to play their games in the dangerous streets. Well would it be if Corporations could *in good time* secure a plot of ground in each proposed street, plant it with trees, and leave it open for the recreation of the district. Future generations will appreciate even more than the present the generous foresight of one of Kidderminster's most energetic sons in presenting to his native town the " Brinton Park " of 24 acres. It has been tastefully laid out, and each succeeding year will add to its beauty. Mr. Brinton was born 25 Jan., 1827, and has been one of the foremost men of his time in raising the special industry of the town to its pre-eminent rank. He has also devoted much time and his great business experience to the public affairs of the borough. He was member of the School Board (1871—1886), Chairman of the School of Art (1863—1889), Borough Magistrate (1856), County Magistrate (1876), and is still Chairman of the Board of Guardians. In 1889 he was appointed High Sheriff of Worcestershire ; and in 1890 was unanimously chosen an Alderman of the County Council. In 1880 he was elected Member of Parliament for Kidderminster (page 84), but retired in 1886 after a serious illness. He has also presented to the town a handsome clock tower and drinking fountain.

John H. Crane, Esq., of Oakhampton, whose family have been for centuries connected with the neighbourhood, and who was High Sheriff of the county in 1888, has made a generous offer to hand over the lovely " Habberley Valley " to the Corporation for the perpetual use of the town.

CHAPTER IX.

The Celebrities.

ICHARD KIDDERMINSTER, D.D., was born here in the latter half of the fifteenth century. When about 15 years of age he was received into the Benedictine monastery at Winchcombe, in Gloucestershire. After four years' study at Gloucester Hall, Oxford, he was recalled to the monastery, and made principal chaplain, and in 1487 was chosen Abbot. He had considerable reputation as a scholar and a promoter of learning, and was a reformer of the discipline of his house. He took the degree of D.D. at Oxford in 1500. He also visited Rome on some business pertaining to his order, and on his return acquired much reputation as a preacher in the beginning of the reign of Henry VIII. In 1515 Abbot Kidderminster contended in a famous debate that "benefit of clergy" should be extended to the minor orders. In 1521 he wrote *Tractatus contra doctrinam Lutheri*. His best work was a *History of Winchcombe Monastery; a List of its Abbots, and its Charters and Privileges*. He died in 1531.

RICHARD JERVYES, born in Kidderminster of mean parents, was apprenticed in London, became wealthy, and was made an Alderman of the City. He purchased the manor of Bedcote Stourbridge in 1538 (*Nash*, ii., 209), and was grandfather of Sir Thomas Jervois, Kt., who sold the manor in 1625 to Nicholas Sparry, Esq.

SIR RALPH CLARE, of Caldwell, eldest son of Sir Francis Clare, was a famous old Cavalier, and might have stood for the portrait of Sir Peveril of the Peak. He was for many years lessee of the manor of Bewdley under the Crown, and represented the borough in the Parliaments of 1623-5-6-8. In 1624 he bestowed a buck upon the Bayliff and Burgesses, when £3 13s. 4d. was spent " for making five pasties thereof, and for other meat provided when it was eaten, and for wine." He was " servant " to Prince Henry, and was made a Knight of the Bath at the Coronation of Charles I. When the charter was granted to Kidderminster in 1636 he was named first High Steward of the new created borough. He was a dignified and courteous gentleman, plain and downright in speech, but kindly in heart and ready to help, the founder of six almshouses, and the donor of money to lend to poor tradesmen. As a zealous Royalist he spent much of his fortune in the King's cause, was taken prisoner at the battle of Worcester, and was committed to Worcester gaol in 1655. As an earnest Churchman he disapproved of Richard Baxter's innovations; but his firmness of principle and courtesy of behaviour led even his great opponent to draw a pleasing picture of the noble old man. " One knight Sir Ralph Clare, who lived at Kidderminster, did more to hinder my greater successes than a multitude of others could have done, though he was an old man of great courtship and civility, and very temperate as to diet, apparel, and sports, and seldom would swear any louder than by his troth, and shewed me much personal reverence and respect beyond my desert, and we conversed together with much love and familiarity, yet having no relish of this preciseness and extemporary praying; his coming but once a day to church on the Lord's-day, and his abstaining from the sacrament, which he refused to receive, unless I would give it to him kneeling and not sitting, as if we kept not sufficiently to the old way, did cause a great part of the parish to follow him, and do as he did. And yet civility, and yielding much beyond others of his party, sending his family to be catechised and personally instructed, did sway with the worst among us to do the like." Sir Ralph is buried in All Saints' church under a slab close to Lady Beauchamp's tomb. The arms are *Three chevrons*, crest *a buck's head cabost*. " The memory of the just shall be blessed. " zealous in his loyalty to his prince, exemplary in his charity to the distressed, and of known integrity unto all men, full of days and fame, he departed this life in the fourscore and fourth year of his age. 21st April, 1670." Caldwell continued in the Clare family till 1777.

JOHN SOMERS, baptized here 26 Nov., 1620, was son of Richard Somers, Low Bailiff of Kidderminster, by his wife Joice Child, a member of an old Kidderminster family (buried in All Saints' churchyard 26 Aug., 1626). He was brought up an attorney, and lived chiefly at the White Ladies, near Worcester, "where he was instrumental and assistant to Bishop Fell in recovering the rents of St. Oswald's Hospital for the poor men and women." He and his wife (Catherine Severne) were buried in Severn Stoke church, where there is a marble monument to their memory erected by their son, John Lord Somers, Lord Chancellor, one of the most famous natives of the county, who defended the "Seven Bishops" and drew up the Bill of Rights. John Somers' elder daughter Mary married Charles Cocks, Esq., M.P., of Worcester, and is ancestress of the present Earl Somers, the Earl of Hardwicke, and Earl Beauchamp. His younger daughter Elizabeth married Sir Joseph Jekyll, Master of the Rolls. John Somers had also a sister Mary, baptized at Kidderminster 8 July, 1624, and married to Richard Blurton, Esq., who purchased the White Ladies. The Registers give the following additional records of the family :—

1658 Sept. 6 married Thomas Sommairs of Worcester and Rebecka Climar.

1664 Feb. 28 buried Rebeckath wife of Thomas Somars of worcester.

1669 buried Ann daughter of John Sumers and Ann.

ROBERT COOPER, M.A., was the son of Robert Cooper, of Kidderminster. He entered as a servitor at Pembroke College, Oxford, where in 1666 he took his degree, and was made Fellow of his College. He proved a good scholar and preacher, and was well skilled in mathematics ; and by the favour of John Lord Ossulton, he became Rector of a parish near Kingston-upon-Thames, Surrey. He wrote *Proportions concerning Optic Glasses* and *A General Introduction to Geography* of much merit. In the 81st year of his age (1731) he put up a monument to his parents in Kidderminster church. (P. 92.)

SIR RALPH CLARE, Knight of the Bath

EDMUND WALLER (1605—1687) is a singular and piquant figure in the seventeenth century—a poet, courtier, and water-drinker among the bibulous Restoration wits. He was born at Coleshill, Herts, of an ancient family. His mother, an ardent Royalist, was connected by blood with Hampden, and by marriage with Cromwell. His father died when he was 11 years old, and at 16 he entered Parliament. Soon he married a rich widow, retired to his estate at Beaconsfield, and studied literature. He was the owner of The Hall, a handsome brick house near Kidderminster church, as well as of the hamlets of Hurcott and Comberton. In 1635 he sold The Hall to Daniel Dobbins, Esq., of London; and a few years later (1643) he disposed of his other property here. Hurcott was bought by George Evelyn, who resold it in 1648 to his famous brother John, of Wotton and Sayes Court, one of the founders of the Royal Society, and author or translator of 30 works, including *Sylva*, and whose *Diary* is so well known. John Evelyn soon afterwards sold it to Colonel John Bridges for £3400. Waller was arrested by order of Pym May 31, 1645, for complicity in a plot against the Parliament. By turning informer he saved his life, but was fined £10,000 and banished. He lived at Paris till 1654, when Cromwell allowed him to return, and he composed a lofty panegyric in his praise. At the Restoration he expressed his joy in a poem "Upon His Majesty's Happy Return." He met the King's complaint that his congratulation was inferior to his panegyric with the famous retort, "Poets, sire, succeed better in fiction than truth." He entered Parliament again, and became the delight of the House by his lively sayings. He died in 1687, aged 82. *(National Biography.)*

ANDREW YARRANTON was born at Larford, in the parish of Astley, 1616. Several members of his family were bailiffs of Bewdley. In his sixteenth year he was apprenticed to a Worcester linen draper. When the civil wars broke out he joined the Parliamentary army, and rose to be captain. In 1652 he began manufacturing iron at Ashley, near Bewdley. At the Restoration he was imprisoned for a time. As soon as he regained his liberty he formed plans for improving inland navigation. His first scheme was to deepen the Salwarpe, and connect Droitwich with the Severn : this was not carried out. His next design was to make the Stour navigable, and join it by a canal with the Trent. Some progress was made with this undertaking. The Registers mention that "Coales were brought by Boates to ye Town on ye 9th of March 1665." Some of the barges used in this navigation have since been discovered imbedded in mud. Yarranton was in advance of his age, and the scheme then came to a stand still for want of money : though it was carried out more than 100 years later by James Brindley at a cost of £105,000. Yarranton's fertile brain was busy devising plans for the good of his country. He introduced clover seed, and supplied it largely to the farmers of the western counties, whence it soon became adopted throughout the country. He then went to Saxony and learnt the art of making tin plates, but some patent was "trumpt up," and he was not allowed to continue his operations. In 1677 he published the first part of his *England's Improvement by Sea and Land : to Outdo the Dutch without Fighting, and Pay Debts without Money*, wherein "he chalks out the future course of Britain with as free a hand as if second-sight had revealed to him those expansions of her industrial career which never fail to surprise us, even when we behold them realised." Inland navigation, harbours, the extension of the iron and woollen trades, the linen manufacture, a public bank, fisheries, a land registry, employment of the poor, a plan for preventing fires in London, &c., all were well thought out by him ; but "his voice sounded among the people like that of one crying in the wilderness." His name and his writings have been nearly forgotten, though Bishop Watson said that he ought to have had a statue erected to his memory because of his eminent public services. The reader will find a fuller account of this remarkable man in Chapter IV. of Dr. Smiles' *Industrial Biography*.

THOMAS FOLEY was born at Kidderminster, and baptized 12 Nov., 1673. He showed great aptitude in learning, and also very much improved himself in the knowledge of men and things by his travels beyond sea for several years. On his return in 1695 he was elected M.P. for Stafford. He distinguished himself in a becoming regard for his religion, his Prince,

THE CELEBRITIES. 155

and his country, in consideration whereof he was (Dec. 31, 1711) created Baron Foley of Kidderminster. He married Mary, daughter and sole heir of Thomas Strode, Esq., serjeant-at-law, by whom he had issue four sons and two daughters. He died 22 Jan., 1733, and was buried at Witley, where an elegant marble monument is erected. A younger brother, Edward Foley, was also baptized at Kidderminster 23 Sept., 1676. He was several times elected M.P. for Droitwich, and died April, 1747. Richard Foley was born here 19 Feb., 1681 : he was one of the protonotaries of the Court of Common Pleas, and M.P. for Droitwich. He died unmarried, 27 March, 1732. Anne Foley, who married Salway Winnington, Esq., of Stanford Court, was baptized at Kidderminster 28 March, 1670. Mary Foley (baptized 14 Jan., 1678) married Sir Blundel Charlton, Bart., of Ludford, near Ludlow.

JOHN JONES, schoolmaster, of Kidderminster, wrote *The New Art of Spelling*, Lond., 1704, 4to.

JOSEPH WILLIAMS, "the Christian Merchant," was born at Kidderminster Nov. 16, 1692, and was son of a "clothier" who lived in Church Street. He was educated at the Grammar School, where he acquired a good knowledge of Latin and Greek. He married (1719) Phœbe, sister of the Rev. Richard Pearsall. He was a man of eminent piety, as is well shown in his life and writings, edited by the Rev. B. Fawcett and Benjamin Hanbury. In 1745 he was one of a band of about 100 volunteers who associated to defend their country against the invasion of the Young Pretender, and who were accoutred chiefly at his expense. He died 21 Dec., 1755, aged 63, and was buried on the north side of Kidderminster churchyard.

THE REV. RICHARD PEARSALL, born at Kidderminster 29 Aug., 1698, was educated at Tewkesbury, and became a minister at Bromyard for ten years, and then at Warminster sixteen years. In 1747 he settled at Taunton, where he died 10 Nov., 1762. He edited the diary of his sister Hannah (Mrs. Housman). He also wrote *Contemplations on the Ocean*. Two volumes of *Reliquiæ Sacræ* of Mr. Pearsall were edited by Thomas Gibbons. D.D., and a brief account of him, with portrait, is in the *Evangelical Magazine* for October, 1810.

JOHN BASKERVILLE was born at Sion Hill, Wolverley. In the Parish Register we find this entry:—" 1706. John ye son of John Baskervile by Sara his wife was baptised January ye 28." When 20 years of age he went to Birmingham, and taught writing and book-keeping. In 1737 he kept a school in the Bull Ring. In 1740 he started at 22, Moor Street, as a manufacturer of japanned goods, by which he made a considerable income. He then took a lease of a small estate of 8 acres, on which he built a house, and " made a little Eden." About 1750 he began type founding; but it was not till 1757 that the famous 4to Virgil appeared—" the first of those magnificent editions which went forth to astonish all the librarians of Europe." *(Macaulay.)* In 1763 was published his famous Bible, one of the finest ever printed. He also brought out fine editions of the Prayer Book, Greek Testament, Milton, and several classical authors. He died 8 Jan., 1775, and, being an infidel, directed his body to be buried in his garden. His works are still prized. " Every book was a masterpiece; a gem of typographic art. Baskerville's type was remarkably clear and elegant. His paper was of a very fine thick quality, but rather yellow in colour. His ink had a rich purple black tint." *(Printers' Register*, 6 Jan., 1876.)

WILLIAM GREAVES, citizen of London, settled in Kidderminster about 1717, and started the manufacture of striped tameys and prunellas, and afterwards of various kinds of figured and flowered stuffs, such as starrets, barley corns, &c., and the trade made a considerable figure in foreign markets. His tomb, of very durable stone, may still be seen in the churchyard. The arms are *an eagle displayed* impaling *a lion rampant*, with inscription:—" Here lie the remains of Mr. William Greaves, citizen and weaver of London, whose generous endeavours for the benefit of the trade of this place procured him esteem while living and his death sincerely lamented. He was a dutiful son, a loving husband, a sincere friend, a loyal subject, and a good christian. He departed this life 28th July 1725 in the 53rd year of his age. Mrs. Elizabeth Greaves his mother 17 Sept. 1729 aged 89."

JOB ORTON, a famous Dissenting divine (1717—1783), was resident at Kidderminster for 17 years. He wrote a life of Baxter, and another of Dr. Doddridge, wherein occurs the epigram on the motto *Dum vivimus vivamus*, mentioned by Dr. Johnson as one of the finest in the English language: —

> "Live while you live, the Epicure would say,
> And seize the pleasures of the present day:
> Live while you live, the sacred Preacher cries,
> And give to God each moment as it flies.
> Lord, in my views let both united be,
> I live in pleasure while I live in Thee."

JAMES JOHNSTONE, M.D., was fourth son of John Johnstone, Esq., of Galabank, an ancient branch of the Johnstones "of that ilk." He was born at Anandale April 14, 1730, and received the degree of M.D. in Edinburgh University 1750. In 1751 he settled as a physician at Kidderminster, where he soon gained a great reputation in his profession. He published *An Historical Dissertation concerning the Malignant Epidemic Fever of* 1756, from which he appears to have been the first to generate hydrochloric acid gas as a means of destroying contagion by pouring sulphuric acid on common salt. In the 54th volume of the *Phil. Trans.* he published the first sketch of his opinions of the uses of the ganglions of the nerves. He attended George the "good" Lord Lyttelton in his last illness, "and was not only his physician but his confessor." He also wrote treatises on *Angina, Scarlet Fever, The Slave Trade, Hydrophobia, &c.*, for which he was voted the honorary medal of the Medical Society. He sent much information about Kidderminster to Dr. Nash for his *History of Worcestershire*. He died at Worcester 28 April, 1802, in the 73rd year of his age. A monument was erected in Worcester Cathedral, but he was buried in Kidderminster churchyard.

JAMES JOHNSTONE, M.D., son of the above and of Hannah daughter of Mr. Henry Crane, of Kidderminster, was born here August, 1754. He was educated at the Grammar School under the Rev. John Martin, and graduated as M.D. at Edinburgh in 1773. Next year he was unanimously chosen a physician to the Worcester Infirmary, and soon reached great eminence in his profession. When called on by the Magistrates of Worcester to visit the prisons, where many laboured under the gaol fever, he went into cells and dungeons full of pestilential contagion, and his life fell a sacrifice to duty. He was seized with the dire contagion, and was conveyed to his father's house in Kidderminster, there to receive the last attention of parental skill and affection. He died 16 Aug., 1783, and was buried in Worcester Cathedral, where on a tablet is an inscription to his memory from the classical pen of Dr. Parr. John Howard, the philanthropist, mentions this sad case as "one incentive to my endeavours for the extirpation of the gaol fever out of our prisons." *(Chambers' Biography.)*

EDWARD JOHNSTONE, M.D., born at Kidderminster 1757, was the third son of Dr. James Johnstone. He settled at Birmingham, where he soon became the first physician of the Midland Counties. He served the General Hospital for 22 years, and acquired the highest professional and social position. He retired early, and enjoyed a ripe old age at Edgbaston Hall. His principal works were on puerperal fever and hydrophobia. He died at the great age of 94 in 1851. *(Timmins' Warwickshire.)*

JOHN JOHNSTONE, M.D., F.R.S., F.R.C.P., &c., was brother of the above, born here 1767. He was not only professionally famous, but scientifically also. He was a personal friend of Dr. Parr, whose life and works he wrote and edited. His works on *Mineral Poisons*, on *Medical Jurisprudence*, and on *Madness: Hereditary and Partial*, are excellent proofs of his skill and knowledge. He died near Birmingham in 1836, aged 69. *(Ibid.)*

THOMAS WRIGHT HILL (1763—1853) was born at Kidderminster. His earliest tastes were scientific, largely influenced by Ferguson's lectures when he was only nine years old. He was first apprenticed to a brassfounder in Birmingham; but the work was uncongenial, and his experience as a Sunday-school teacher under Dr. Priestley led him to devote himself to teaching. He established first the Hill Top School in Birmingham, and afterwards the Hazelwood School at Edgbaston, where many eminent men received their early training, and pupils came to him from all parts of Europe. He had a very remarkable and original power of interesting boys. He made his school a small republic, and trained the boys for the work of life. He encouraged manual labour, as well as games and sports. He not only proposed a magazine, but the boys printed and illustrated it also, and many etchings and early lithographs were produced. His five sons trained by him had most successful careers. The third was Sir Rowland, of the Post Office; Matthew Davenport was an eminent jurist; Edwin, at the Stamp Office, made many inventions; Frederick was an inspector of prisons; and Arthur carried on the school at Bruce Castle, Tottenham, after Hazelwood was closed. He died in 1853, full of honours as well as years, and has been remembered by three generations of pupils and friends, who owe to his teaching and example the culture and success of their lives. *(Timmins' Warwickshire.)*

LANT CARPENTER, LL.D., born at Kidderminster 2 Sept., 1780, was third son of George Carpenter (died 12 Feb., 1839, aged 91), carpet manufacturer, by his wife, Mary Hooke (died 21 March, 1835, aged 83). Ann Lant was the maiden name of George Carpenter's mother. The father failed in business, and removed from Kidderminster, but Lant was left behind with his mother's guardian, Nicholas Pearsall, who adopted him with a view to his becoming a minister. Pearsall was a strong Unitarian of much practical benevolence, and had founded a school in Kidderminster, at which Lant received his early education. In 1797 he entered the Dissenting Academy at Northampton under John Horsey. This was broken up, and he then went to Glasgow University. In 1801 he became assistant in the school of his connection, the Rev. John Corrie, at Birch's Green, near Birmingham. From 1802 to 1805 he held the librarianship of the Liverpool Athenæum. On 9 Jan., 1805, he accepted a co-pastorate at George's Meeting, Exeter. He brought out next year a popular manual of N.T. Geography.

Applying to Glasgow in 1806 for M.A. by special grace, he was at once made LL.D. In 1817 he removed to Lewin's Mead Chapel, Bristol, on the retirement of Dr. Estlin. The congregation was large and wealthy, but had lost cohesion. Carpenter drew its various elements together, developed its religious and philanthropic life, and gave it a hold upon the neglected classes of society. Of Carpenter's own catechumens, a considerable number, including some of his favourite pupils, ultimately joined the Church of England. Many of the sterner Unitarians regarded his influence as too evangelical. The rite of baptism he rejected altogether as a superstition, substituting a form of infant dedication. In 1833 the Rajah Rammohun Roy, in whose monotheistic movement Dr. Carpenter was strongly interested, died at Bristol, and he preached his funeral sermon. He gave up his school in 1829. James Martineau was one of his pupils. No master was ever more adored by his scholars, or more effective in the discipline of character. Till 1836 he took a leading part in all public work in Bristol, and was one of the chief organisers of the Literary and Philosophical Institution in 1822. By 1839 his constitution was completely exhausted under his unsparing labours. He was recommended to travel on the Continent, but was drowned on the night of 5 April, 1840, while going by steamer from Leghorn to Marseilles. He was not missed till morning, and it is supposed that he was washed overboard. His body was cast ashore two months afterwards near Porto d'Anzio, and was buried on the beach. He married 25 Dec., 1805, a daughter (died 19 June, 1856) of James Penn, of Kidderminster, and had six children, of whom the eldest was Mary, the distinguished philanthropist, the chief organiser of industrial schools and the friend of Indian education. The fourth was Dr. W. B. Carpenter, F.R.S., Registrar of London University, and a famous physiologist, who left five sons, including W. Lant Carpenter, B.Sc., and Dr. P. H. Carpenter, F.R.S. The youngest son, Philip Pearsall Carpenter, B.A., was at first a minister at Warrington, but is best known as a conchologist. The other son, Russell Lant, was his biographer. Dr. Lant Carpenter's works were—(1) *Unitarianism the Doctrine of the Gospel*; (2) *Systematic Education*; (3) *An Examination of the Charges made against Unitarians by Rt.*

THE CELEBRITIES.

Rev. Dr. Magee ; (4) *Principles of Education ;* (5) *A Harmony of the Gospels ;* and (6) *Sermons on Practical Subjects.* [These facts are chiefly taken from the *National Biography.*] A marble monument is erected to his memory in the New Meeting, Kidderminster.

SIR JOSIAH MASON, Kt., was born in Mill Street 23 Feb., 1795, of humble parentage. The family apparently had been long settled in Kidderminster, for the name occurs in the Registers as early as 1559. The future philanthropist had a hard uphill struggle, and was obliged to commence his industrial career at the age of eight by selling cakes and vegetables in the streets. When about 21 years old he removed to Birmingham, where after several trials and disappointments prosperity at length dawned upon him. His greatest difficulty was to save his first five pounds: when this was done the rest was comparatively easy. Through the kind offices of Mr. Heeley, a steel toy manufacturer, he was engaged by Samuel Harrison to superintend a manufactory for the production of split rings, of which, when only twelve months had elapsed, he became the purchaser at the price of £500, a sum he was enabled to pay out of the profits of the first year. Harrison had made for Dr. Priestley the first steel pens recorded. Mason saw that these rude efforts could be improved, and that pens could easily be made by machinery. In conjunction with Mr. James Perry, he took up this new branch of industry, which prospered wonderfully, and laid the foundation of a splendid fortune for the Kidderminster carpet weaver's son. About 1840 he joined the Messrs. Elkington, and brought £80,000 to aid in developing their patents for electrotyping. Wealth flowed in upon him, until the very disposal of it in the future became a subject of anxious deliberation between himself and his wife (Annie Griffiths), for they were childless, and he had not a relative in the world. So they resolved to make desolate orphans heirs to part of their accumulated wealth; and the friendless widows and homeless spinsters were not forgotten. In 1858 he established at Erdington an almshouse for 30 women and an orphanage for 50 girls. Soon after rds a new orphanage was erected in the same village at a cost of £60,000, and endowed with property worth £200,000. In 1874 it was enlarged so as to render it capable of accommodating 300 girls, 150 boys, and 50 infants. The original orphanage has been devoted to the purpose of an almshouse, with which is combined a home for girls who have gone into domestic service from the orphanage, but are temporarily out of a situation. Some of the orphans are always to be chosen from Kidderminster. The "Mason Science College" in Birmingham was opened 23 Feb., 1880. About £60,000 was spent on the building, and the total endowment is estimated at nearly £250,000. Sir Josiah, upon whom the Queen bestowed the honour of knighthood in 1872, died 16 June, 1881, in the 87th year of his age. He was buried in a mausoleum by the side of his wife in the orphanage grounds at Erdington. A marble statue of him is erected near his College in Birmingham. (*Worcester Journal, Kidderminster Shuttle*, &c.)

SIR ROWLAND HILL, K.C.B., D.C.L., F.R.S., &c., was born Dec. 3rd, 1795, in Blackwell Street, Kidderminster, in a house that had belonged to at least three generations of his family. In the time of Edward I. John Hill *(de Monte)* held a messuage and half a virgate of land in Comberton. The name appears in the Registers in 1539—the first year recorded. The distinctive Christian name also occurs in 1628, June 3d :—" Baptized Marryan daughter of Rowland Hill and Mary." From his father, Thomas Wright Hill, Sir Rowland is thought to have acquired the largeness of his conceptions, but from the judicious training of his mother (Sarah Lea) he imbibed more important qualities—firmness and shrewdness, patience and prudence. When he was five years old the French war ruined his father's manufacture, and he left Kidderminster for Wolverhampton. In 1802 Thomas Hill gave up trade, and started a school at Hill Top, Birmingham. Here Rowland was a school-boy, but in his twelfth year he became an assistant master. The straightened circumstances in which his family found themselves in his early days did much to develop in him the important quality of self-help. He worked at mathematics, navigation, astronomy, architecture, electricity, &c., with great zest. " Most of all was he indebted for that first of all know-

SIR ROWLAND HILL, K.C.B., D.C.L., F.R.S., &c

Born at Kidderminster Dec. 3, 1795

ledge, the knowledge of self, to an eminent physician, Dr. Johnstone (see page 158), who had engaged him to give lessons to his son. 'I heard matters talked of which I could not in the least understand. This discovery of my ignorance was at first very painful to me, and set me to work very hard.'" In conjunction with some friends he formed a "Society for Scientific and Literary Improvement." In 1822 Rowland and his elder brother Matthew brought out *Plans for the Government and Liberal Education of Boys in Large Numbers. Drawn from Experience.* In this work is set forth a complete scheme for the government of a large school on a novel plan. He gave his pupils a constitution, and established a court of justice, of which the boys were themselves the officials. When a boy above 12 left the school a sub-committee drew up his character, entered it in a book kept for the purpose, and it was read aloud before the whole school. Counters were given for "voluntary labour," so as to stimulate all tastes—working the printing-press, penmanship, drawing, etching, painting, music, modelling, learning orations and poetry, reports of lectures, debates, &c., composition in prose and verse. Fights were common at first. The plan adopted as a remedy was this: For six hours every attempt was made to appease the boys: if all was in vain the other boys were kept in school while the two combatants settled the matter in the presence of a master as marshal of the lists. Fighting was soon unknown. The system was of a highly stimulating character, but from Rowland's eagerness and great inventive powers the rules of the school were in a state of continual flux. The publication of *Public Education* aroused much attention to their work. Distinguished philosophers, such as Jeremy Bentham, Joseph Hume, Grote, Brougham, De Quincey, Malthus, Dr. Gilchrist, &c., crowded to the scene, and the school almost at one bound sprang into fame. The book was translated into foreign languages, and a similar system was tried in other lands. Men of rank and learning sent their children to be educated at "Hazelwood"—a house which the Hills had built when Hill Top became too small for the increased number of scholars. In 1826 a sucker from Hazelwood—now well known as the Bruce Castle School—was planted in London. Here Rowland brought home his bride,

Caroline daughter of Mr. Pearson, of Wolverhampton, and here he spent the first six years of his wedded life. Nothing in the biography of the Hill family is more interesting than the wonderful feeling of unity and the spirit of co-operation which prevailed among them. " As they trusted each other for aid in case of need, so at all times did they look to each other for counsel. The affairs of all were known to each. At every important turn each sought the judgment of all." By 1833 the strain of teaching had begun to tell so severely upon Rowland's health that he had to give up the work and travel abroad. The territory of South Australia—then a waste—was about to be colonised under the auspices of Mr. E. G. Wakefield, who offered him the post of secretary in England. This he accepted, and occupied it for four years with " conspicuous success." His brother Matthew had been elected Member for Hull, and aided materially in getting an Act of Parliament authorising the colonisation. In January, 1837, Rowland drew up the famous pamphlet on *Post-office Reform*, which brought him into contact with the Chancellor of the Exchequer, Mr. Spring Rice. All his knowledge of the postal service was derived from Parliamentary reports. The charge for conveyance of a letter from London to Edinburgh was 1s. 1½d. ; but from Hill's calculations it appeared that the actual cost for this distance of 400 miles was to the Government only one thirty-sixth part of a penny. " Hence," he says, " I came to the important conclusion that the existing practice of regulating the amount of postage by the distance over which an inland letter was conveyed, however plausible in appearance, had no foundation in principle ; and that consequently the rates of postage should be irrespective of distance. I scarcely need add that this discovery, as startling to myself as it could be to any one else, was the basis of the plan which has made so great a change in postal affairs." In his pamphlet he advocated the use of stamped covers for the prepayment of letters a plan first suggested by Mr. Charles Knight. For the benefit of illiterate persons Rowland made the happy suggestion of the adhesive stamp, now used throughout the world : " A bit of paper just large enough to bear the stamp, and covered at the back with a glutinous wash, which the bringer might, by applying a little moisture, attach to the back of the letter." Hill's scheme of penny postage was at first treated by the heads of the Post-office with contempt. The Postmaster-General declared that "of all the wild and visionary schemes which he had ever heard or read of, it was the most extraordinary." For two years the strongest opposition was given to the plan; but public opinion soon began to speak out loudly in its favour, and in May, 1838, a deputation, consisting of 150 Members of Parliament, urged the Prime Minister, Lord Melbourne, to adopt it. On 17 Aug., 1839, the Bill for establishing the Penny Postage received the Royal assent, and on Sept. 16th following Mr. Hill received an appointment in the Treasury, at a salary of £1500, to enable him to carry it out. On 10 Jan., 1840, the penny postage was extended to the whole kingdom. The issue of stamps, or "bits of sticking plaster for dabbing on to letters" as they were derisively called, began on May 1st. The "Mulready envelope" caused so much ridicule that nearly all the issue was destroyed. Difficulties innumerable sprang up connected with the forgery and incomplete obliteration of stamps, the cumbrous routine of the old officials, the increased expenditure caused at first by the introduction of railways, &c.; but Rowland Hill's energy and inventive genius surmounted them all. In 1842, owing to a change in the Ministry, he was dismissed from his office. He was soon appointed managing director and then chairman of the Brighton Railway Company, of which the affairs were in an unsatisfactory state. When he took office in 1843 the £50 shares were as low as £35. In 1845 they had risen to £75. At his suggestion two institutions were adopted till then unknown, viz., excursion trains and express trains. In 1846, as a national benefactor, he was presented with a cheque for £13,000, and in the same year was reinstated in the Post-office as secretary to the Postmaster-General. In 1854 he was appointed sole secretary to the Post-office. In 1857 he was elected a Fellow of the Royal Society, and early in 1860 Her Majesty conferred upon him the honour of Knight Commander of the Bath. In 1864, owing to ill-health, he retired. Parliament granted him £20,000 and an annual pension of £2000, "not merely as a meritorious public servant, but as a benefactor of his race; and feeling that his fitting reward is to be found not in this or that amount of pension, but in the grateful recollection of his country." The rest of his life was spent in quiet retirement, and when he died 27 August, 1879, he was buried in Westminster Abbey. His interesting biography, in two volumes, written by his nephew, George Birkbeck Hill, D.C.L., was published in 1880. Birmingham, where he spent his youth and early manhood, has set up his statue; and a similar honour was done to him in his native town of Kidderminster at a cost of £1800, contributed by 200,000 people chiefly in penny stamps. The statue was executed by Mr. T. Brock, R.A., and unveiled in June, 1881, by the Mayoress (Mrs. H. R. Willis), when an eloquent eulogy was pronounced by Sir Rupert Kettle. A charity for the relief of the widows and orphans of the servants of the Post-office will keep his memory green. "But so long as men keep warm feelings, and the name of home has still its charm ; so long as there are sorrowful partings and hearts that need comforting ; so long as our high aim is towards peace on earth, good will toward men, Rowland Hill is not likely to be forgotten. For he has done almost more than any other man to bring near those who are far off, to bind the nations together, and to make the whole world kin."

WILLIAM LEA, M.A., son of William Lea, Esq., of Kidderminster (p. 91), was born at Stone House 19 Nov., 1819. He was educated at Rugby and Brasenose College, Oxford, B.A. (2nd Class *Lit. Hum.*) 1842. In 1849 he became Vicar of St. Peter's, Droitwich, which he resigned in 1887. In 1881 he was made Archdeacon of Worcester, and filled the office with conspicuous tact and ability. For more than 40 years he earnestly promoted the cause of education in the diocese as secretary of the Worcester Board of Education and hon. secretary of Saltley College. He was also a great authority upon fruit growing, recommending it especially to cottagers. In addition to his published *Charges*, he wrote *Catechisings on the Book of Common Prayer, On the Life of our Lord, Sermons on the Prayer Book Preached in Rome, Small Farms*, and *Church Plate in the Archdeaconry of Worcester*. He was also collecting materials for an account of the church fonts in the Archdeaconry. He died at "Orchardlea" 24 Sept., 1889, and was buried in St. Peter's churchyard, Droitwich.

HUMPHREY PRICE, born at Kidderminster, and educated at the Grammar School, was afterwards minister of Christ Church in Needwood. He was a man of exceedingly benevolent disposition, but somewhat eccentric and misguided in his chivalrous support of the cause of the weavers during the great strike of 1828. Nearly 2000 looms were standing idle from March till the end of August, entailing a loss upon the operatives of about £50,000. This produced great distress in the town; Mr. Price composed a pathetic poem, "A Kidderminster Weaver's Wife's Dream," and also published highly inflammatory letters addressed to John Woodward, John Broom, James Hooman, and George Hallen (High Bailiff), which were considered to be the cause of some riots which ensued. J. Bowyer, of The Copse, and "Oppidanus" replied to these letters (printer, T. Pennell, High Street). Sir James Scarlett moved in the King's Bench for a rule to show cause why a criminal information should not be filed against the Rev. H. Price. He was tried at Hereford, and sentenced to twelve months' imprisonment. In the end the men returned to work at lower wages, and received 20s. each as a present.

REBECCA SWAN was the last of the Kidderminster witches. She lived in Church Street, where a signboard made known her qualifications:—"Town and Country Letter Writer to All Parts. Gives Advice in all Periods. No need to Apply without recommendation. I have been wrongfully used. Wishes to do justice, love mercy, and walk humbly with God." A number of fine cats assisted her in her extensive trade of fortune-teller and recoverer of stolen property; but when herself robbed of twelve half-crowns and six gold rings her mystic art failed to regain the articles. She was burnt to death while intoxicated on a tempestuous night in November, 1850, when all her cats mysteriously disappeared. Richard Baxter was a believer in witchcraft, and from the *Townsend MSS.* it appears that in 1660 four persons accused of the black art were brought from Kidderminster to Worcester gaol. "The eldest daughter had said that if they had not been taken, the King should never have come into England; and though he now doth come, yet he shall not live long, but shall die as ill a death as they; and

v

that they would have made corn like pepper. Many great charges were made against them but little proved ; they were put to the ducking in the river ; they would not sink, but swam aloft. The man had five teats, the mother three, and the eldest daughter one. When they went to search the women none were visible : one advised to lay them on their backs, and keep open their mouths, and they would appear ; and so they presently appeared in sight."]

GEORGE GRIFFITH served his first clerkship in a corn merchant's office in Bewdley, and was afterwards resident for many years in Kidderminster. Quite early in life he became possessed with two ruling passions—verse making and the reformation of grammar schools. His writings were very voluminous, chiefly in "history, history-romance, drama satire, and a miscellaneous worship of the Muse." His chief publications were *The Free Schools of Worcestershire*, *Life of George Wilson, Charles II., Going to Markets and Grammar Schools*, and *Records in the Midland Counties*. He died in 1883, and was buried at Ribbesford.

THOMAS HELMORE, M.A., was the son of the Rev. Thomas Helmore, minister of the New Meeting (1810—1818). He graduated at Hertford College, Oxford, and was ordained by the Bishop of Lichfield in 1840. From 1842 to 1846 he was Vice-Principal of St. Mark's College, Chelsea. In 1847 he was made Priest-in-Ordinary to her Majesty's Chapels Royal. He was a prolific writer of church music, and was the originator and principal editor of *The Hymnal Noted, Manual of Plain Song, Carols*, &c. He died July, 1890, aged 79, and was buried in Brompton cemetery.

DR. G. CUSTANCE, born in Kidderminster, was the author of a *History of the Church in England*.

EDWARD BRADLEY, B.A., more widely known as "CUTHBERT BEDE," was born in the topmost house in Swan Street, Kidderminster, on 25 March, 1827. His father was a surgeon, and Edward was educated at the Grammar School under the Rev.

W. Cockin. Whilst still a school boy he was a member of the local *Athenæum*, and contributed a large number of original compositions in prose and verse to its " Manuscript Magazine." Many of them are illustrated in his facile style with pen-and-ink sketches. At Durham University, where he graduated in 1848, he was Thorpe and Foundation Scholar. In 1850 he was ordained, and held successively the benefices of Bobbington in Staffordshire, Denton (Hunts), Stretton, near Oakham, and Lenton, near Grantham, which he retained up to the time of his death, 12 Dec., 1889. His celebrity mainly rests upon his famous book, *Verdant Green* (1854), a humorous story of Oxford University life. His other works were *Photographic Pleasures, Nearer and Dearer, Fairy Fables, Happy Hours, Glencreggan, Humour, Wit, and Satire, Curate of Cranston, Tour in Tartan Land, The White Wife, The Rook's Garden, Matins and Muttons, Little Mr. Bouncer,* and *Fotheringhay and Mary Queen of Scots*. He was also a regular contributor to *The Queen, Notes and Queries, Society*, &c. A large water-colour view of the interior of Kidderminster parish church, sketched by him before its restoration, is in the chantry. He took a deep interest in the history and antiquities of his native town ; several of his early sketches were presented by him to the Museum, and have been framed at the expense of G. W. Grosvenor, Esq. Mr. Bradley married a daughter of William Hancocks, Esq., of Blakeshall House, Wolverley, and leaves several children. His brother is a well-known Worcestershire writer under the *nom de plume* of " Shelsley Beauchamp." An ancestor, the Rev. John Bradley, was Rector of Ribbesford from 1725 to 1730.

DANIEL WAGSTAFF GOODWIN was born at Holt in 1821, and was son of John G. Goodwin, Alderman and Mayor of Worcester. In 1845 he came to the ancient Town Mills of Kidderminster, where he adopted the latest improvements in machinery and apparatus, and by unremitting attention to business achieved much success. He was chosen to nearly all the offices of honour and trust in the town, such as Alderman, Mayor, County Councillor, Churchwarden, Chairman of the Chamber of Commerce, &c. He was of simple, quiet manners, but displayed abundant common-sense and public spirit. He gave the site and was the chief promoter of the Schools of Art and Science: and shortly before his death he had anonymously offered £500 towards building a new Free Library. He also erected a useful and handsome drinking fountain at the Blakebrook entrance of the town. He died 25 March, 1890, and is buried in St. John's churchyard.

WILLIAM HENRY SIMCOX was son of George Price Simcox, of Kidderminster, and his wife Jemima (Haslope). He was educated first at Kidderminster Grammar School, under Dr. Sheppard, whence he won an open exhibition at Marlborough College. In 1860 he was elected scholar of Balliol College, Oxford; in 1863 he was First Class, Moderations; 1864, First Class *Lit. Hum.*; 1865, Craven Scholar and Gainsford Greek Prose Prize; 1867, Theological Scholar and English Essay; 1868, Arnold Historical Essay and M.A.; Fellow of Queen's College 1864—1870. In 1866 he was ordained. He was Rector of Weyhill, Hants, 1869—1885, and of Harlaxton, Lincolnshire, 1885—1887. He died in 1889, aged 48. He wrote *Beginnings of the Christian Church*, 1881, and edited *The Orations of Demosthenes and Æschines on the Crown*, 1872, and *Tacitus' Histories*, 1875.

GEORGE AUGUSTUS SIMCOX, elder brother of the above, was likewise born in Kidderminster, educated at the Grammar School, and has had a brilliant university career. In 1858 he won an open scholarship at Corpus Christi College, Oxford; 1860, First Class Moderations; 1861, Ireland Scholar; 1862, First Class *Lit. Hum.* and Craven Scholar; 1864, Latin Essay and Fellow of Queen's College. He has written a *History of Latin Literature*, 2 vols., Longmans (1883), &c.

CHAPTER X.

The Manufactures.

ADON'S *Formulare Anglicanum* (*Nash*, ii., 42) contains the earliest reference to manufactures in the town: it is the release of a messuage and land in Wich, made by one Alured, son of Ketelbern, a *fuller* of Kidderminster. The deed is without date, but Hugh le Poer, one of the witnesses, was under sheriff in the eighth, fourteenth, and nineteenth years of Henry III. Taking the latest period, we get 1235 as the date when the clothing trade was undoubtedly in operation here.

In the *Wanley MS.* mention is made of Alured the Fuller as holding land "on which the Hospital was formerly situated, near the great Mill of Kidderminster." Other deeds of the time of Henry III. refer to "Margery widow of Richard the Fuller," and "an annual rent of 2s. to be paid by Simon the Fuller my man." One of the earliest fulling-mills set up in England was that at Bradford-on-Avon, in Wiltshire, a few miles from Maiden Bradley. Its advantages would not escape the keen eyes of the monks; and before long they were the owners of a fulling-mill worked by water power at Mytton, in the tenancy of William de Stour. (Page 21.)

Before 1334 the manufacture of cloth was so well established that regulations were made respecting it.

"FOR THE MAKING OF WOOLLEN CLOTH.

"Alsoe we woll that no manner of man within the Manner and Burrow off Ketherminster shall *make* any woollen cloth

Broad nor Narrow without the Baylieff's Seall in payn of xxs. for every defaulte, the one haulfe to the prince and the Lord and the Other to the Bayliefe."

From the wording of the above there can be no doubt that the cloth was made in the town itself. Kerseys were probably made here also, but the following regulation relates only to the *sealing* of such as were exposed for sale :—

"FOR THE SEALING OF CARSEIES.

"Alsoe wee woll that noe man nor woman shall Bring to the ffayr or Markett Any Carseies for to sell to sale without a seall for dought off the Catchpowles for all such Carseyes or Cloth are fforfeyted, the one halfe to the prince and the lord And the other halfe to the baylyffe and his Catchpoles."

Wool was abundant in England, and the prosperity of the Flemish burghers depended entirely on this important raw staple. In the valuation of the Rectory of Kidderminster, made in 1335, the tithes of wool amounted to the large sum of £4— three times the value of the hay and four times that of the oats. The tithe of lambs was 13s. 4d., whilst that of calves was only 12d. The sheep, however, were small, and each fleece averaged only 1¼lb. (*Rogers.*) The foreign wars of the Edwards and the Henrys were carried on almost entirely by the tax on wool. The heavy export duty on this article induced many Flemings to take up their residence in England just as in our own times carpet manufacturers have gone to the United States. From the names of some old Kidderminster Burgesses we may conclude that a few of them found their way here ; we have for instance Delph, Fleminge, Holland, and Flanders.

Flax was extensively grown in this district in the middle ages, and in 1335 the tithe was valued at 13s. 4d. Its importance will be understood when we remember that cotton was unknown. Leather was very largely used for clothing, but Bewdley was the chief seat of the tanneries, having an abundance of oak bark from the Wyre Forest.

In 1533 the cloth trade of Worcestershire was passing through a crisis ; and a paternal government interfered to protect the towns from ruinous competition, though in a manner somewhat contrary to our modern ideas of political economy. John Leland about this time records: "The Towne standeth most by cloathinge." The Act 25 Henry VIII., cap. 18, runs thus:—

"i Sheweth unto the King our Sovereign Lord, and to the Lords Spiritual and Temporal, and to the Commons in this present Parlt assembled, the Citizens, Burgesses, and Inhabitants of the City of Worcester, and the towns of Evesham, Droitwich, Kederminster, and Bromisgrove within the County of Worcester. That where the said City Boroughs and Towns have been in times past well and substantially inhabited, occupied, maintained, and upholden by reason of making of woollen Cloths, called long Cloths, short Cloths, and other Cloths, as well whites, blues, and brown blues, and the poor people of the same Towns and of the country adjoining to them, daily set a work, as in spinning, carding, breaking, and sorting of Wools, and the Handicrafts there inhabiting as Weavers, Fullers, Sheremen and Dyers, have been well set a work, and had sufficient living by the same, until now within few years passed, that divers persons inhabiting in the hamlets, thorps, and villages adjoining to the said towns, for their private wealths, singular advantages and commodities, nothing regarding the maintenance and upholding of the said Towns, ne the commonwealth of the said handicrafts, ne the poor people which had living by the same, have not only ingrossed and taken into their hands divers and sundry farms, and become farmers, grasiers, and husbandmen, but also do exercise the mysteries of cloth-making, weaving, fulling and sheering within their said houses to the great decay and ruin of the said Towns.

"ii For remedy whereof and for the amendment and good advancement of the said towns be it enacted . that after Sept 30, 1536 only such persons inhabiting within the towns of Worcester, Evesham, Droitwich, Kederminster, and Bromisgrove shall make any manner of woollen cloths to be sold upon pain of forfeiture for each Cloth xls.

"iii No higher rent shall be imposed for houses in the said towns than was given within 20 years next before the making of this Act.

"iv Persons may make cloaths for their own wearing, their children or servants wearing.

"v That in every town there be due search made of every such cloth beforesaid there made, and that they be meted both length and breadth, being wet from the mill, before they be set upon the rack and dried (2) and that they shall be sealed with the seal of the searcher of the same town, which seal shall have a stamp containing the true numbers for the length and breadth of the same cloth being wet, on pain of forfeiting for every cloth put to sale, not having the said seal of the searcher xxs. (1) and the searcher shall have for the sealing of every cloth a peny, and not above."

In 27 Hy. VIII., cap. 12, is a further " Act for the true making of cloth."

In 4 and 5 Philip and Mary, cap. 5, § 2, it is enacted that every white cloth and clothes commonly called long Worcesters shall weigh 75lb. at the least.

From the Borough archives we extract the following :—

" Ordinances and By-lawes agreed uppon, and made at Kidderminster, under ye Common Seale of ye said Burrough, by John Elsmore the nowe Baylive, and the Major part of the Capitall Burghesses thereof, Assembled to y^t end in the Guildhall of that Burrough the xxiijrd day of August, A.D. 1650.

" 1 Imprimis whereas the Burrough of Kidderminster aforesaid hath bine, and is an Auncient Burrough and hath auntientlie had in it divers Fraternities, Companies, or fellowshipps of ye Tradesmen and Inhabitants thereof known by severall names—That is to say, the Societie or Companie of Weavers, The Societie of Taylors The Societie of Smithes and the Society of Shoemakers. And whereas also the said severall Fraternities, Societies, Companies, or Fellowshipps, have each and every of them had two persons respectively elected yerelie out of the said severall Fraternities, upon the Munday next after Midsummer day, by ye greater of the said respective Fraternities, which are called, and so auntiently were called, by the name of Wardens of the said severall Fraternities, which said Wardens were, and are for ye next yere following their eleccion to doe ye best of their skill, and power, and to execute and accomplish all things whatsoever by all good wayes for ye maintenance, and continuance of good Orders for the generall good of ye said Burrough, and for ye particular good and benefit of their respective Fraternities or Societies. It is therefore now agreed upon and ordeigned by ye foresaid John Elsmore Baylive of ye said Burrough, and ye Major part of ye Capitall Burghesses thereof, That the said severall Fraternities, Societies, Companies, and Fellowships still continue, be, and remayne as before they have bine.

" 3 Item it is ordeyned That at every such Eleccion such person of the severall Fraternities as shall last come before Eleven of ye Clock to the place of ye Assembly is, and shalbe made for the yere then next following a Beedle or messenger unto ye sayd respective Wardens, to summon ye said respective Fraternities together as often as he shall by the sayd respective Wardens be commanded penalty 3^s. 4^d.;

" 5 It is ordeyned that no person of any of the particular trades belonging to any of the said Fraternities shall set up any shop or house of trading within the said Borough or exercise any of the said Trades unless he be first admitted into one of the said Fraternities by the respective Wardens and Companies, paying for his admittance such reasonable summe as shall then be agreed upon by him and them, and not exceeding Twenty Shillings; the one halfe to goe to ye said Baylive and Capitall Burghesses for the use of the said Burrough, and ye other halfe to ye use of the said respective Fraternities. And it is further ordeyned that no person shall exercise any of the said Trades there unlesse he hath bine bound an Apprentice to ye same by the space of Seaven yeares penalty Ten Pounds.

"14 Item for asmuch as the Society of Weavers of the Stuffes called Kidderminster Stuffes have received of late much dammage in their reputacion of trading by the Covetousnes and irregularity of some others of ye same profession and Trade within ye said Burrough who for their own advantage have driven a privat Trade of ye same Stuffes deceitfully made both for measure and workmanship, By which means a scandall is fastened upon ye said Trade, the Traders therein much disparaged, the Trade decayed, and the poore increased, who formerly by their Labour therein were supported and mainteyned. For the regulating hereof and to th'end ye said Trade, and profession may regaine its credit (now so much impayred), the poore as formerlie set on worke, and releeved, and that each man may in love and charity live neighbourly one with another. It is therefore thought fit, and ordeyned that from henceforth no Master of and in the said Trade of Weavers, nor likewise of any the Trades belonging to ye severall Companies or Fraternities as aforesaid shall take any Apprentice to any their severall trades but he shall first acquaint ye Wardens of the said severall Fraternities Companies and Fellowships therewith, who shall take care to have him bound according to ye Lawes of ye Realme, And shall enroll his name, age, and time of his service in their book, for which they shall be allowed 2sh. 6d. and not above, to be payd by him or her that shall procure the same Apprentice to be bound as aforesayd. And likewise yt all and every Master of the said Trade of Weaving within the sayd Burrough be required to take no Apprentice to ye foresayd trade for ye space of Seven years after ye Confirmacion hereof according to ye Statute in that behalf made, except only poore boyes necessarily cast upon the Towne (if so many there be) or a Townsman's owne sonne, if any such be; And also not to take an Apprentice till he that taketh him hath been a Master at ye sayd Trade one whole yere; And that to and for each Apprentice that any man shall take in ye sayd Trade he doe keep Two Journymen, which shall be such, and none others, and so qualified, as ye Lawes of this nation doe allow of, and that shall be approved of to worke in the said trade by ye sayd Fraternitie Societie Company or Fellowship of Weavers. And that in case any Tradesman within the said Burrough shall fall into decay having an Apprentice The same person so decayed shall not take money to make his sayd Apprentice free; But with the consent of ye same Fraternitie, Company or Society shall turne him over to some other of the same profession, and trade to work out the residue of his time then undetermined

w

"15 Item it is thought fit, declared, and agreed upon, That for and during the space of three years next after the confirmacion of these present Ordinances as aforesaid, no one Master of the sayd Trade or Fellowship of Weavers doe keep at work at once any more Loomes of Linsey Woolseyes than onelie three, except he be (for good causes by him alleaged, and so approved) admitted and alowed to keepe more by the Wardens and Fellowshipp of the same profession at their comon hall, or meeting. Nor shall any person setting up the sayd Trade of Weaving of Linsey Woolseys, and other stuffes made of Linnen and Woollen within the sayd limit of time in the sayd Burrough be permitted to worke upon more than one Loome till the sayd time of three years be expired, nor to weave unto or for any that is not free of the sayd Trade. And that each Loome shall if conveniently it may weave a piece a week of six quaters wide and Twentie fower yards long, for which peece the Journyman that workes thereupon shall weekly have five shillings during the sayd time and so proportionally for other breadths and lengths."

The charter of Charles I. (1636) recites that Kidderminster is an ancient borough of great commerce for the working and manufacture of cloths. Baxter says :—" My people were not rich ; there were among them very few beggars, because their common trade of stuff weaving would find work for them all, men women and children, that were able, and there were none of the tradesmen very rich, seeing their trade was poor, that would but find them food and raiment ; the magistrates of the town were few of them worth £40 per annum, and most not half so much ; three or four of the richest thriving masters of the trade got but about £500 or £600 in twenty years, and it may be lost £100 of it by an ill debtor. The generality of the master workmen lived but little better than their journey men, but only that they laboured not quite so hard."

In 23 Charles II. (1671) an Act was passed for regulating the manufacture of Kidderminster stuffs :—

"Whereas divers abuses and deceits have of late years been had and used in the making of stuffs, called Kidderminster Stuffs, within the borough and parish of Kidderminster, tending to the debasing of the said manufacture, and to the great prejudice of the publick.

"For the prevention of which abuses and deceits, may it please your Majesty that it may be enacted : that there shall be chosen one president, four wardens and eight assistants, all which shall be master weavers within the said Borough the first Monday after Pentecost, in the year of our Lord

1671, and from thenceforth yearly and every year, by the master weavers of the said borough or the greater part of them then present.

" And for the regulation and good government of the said trade and manufacture, the said President, Wardens and Assistants or any seven or more of them whereof the President and three or more of the said Wardens are to be present, shall and may from time to time meet and consult together for the good and benefit of the said trade and manufacture and for the due execution of the powers and authority given by this Act, and to make and ordain Bye-laws Rules and Ordinances for the better regulating of the said trade and manufacture, and the artificers of the same; and to make seals from time to time for sealing of the same stuffs: which Bye-laws Rules and Ordinances being ratified and confirmed by the Justices of Assize for the County of Worcester for the time being, shall be published at least twice in the year, at two publick assemblies for the said trade and manufacture and by the several persons using the same within and under the said Regulation. And the said President, Wardens and Assistants or any seven or more of them shall have and hereby have power to impose a fine or penalty upon any person or persons using the said trade, or that shall be under the regulation thereof, as shall not conform to such Rules so made. Provided that the said fine or penalty upon any person for not conforming as aforesaid shall not exceed forty shillings for any one Offence.

" And for the better regulation of the said trade and manufacture, and the avoiding of fraud and deceits therein; be it further enacted by the authority aforesaid, that all linen yarn reeled, and usually bought and sold, or estimated by the lea to be hereafter used by any of the said artificers and stuff weavers within the said borough or parish of Kidderminster or liberties thereof shall be made without fraud or deceit, and be openly bought and sold in some publick market place on the market day within the said borough to be appointed by the Bayliff of the said borough for the time being: and before the same be exposed to sale, shall be reeled on a reel four yards about, every lea of the said yarn containing two hundred threads. And in case any person or persons shall hereafter sell or expose to sale any the yarns aforesaid, made or reeled in any other manner then as aforesaid; it shall and may be lawful to and for the said President, Wardens and Assistants to seize and carry away all such deceitful and defective yarns, which said yarns within twenty days after such seizure shall be tried by a jury of twelve honest and able artificers of the said trade who shall be from time to time impannelled and summoned by a precept under the hands and seals of the Bayliff and any one Justice of the Peace of the said borough to appear at the *Guild-hall* of the said borough to try whether the said yarns be made and reeled according to the true intent and meaning of this act. And if the said jury impanelled and sworn as aforesaid shall find any of the said yarns not made and reeled according to the intent and meaning of this act, that then the said Bayliff and Justice of the peace of the said Borough shall impose such fine upon the owner of such defective yarns in their discretions shall be thought meet not exceeding the value of the moyety of such defective yarns : which said fine the owners of the said defective yarns shall pay to the said President for the time being (to be disposed of as the said President, Wardens, and Assistants or the *major* number of them shall seem meet at their next publick meeting within thirty days after the said tryal) and in default thereof the said yarns to be sold by the President or any two of the said Wardens and the overplus of the moneys thereof coming after the fine or fines deducted to be restored to the said owner or owners upon demand.

" And be it further enacted by the authority aforesaid, that all sorts of clothes and stuffs woven with wooll onely, or of wooll and other materials within the said borough or parish of *Kidderminster* or the liberties thereof shall be under the Power, Government, and regulation of the said President, Wardens and Assistants, in such manner, as by this act, and the Bye-laws and ordinances made or to be made by vertue thereof or by the laws or statutes of the Realm, are or shall be established.

" And that all clothes and stuffs made or to be made under the regulation aforesaid before the same shall be exposed or put to sale, shall be brought to some convenient place within the said Borough to be appointed by the said President and Wardens to be viewed and searched by the said President, and any one of the said Wardens, or by any two of the said Wardens, and if the same shall be found to be well and sufficiently made and wrought, according to the rules and ordinances of the said trade and manufacture : then all such clothes and stuffs shall be by the said President and any one of the said Wardens sealed and allowed accordingly ; and if upon such search and view any clothes or stuffs shall be found or conceived not to be well and sufficiently made and wrought according to the rules and ordinances of the said trade : then such clothes and stuffs shall be seized by the said President and Warden, or any two of the said Wardens, and be brought to tryal and the owner or owners fined in such manner and form as in this present Act is before limited and appointed for the tryal of defective linen yarn.

" And be it further enacted by the authority aforesaid : that the said President, Wardens and Assistants, or any two or more of them, shall have and hereby have power and authority to enter into and search the houses and work-houses of any artificer, under the regulation of the said trade, at all times of the day, and usual times of opening of shops and working ; and into the shops, houses and warehouses of any common buyer, dealer in, or retayler of any of the said clothes or stuffs, and into the houses and work-houses of any dyer, sheer-man and all other workmen's houses and places of sale or dressing of the said clothes, stuffs, and yarns and may there search and view the said clothes stuffs and yarns respectively, whether they be made and wrought according to the laws, orders, and ordinances of the same trade and if any cloths stuff, or yarns shall be found faulty or defective to seize and carry away the same to be tryed by a jury as afore in this Act is appointed.

"And be it also enacted by the authority aforesaid, that it shall not be lawful for any person or persons to buy any piece or pieces of clothes or stuffs, made, or to be made within the said borough or parish or liberty thereof, before the same be sealed as aforesaid, and if any piece or pieces of such cloth or stuff, shall be found in the possession of any person or persons unsealed (except in the possession of the first owner or maker thereof) the person or persons in whose custody the same shall be found, shall be adjudged guilty of deceit shall forfeit for every such piece of cloth or stuff so found in his or their possession unsealed as aforesaid, the sum of four shillings, and the maker and seller of the same who shall deliver the same out of his or their possession before the same be sealed, shall likewise forfeit for every such piece other four shillings to the use of the poor of the same trade.

"And if any person shall counterfeit any seal of the said trade or shall seal any piece of cloth or stuff made under the regulation of the said trade with any counterfeit seal, or shall remove a seal of one piece and set it unto another piece which hath not been sealed, as before in this Act is appointed to be sealed ; every person so offending and being thereof convicted by his own confession or by the oath of two or more witnesses, shall forfeit for every such offence the sum of twenty pounds.

"And for the better providing that poor journeymen who have served in the said trade, and are not able to set up for themselves may be imployed in work ; it is hereby enacted, that every person under the regulation of the said trade, who shall imploy two apprentices in the said trade, shall likewise imploy and set on work two journeymen in the said trade during the time he shall have or imploy two apprentices upon pain that every person shall forfeit for every moneth so offending as aforesaid the sum of twenty shillings.

"And be it enacted by the authority aforesaid, that the one moiety of all fines, forfeitures and penalties before in this Act mentioned, other than such as are expressly otherwise appointed shall be to the use of the Kings Majesty his heirs and successors, the other moiety to the use of the poor of the said trade ; and shall and may be levied by distress and sale of the goods and chattels of the offender or offenders by warrant under the hands and seals of the Bayliff and one of the Justices of Peace of the said borough, or be recovered by action of debt bill, plaint or information in any of his majesties courts of record wherein no essoin, protection, or wager of law shall be allowed.

"And be it also enacted that all Bayliffs, Justices, Sheriffs, Constables and all other officers shall be aiding and assisting to the said President, Wardens and Assistants or any of them, as often as they shall be thereunto required and in all Actions and Suits that shall be brought against any person or persons for what he or they shall do in persuance or in execution of this Act or any of the authorities hereby given, the person or persons so sued or

180   A HISTORY OF KIDDERMINSTER.

molested shall or may plead the general issue of not guilty and give the special matter in evidence and shall recover double costs in any such case if the verdict pass for such person or persons or that the plaintiff or plaintiffs be *Nonsuit* therein or forbear further prosecution or suffer discontinuance; for which costs the said person or persons shall have the like remedy as in any case where costs by the law were given to the defendants.

" In the Savoy

" Printed by the Assigns of John Bill
and Christopher Barker, Printers to the Kings
Most Excellent Majesty 1671."

In 1677 the number of looms of all sorts was 417; master weavers, 157; journeymen, 187; apprentices, 115. Only one of the masters had seven looms; most of them had two or three.

In the parish accounts of St. Michael's, Worcester, for the year 1623, eight yards of Kidderminster stuff at 1½d. a yard were bought for the clothing of two pauper lads.

At the Restoration 14 yards of "Kidderminster stuff," value £3 7s. 6d., were purchased for Worcester Cathedral. At Wenlock, in 1687, it was resolved to have a carpet of "Kidderminster stuff" for the Council Chamber. Judge Jefferies alluded to the distinctive trade of the town when he inveighed against poor Baxter's "linsey-woolsey doctrine." The linsey woolseys, or "Kidderminsters," were printed linseys in use for hangings of rooms and beds. When this industry declined, the manufacture of a rough cloth called frieze, chiefly sold to the Dutch, was taken up. In the early part of the eighteenth century cheneys and ratteens were made. On the decline of the clothing trade the town was reduced very low for want of business, yet a few employed themselves in making worsted stuffs, or stuffs composed of worsted and silk mixed, called Spanish poplins; the breadth of these was half a yard. *(Nash.)* Other fabrics manufactured here were arras, woollen camlet, glossanett, Irish poplin, and several kinds of crape.

About the year 1717 Mr. Greaves, of London, encouraged a manufacture of striped tameys and prunellas. In 1748 yard-wide silk and worsted stuffs were made to great advantage. In

THE MANUFACTURES.

1755 was established a manufacture in silk alone, figured and flowered for women's cloaks. "The invention of quilting worsted in looms for bed-quilts and petticoats, in imitation of Marseilles quilting, is to be ascribed to the Messrs. Pearsall, and is executed by those ingenious weavers Freestones, who have likewise invented a loom for weaving nets of all kinds."

In 1772 there were 1700 silk and worsted looms at work. In 1767 a journeyman's wages were from 10s. to 12s. a week.

In 1776 an advertisement in *Berrow's Journal* announced that on Feb. 3rd (Bishop Blaze) the Woolcombers of Kidderminster intended making a grand Cavalcade round the town dressed in the following manner, viz. they will be completely dressed with Caps and Sashes *of their own manufacture :* to be preceded by an Orator, then the God Jason bearing the Golden Fleece, a Shepherd and Shepherdess, the Patron Bishop Blaze in a single-horse chair, attended by two Pages ; the Woolcombers on Horse-back two and two : Band of Music. To start from the Rose and Crown about 10 a.m.

On 27 Feb., 1794, the woolcombers presented a petition to Parliament setting forth their certain ruin by the invention of a machine, which, when worked by one person and four children, would do as much as thirty men.

At the time of the American War of Independence trade had been so bad that nearly the whole of the 87th Regiment and part of the 88th were raised in Kidderminster : few of them ever came back.

By 1831 the silk and worsted looms had decreased from 1700 to 340. Bombazine was being made, but not so much as formerly.

"The old order changes, giving place to new," and any manufacturing town that is content to rely on its present success, without making constant efforts to improve its industries and develop new ones, will soon find itself left behind in the race. Fortunately for Kidderminster, at nearly every period of its history it has had men of sagacity, enterprise, and forethought, who could read the signs of the times. In 1735 the first carpet factory was erected on Mount Skipet, Kidderminster. From an article by Mr. Joseph Mears, of *The Sun*, we learn some interesting details of the early history of this important industry, with which the fortunes of the borough are now so closely interwoven. A local poet mentions the names of Pearsall and Broom as those of the founders of the carpet trade. It is probable that to Pearsall belongs the honour of weaving the first "Kidderminsters," a flat carpet, now made chiefly in Scotland, though keeping the old name. The master weavers in the town, however, had carefully noted what had been done at Wilton, Wiltshire, under the patronage of Henry Herbert, ninth Earl of Pembroke. That nobleman had been a traveller for years through Flanders and France, and had inspected splendid products of the Continental carpet looms, and had patriotically resolved to have weavers, artists, managers, and everybody essential to the use of the carpet trade near his Wilton mansion. He therefore persuaded Anthony Duffory, Pierre Jernaule, and others to leave France for England, and in 1745 those famous weavers began at Wilton to revolutionise the carpet trade of the empire. In 1755 Axminster began to work side by side with the industry of Wilton. It was a trying hour for carpet masters on the banks of the Stour—everything depended on a bold and rapid resolve to wrestle with Wilton for the cut carpet market. Three years had proved that Kidderminsters could not hope to compete with Wiltons, and instead of pausing to see what the next three years would bring forth, a brave townsman quitted Kidderminster and crossed the Channel, determined to make or mar his fortune as a carpet weaver. JOHN BROOM, a middle-aged man of enterprise, whose tomb may still be seen in the old churchyard, travelled first to Brussels and next to Tournay, studying with desperate earnestness the "mystery" of Brussels carpeting, and bent on finding for Kidderminster a first-class adept in the Brussels trade. At Tournay he made the acquaintance of just the weaver he wanted, and losing no time in embarking with him for England, Mr. Broom settled his Belgian stealthily in the neighbourhood of Mount Skipet. In an upstair room master and man built forthwith the first Brussels loom A.D. 1749, and they worked the machine with as much secrecy as though they were counterfeiting coin. Gradually the secret carpet weaving was on everybody's lips, though as yet none but Broom and his Belgian could pretend to produce a Brussels. But as the weavers drove their loom by candle-light as well as by sunlight, another manufacturer in the town engaged a workman night after night to climb a ladder and watch their proceedings, until he was able to bring out a Brussels loom. The plot succeeded, and a second firm—or, rather, several firms—were the consequences of the conspiracy. The trade expanded so much that, in 1753, Lord Foley laid out new streets and built 200 new houses. The master weavers of Wilton were so alarmed by the rising carpet trade at Kidderminster that they resolved to sink large sums over and above their common profits in order to crush it. But the Brussels carpeting had taken root, and in less than fifty years it was found to flourish exceedingly, and became the chief industry of the town. In 1807 the silk and worsted looms had decreased from 1700 to 700, while the carpet looms had increased from 250 to 1000. But nearly all other weaving except that of carpets was swept away in 1825, when Jacquard machines were introduced for the manufacture of carpets by Messrs. Lea, Broom, and Sons. In 1828 a severe competition arose with the Scotch manufacturers. Wages were reduced, and a ruinous strike ensued. In 1830 the ill-feeling between masters and men culminated in some very serious riots. By 1838 there were 2020 carpet looms—1765 for Brussels, 210 for Kidderminster, and 45 for Venetians. There were 24 employers and 4016 weavers in the town. It would appear, however, that the manufacturers had not the same enterprising spirit that distinguished their forefathers. When the celebrated Mr. Whytock invented and patented his new fabric called tapestry or printed Brussels, he offered to sell the patent to the carpet masters of the town, but they would not purchase it. A similar thing happened when Mr. Bigelow, of Massachusetts, offered to Kidderminster the sale of his power loom, first shown in the Great Exhibition of 1851, and afterwards erected on trial at the Hoobrook mill. Eventually the Messrs. Crossley, of Halifax, at the price of £10,000, became the purchasers of the Patent Rights for Great Britain, with the result that for a period they almost monopolised the trade. They offered the invention to

Kidderminster on payment of a royalty, and the privilege was soon secured by Messrs. Worth, Brinton, and Jecks Dixon.

The firm of Messrs. Pardoe, Hoomans, and Pardoe saw the fatal mistake that had been made in the rejection of the power loom, and they did what they could to make amends by applying it to the manufacture of tapestry carpets in this town in 1851; while Messrs. James Humphries and Sons applied steam power to the manufacture of Brussels carpets in 1852. The development of the movement for the introduction of the power loom was exceedingly rapid, and the late Earl of Dudley gave it an immense impetus by erecting spacious works, with steam power and plant, in what is now known as Green Street. In this way many of the manufacturers were allowed to have their work carried on in what was popularly known as "Lord Ward's shed." Power looms were placed there by Messrs. H. Woodward and Sons, Morton and Sons, Samuel Fawcett, Thomas Humphries, and John Lloyd Dobson. The population, which had decreased nearly 4000 in the decade 1851 to 1861, began rapidly to rise again, and the trade increased to an enormous extent. Many acres of ground were soon covered with large and well-appointed factories, affording employment to thousands of workmen, and keeping the builders busy in the erection of new streets. The railway was opened in 1852.

In 1854 George Price Simcox (firm formerly Lea and Simcox) obtained a patent for printing a twill fabric which was woven plain colour, then printed with blocks, and called "Beaver Carpet." Works were erected on the Worcester Road for weaving and printing this fabric, and are still called the Beaver works. The carpet was not a success, and was followed by a one-frame white Brussels fabric printed with a pattern from blocks in the same way as the beaver carpet. This firm also introduced a low quality Brussels carpet called "Stouts:" it was made by hand in some factories at Mount Pleasant, now occupied by Messrs. Tomkinson and Adam.

A most important development of the trade, and one of far-reaching influence on the future fortunes of the town, was the introduction into England in 1878 or the Royal Axminster power-loom. Messrs. Tomkinson and Adam acquired the patent rights for Great Britain, and the first looms were erected in their factory on Arch Hill. They also granted licenses for the use of the patent to Messrs. Southwell of Bridgnorth, J. W. and C. Ward of Halifax, and H. J. Dixon and Sons, Woodward and Grosvenor, and Morton and Sons, of Kidderminster. This loom was invented by Halcyon Skinner, and became the property of the Alex. Smith and Son's Carpet Company, Yonkers, New York. The power Chenille Axminster setting loom was invented by Mr. William Adam ; and in 1880 the firm of Tomkinson and Adam licensed James Templeton and Co. and J. Lyle and Co., of Glasgow, and R. Smith and Sons, of Kidderminster, to use the patent. The first looms were erected at " The Sling " in the shed formerly used as a tapestry weaving shed by Messrs. Pardoe, Hoomans, and Pardoe. The American patent was disposed of to the Alex. Smith and Sons' Carpet Company, Yonkers, New York. The great Jubilee banquet of 1887 was held in a new shed built by Tomkinson and Adam at Mount Pleasant.

In 1889 an attempt was made to combine nearly all the carpet factories of the town into one huge undertaking under the control of a " Syndicate." The large scheme fell through, but led to the combination of some firms, and the transformation of others into limited liability companies. The value of the carpet factories here now is estimated at fully £2,000,000. The " Carpet Manufacturing Company " is a combination of two very successful undertakings—" Morton and Sons " (founded 1809) and " Richard Smith and Sons " (founded 1855)—which owns 702 looms for Brussels, Axminster, Royal Axminster, Chenille, and other carpets.

The firm of " John Everard Barton and Sons " has been in existence for over 100 years. In 1807 a deed of partnership was drawn up between Charles Wright, George Gower, and John Gough. Later on the firm became " Wright, Crump, and Crane," relatives of the founders. In 1855 John Everard Barton and Thomas E. Crane took over the business, and carried it on together until Mr. Crane's death in 1865. Mr. Barton died in 1885, and was succeeded by his sons.

The famous firm of "John Brinton and Co." employs 1500 hands, producing Brussels, Wilton pile, tapestry, and velvet carpets, and hosiery and carpet worsteds. Mr. William Brinton, grandfather of the present head of the firm, began in the carpet trade in 1784. His son Henry, in 1821, started the existing works on some small premises originally owned by him, and which have since been so much extended that six acres of land are covered by the buildings of the company. In 1848 Mr. Henry Brinton took his third son (the present head) ard another son (Henry) into partnership. Both the Henry Brintons died in 1857, and the survivor, Mr. John Brinton, carried on and developed the business in a marvellous manner, until in 1880 he merged it into a limited liability company, of which he continues to hold the chief management.

"Henry Jecks Dixon and Sons" was founded by Mr. Bowyer, who was joined in 1823 by Mr. H. J. Dixon. In 1886 it was formed into a limited company. Besides Brussels, Wilton, and Axminster carpets, this company manufactures saddle bags, moquettes for furniture coverings, carriage linings, &c.

"Woodward, Grosvenor, and Co. (Limited)" is an old-established firm owning the Stour Vale Mills, and manufacturing high-class Brussels, Wilton, and Royal Axminster carpets.

"Edward Hughes and Sons" (founded 1850) produces Patent Aubusson carpets and beam rugs, in addition to all the best varieties of carpets. The premises at Worcester Cross, now occupied by the firm of "H. R. Willis and Co.," were built by Mr. James Holmes, who had previously been partner in "Butcher, Worth, and Holmes," of Callows Lane. Mr. Holmes afterwards sold the works to Messrs. John Crossley and Sons, of Halifax, and became their manager. In 1869 the premises were purchased by Mr. H. R. Willis, who has considerably improved and extended them. His "speciality" is superior Brussels and Wilton carpets. "Messrs. M. Whittall and Co." (1868) make Brussels and Wilton carpets and Patent Afghan

squares. The "Chlidema Company" manufactures a carpet
or seamless border without mitre, cross-join, or false shading.

Other well-known manufacturers (1890) of all the best kinds
of carpets are Messrs. John Bennie and Co., of the "Jubilee
Works,' Exchange Street; W. Green and Sons, New Road
and Mill Street; W. J. Bannister, Hartlebury Road; C. Harrison and Son, Stourport; Humphries and Sons, Mill Street;
Naylor and Lloyd, Mill Street; T. and A. Naylor, Green Street;
G. W. Oldland and Co., New Road; Potter and Lewis, New
Road; Purdey and Co., Vicar Street; M. Whittall and Co.,
Exchange Street; and T. B. Worth, Stourport.

Mr. Thomas Lea, M.P., has extensive mills for spinning all
kinds of worsted yarns for the carpet, hosiery, furniture, and
clothing trades. The same industry is carried on by Mr. Edwd.
A. Broome, of the Castle Mills, and Messrs. Watson Brothers,
Pike Mills. Mr. Richard Watson, whose family has been connected with the trade of Kidderminster for upwards of 200
years, and Mr. Samuel Broom, commenced worsted spinning at
Drayton Mill in 1843. In 1847 Mr. Broom retired, and in 1854
Mr. Joseph Naylor joined Mr. Watson. In 1859 the Pike Mills
were built, and Drayton Mill given up. Mr. Watson retired in
1873, and his son, R. Talbot Watson, joined Mr. Naylor, and
subsequently J. Harold Watson and Mr. Naylor's sons, Thos.
F. and Arthur Naylor, were admitted partners. The partnership was dissolved in 1883, when R. T. and J. H. Watson
carried on the worsted spinning, and T. F. and A. Naylor took
up the woollen spinning and carpet manufacturing, which had
been added to the business in 1868. The Pike Mill was totally
destroyed by fire on July 1st, 1886, but was rebuilt and work
resumed in September, 1887.

Messrs. Crowther Brothers carry on extensive iron manufactures at the Stour Vale and Falling Sands works. At
Stourport and Wilden are the Anglo-American Tin Works.
Stourport also has vinegar works, and does some boatbuilding. Other industries carried on in Kidderminster are
maltings, breweries, wire works, brickfields, tanyards, &c.
The paper manufacture at Hurcott is of long standing; the

Registers record the burial of Robert Gough Aug. 20, 1653, "whoe dyed at Hurcoate papar myll."

For six centuries and a half the looms have been busy at Kidderminster in the manufacture of textile fabrics of various kinds. When the demand for one product passed away another product took its place. In this way the town has more than held its own in the manufacturing world. With one or two exceptions a good understanding has existed between those who have risked their capital in the development of the various industries and those who have co-operated with them by manual labour. Whilst other nations are straining every nerve to drive England from her pre-eminent position, it was short-sighted policy on the part of some of the weavers that led them a few years ago to oppose the introduction of a new manufacture by Messrs. Jecks Dixon.

The striking improvement in artistic skill that has characterised the last quarter of a century has now enabled native talent to supply the designs required by the carpet trade, whereas in former years Frenchmen were generally employed for the work. In this respect the local School of Art has done most valuable service. The scientific teaching of chemistry and dyeing recently started will no doubt have equally beneficial results, and enable the town to keep abreast of every development in the future.

CHAPTER XI.

The Neighbourhood.

CLENT.

(By John Amphlett, Esq.)

HIS parish is situated at the highest part of the range of high land that forms the north-eastern boundary of the valley of the Severn. Among these hills, which attain a height of over 1000 feet, rise the head waters of the stream which, flowing through Hurcott and Broadwaters, joins the Stour at Kidderminster, after a course of some seven miles. The name of Clent, no doubt, is Danish, though it would be more applicable from its meaning to jagged precipices than to rounded outlines such as those of the Clent hills. It is true that the legend of St. Kenelm would assign the name of Clent to this locality in 821, the year of his murder, while the Danes did not come into England until 30 or 40 years after. But the legend is told us not in contemporary writings, but in histories compiled by monks who lived 300 or 400 years after the event, by which time the Danish name would have become well established.

The earliest mention of Clent, apart from its connection with St. Kenelm, whose legend is so well known, is that in the year 1016 it was bought, with Kingswinford and Tardebig, from Ethelred II. by Ægelsi, Dean of the church at Worcester, for 200 pounds weight of silver. During the disturbances consequent upon the seizure of the English Crown by Canute, the Sheriff of Staffordshire, whose name was Ævic, "quidam malignus homo" says the chronicler, took possession of these villages. It was from the fact that the levies due to the Crown were paid to the Sheriff of Staffordshire that Clent, with the adjoining village of Broom, then portion of the manor of Clent, came to be considered within that county. But at the time of Domesday its ancient connection with Worcestershire had not been forgotten, and it gave its name to a large hundred in the northern part of that shire. In later days it has come back to Worcestershire again, having been made a portion of that county by a Boundary Act passed after the first Reform Bill of 1832.

At the time of Edward the Confessor and of Domesday, Clent was a manor belonging to the King, and it remained in the possession of the Crown till the time of John, who exchanged it with Ralph Somery, Baron of Dudley, for the manor of Stow-heath, near Wolverhampton, reserving to himself a small chief rent. For 120 years the manor remained with the Someries, when it passed through a female to Lord Bottetourt, and after his death to his granddaughter, the wife of Lord Burnell. When she died childless there were several claimants for it, and after much litigation an agreement was come to by which Clent became the property of the Earl of Wiltshire.

During the Wars of the Roses the Earl of Wiltshire's estates were confiscated, and the manor of Clent fell into the possession of the Staffords, of Grafton Manor; but on the accession of Henry VII. it was restored to Thomas Butler, the late Earl of Wiltshire's brother. From him it descended to Ann wife of Sir John St. Leger, of Annary, in Devonshire, aunt of Anne Boleyn, the ill-fated Queen of Henry VIII.; and her grandson, another Sir John, sold it in 1564 to Sir John Lyttelton, of Frankley, in whose family it has since remained.

There is another small manor in the parish, consisting of Calcott Hill farm, the glebe land, and one or two other fields. It is known as Church Clent Manor, or the King's Holt. Its history is obscure, but it in some way originated with the neighbouring Abbey of Halesowen, whose property it was at the dissolution of that monastery. Afterwards it remained some

THE NEIGHBOURHOOD.

time in the possession of the Crown, whence its second name; and then was granted to the notorious John Dudley, Duke of Northumberland. When this nobleman lost his head, his possessions again came to the Crown. Church Clent was, after some time, sold, since which it has passed through the hands of several proprietors.

No church is mentioned as being in the parish at the time of Domesday, and we do not hear of a Rector of Clent till 1205. The parsons of Clent were Rectors till 1345, when, following a usual proceeding with such establishments, the Abbey of Halesowen took possession of the great tithes of the parish, and deputed a Vicar to serve the church. After the dissolution the advowson and the tithes were granted to the Duke of Northumberland, and after his attainder were sold by the Crown. Before very long a dispute arose concerning them, and both advowson and tithes got into Chancery. By some means the tithes came out of this Court, and after passing through several owners were bought by the Amphletts; but the advowson still remains in the patronage of the Lord Chancellor.

The present church is dedicated to St. Leonard, and was thoroughly restored in 1866. The first parson of Clent is called " Master Herbert of St. Peter's," so that the first church has either disappeared or the present one has changed its patron saint. It should be noted, however, that the church of Broom, a parish which formerly formed part of the manor of Clent, is dedicated to St. Peter. Little original work remains in Clent church, but the tower and chancel are comparatively untouched. The south arcade is Early English, and the roof of the chancel is of typical Early English work. Strange to say, nevertheless, the roof rests on walls of the most debased Perpendicular work at least 300 years later in date, and so must have been transferred to its present position from some other part of the church. The tower is of plain Perpendicular architecture of late date. The north aisle is quite modern, of the date of the restoration in 1866. One of the most curious things about the church is the orientation of the chancel, the axis of which in reference to the axis of the nave bends considerably

Y

towards the south. Instances of orientation are not uncommon, but the bend is usually towards the north. The registers begin in 1562, and are fairly continuous to the present date. The earliest legible inscription in the churchyard is 1691.

There are few antiquities in the parish. The four stones on Clent Hill are quite modern, all tales to the contrary notwithstanding. They were erected by the first Lord Lyttelton about 1760, and formed part of a general scheme for the decoration of the neighbourhood carried out by that nobleman. It is sometimes said that the stones stand each in a different county, but this statement has no foundation in fact. All over Clent Hill the traces of old hedge banks may be seen, showing that cultivation was at one time more extensive on the slopes than at present. It is probable that the land went out of cultivation at the time of the Black Death in 1348. One of these hedge banks, running up the hill near the road from Clent church to St. Kenelm's, is called St. Kenelm's furrow, and there is a legend attributing it to the running away of an old woman's cow, dragging the plough behind it, through her persistence in working on St. Kenelm's day.

There are records of the enclosures of two commons in the parish—Calcott Hill about 1678, and Clent Lower Common in 1788. On Clent Lower Common, called formerly also Clent Heath, there used to exist several barrows, which were explored during the last century, and bones were discovered in them; faint traces of them still remain. Of the remaining common land in the parish, altogether about 260 acres, 170 acres on Clent Hill were placed under the control of a body of conservators, and dedicated to the public by Act of Parliament in 1880; and in spite of the poor accommodation and the comparative difficulty of access, increasing numbers of visitors in each year come to this parish to enjoy the bracing air, the open commons, and the distant views.

WOLVERLEY.

OR more than a thousand years this pretty village has pertained more or less completely to the Bishops and Cathedral of Worcester. In the Saxon charters the name is spelt in eighteen ways. The earliest name apparently was Seckley—" Secceslea, which the country people call also Uulfordilea" (*Heming*, p. 410), most likely from the droves of wolves that had then their lairs in these wild regions. Originally forming part of the district of Sture-in-Usmere, it was given by Bishop Dencherht to Kenulph, King of Mercia, in 816, and restored to Aelhun, eleventh Bishop, fifty years later, by King Burhred. As we have seen (page 71), it was ravaged and seized by the Danes, but was afterwards given back to Worcester by Earl Leofric, at the intercession of Lady Godiva. The charter invokes the fate of Judas Iscariot on all who should presume to infringe this gift. The Cullecliffe (Cookley) portion was given by King Edgar (964) to Earl Beorthnots and his heirs, which land William the Conqueror gave to Worcester 1066. The bounds are marked as " From the river Usmere to Mount Heseeande, thence to Cuthred's tree, thence along the dyke to Stour, &c." The Horsebrook, Keningford, Kinver-stone, Hoccanstige Road, Merewell Spring, Meredeune, Indosse, Stapol, and Mount Litlandune are also mentioned in the bounds.

In Domesday we read :—" The church of Worcester holds Ulwardelei ; there are five hides. In demesne are two ploughs and four villeins, and five bordars with four ploughs. There is a priest having half a carucate, and one freeman having one hide, and paying two sextaries of honey ; there are six slaves, some men and some maids, and a mill of six shillings. In the time of King Edward it was worth £4 ; at the survey 40s."

King Stephen gave leave to the monks of Worcester " re-edificare Burconam terram suam apud Wlverdela." King

A HISTORY OF KIDDERMINSTER.

John (1208) granted to them here Soc and Sac, Thol and Theam, and Infangethef, with judgment of fire and water, of gallows and sword, fines for murders, &c., freedom from attendance at the Hundred and County Courts, &c.

In 1240 the monks cultivated for themselves two carucates of land, which they had previously let for £4 yearly. They also held the mills, which used to pay 10s. The fulling-mill was let for 13s. 4d. Twelve freemen held lands chiefly in virgates. There were eight cottars: three paid a rental of 1d. a quarter; four paid three farthings a quarter; and "The smith makes the iron of one plough for his own land, and for another receives 10d., and for a bill 8d." Five villeins, holding half a virgate each, paid 10½d. a quarter. *(Reg. Prior. Wig.)*

The Rectory of Wlverslawe was given to the Priory of Worcester by Bishop Roger, who died 1179. The reasons assigned afterwards by the monks as a pretext for its impropriation were the ruinous condition of their buildings and the cathedral tower, and the heavy law expenses they had incurred in defending their rights. Pope Clement issued a bull in their favour from Avignon, and the ordination was made in 1354 by John Bishop of Hereford, "having special power from the Apostolic See."

The Register begins with the year 1539, when there were 17 baptisms, 9 burials, and 3 marriages. In 1563 a return gives 72 families. In 1776 there were 120 houses and 500 inhabitants. In 1881 the population had increased to 3343. The oldest family in the parish was the Attwoods (page 95), of which the elder branch became extinct in 1726. The Sebrights go back as far as Henry III. William Sebright, Esq., in 1620, founded and endowed a grammar school, and left money for repairing the church and four bridges, &c. Colonel Sir F. Winn Knight, K.C.B., of Wolverley House, and Major A. T. Hancocks, of Wolverley Court, are the representatives of families of long standing here. John Baskerville (p. 156) was born in this parish.

The Enclosure Act was passed in 1775, but Nash mentions 1456 acres of common land as still unenclosed in 1782. The old church of St. John the Baptist was pulled down in 1769, and a new one, built of brick, was opened 20 Sept., 1772. In 1882 the chancel was restored by the Ecclesiastical Commissioners. The altar table and cloth were given by Mr. and Mrs. E. J. Morton, of Heathfield; the pulpit is a memorial to Mr. John Saunders, of Sion Hill; and the east window is erected in memory of Mr. William Hancocks. In the nave is a fine mural tablet by Flaxman in memory of Helen Charlotte wife of Mr. John Knight, of Lea Castle. The nave was thoroughly restored and beautified in 1889. The Vicarage, in the patronage of the Dean and Chapter of Worcester, is valued at £300 with residence, and is now held by the Rev. C. B. Rowland, M.A., St. John's College, Oxford. Edmund Green, Abbot of Hales Owen, was Vicar 1510—1520. The well-known linguists and antiquarians, Dr. Hickes and Dr. Hopkins, held this benefice in the seventeenth century.

HAGLEY.

OPE and Shenstone, Thomson and Gray, have sung in famous verse the beauties of this charming spot. But a still greater renown arises from its being the home of the distinguished family of Lyttelton, which has shown for generations how the feudal leaders of mediæval times can adapt themselves to modern circumstances, and still take the lead in all that is best for their country. The late Lord Lyttelton (George William, fourth Baron) will be long remembered for two great improvements wrought by his influence, viz., the reformation of grammar schools and the increase in the Episcopate.

There are Roman and British remains in this parish. On Wichbury Hill is a large camp occupied by the Romans before fighting the Britons who were posted on the Clent Hills. An earthen pot full of Roman coins was taken out of a pool close to the hill. Sepulchral urns have also been found. The Roman Road is now called the King's Headland.

Hagley is mentioned in Domesday as one of 14 Worcestershire manors of William Fitz-Ansculph, of Dudley. There were 5½ hides, having one plough in demesne, a priest, five villeins, ten bordars, with five ploughs, and land sufficient to employ eight more, two serfs, and a wood. Before the Conquest Godric, a thane of King Edward, held it—now Roger under Fitz-Ansculph.

The Paganels and Somerys succeeded Fitz-Ansculph. In the time of Henry II. William de Haggaley held it as a knight's fee of Gervase Paganel. In 24 Edw. III. Edmund de Hagley gave up the manor and advowson to his lord paramount, Sir John Botetourt, for 100 marks. Twenty-three years later Henry de Haggaley, heir-at-law to Edmund, recovered the manor: he was High Sheriff in 1398—9 and 1403. In 1411 he sold it to Thomas Walwyn, who alienated it to Jane Beauchamp, Lady Bergavenny, and she devised it to her grandson, Sir James Boteler, son and heir of the Earl of Ormond, created Earl of Wiltshire in his father's lifetime. He was a Lancastrian, was taken prisoner at Towton, and beheaded. The confiscated land at Hagley was granted by Edward IV. to Fulke Stafford, but it soon reverted to the Crown, and was granted to Queen Elizabeth Woodville. In 18 Edw. IV. the King and Queen conferred it upon the Abbot and Convent of Westminster, for two monks to celebrate masses for the repose of their souls. But soon Thomas Butler recovered the forfeited lands of his brother, the Earl of Wiltshire, and his great-grandson, Sir John St. Leger, sold them in 1564 to Sir John Lyttelton, of Frankley, Kt., in whose family they still remain. In 1600 John Lyttelton, Esq., was implicated in the Essex rebellion, for which he was tried, condemned, and imprisoned. His estate was forfeited, and complete ruin threatened the family, when his noble wife Muriel, daughter of Lord Chancellor Bromley, came to the rescue. She threw herself at the feet of King James I. at Doncaster, and obtained a grant of her husband's estate, and soon an Act was passed whereby Mr. Lyttelton's attainder was reversed. After the Gunpowder Plot

THE NEIGHBOURHOOD.

two of the conspirators, Stephen Lyttelton and Robert Winter, were concealed in the old Hall at Hagley, but were betrayed by an under-cook.

The present Hall was erected by George first Lord Lyttelton. The oldest part of the Church of St. John the Baptist is of the time of the Somerys, about Henry III., but it has been much enlarged. About 1858 it was restored at a cost of £2300, as a county testimonial to the high character of the fourth Baron Lyttelton. Afterwards a tower and spire were added from the designs of Mr. J. E. Street.

The Registers commence in 1538. The present Rector is the Rev. W. C. Gibbs, M.A., of Jesus College, Cambridge. The patron is Viscount Cobham, who lately inherited this title from one of Marlborough's famous generals, at the death of the Duke of Buckingham and Chandos.

STONE.

RSO D'ABITOT, in Domesday, held Stanes in Creslau (now Halfshire) hundred, containing six hides; Turni and Euchil held it for two manors. Herlebald held it of Urso. In demesne are two ploughs and seven villeins, and fifteen bordars with six ploughs. There are four slaves and a mill of three oræ; one lewe and a half of wood. In the time of King Edward it was worth 40s., now 30s.

Emmeline, Urso's daughter and heir, carried the manor to her husband, Walter de Beauchamp. Some time after it belonged to Ralph de Somery. A family, "de Stanes," flourished here as early as Henry II., taking their name from the place. Thomas Foliot inherited the property in the time of Edward III., by his marriage with a daughter of Richard de Stone. Sir John Foliot sold it to Sir William Courteyn; it afterwards passed to the Rushouts, and then to Mr. Cox, attorney, of Kidderminster, whose daughter sold it to Mr. John Baker. Mr. James Holcroft, of Stourbridge, is now lord of the manor.

The hamlet of Dunclent, in the time of the Conqueror, was the land of St. Guthlac, and was held by Nigel. It afterwards became the property of the Beauchamps, and was held under them by the Dunclents. (Pp. 55, 64.) Later on it came to the Barons of Abergavenny. Edward Broad, of Dunclent, had much influence at Kidderminster in the time of Charles I. From the Foleys it passed with the other estates to Lord Ward, and the Earl of Dudley is the present owner. The "Monks' furlong" formerly belonged to the Abbot of Bordesley. Henry VIII. gave it to John Maynard, who conveyed it to Edward Broad.

The church of St. Mary, consecrated by Bishop Gifford in 1269, and originally dependent upon Chaddesley, was appropriated to the College of Warwick. Thomas Forest, in 1511, left land for the Lady Chapel. (Page 68.) The church was almost entirely rebuilt in 1831. The Register dates from the year 1601.

CHADDESLEY CORBET.

DDEVE, a woman, held Cedeslai of the King at the time of the Domesday survey. She had held it in the reign of Edward the Confessor. There were 25 hides with eight corn farms. Ten of these hides were free from geld, as appeared by the testimony of the county. In demesne were three ploughs and 33 villeins, and 20 bordars, and two priests with four bordars. Among them all they had 25 ploughs. The number of bondmen and bondwomen was eight. Three mills paid 12 seams of corn. Two houses in

Worcester paid 12d. In Wich five salt pans paid 21s. 4d. There was a wood of two lewes, and another wood of one lewe. T.R.E., and at the time of the survey, it was worth £12.

Chaddesley was formerly included in Pyperode Forest, the name of which still survives in Peper Wood. The Corbets afterwards came into possession of this parish. Edward I. issued a mandate "to our beloved and faithful Peter Corbet" to take and destroy wolves wherever he could find them within the counties of Gloucester, Worcester, Hereford, Salop, and Stafford. From the Corbets Chaddesley passed to the Beauchamps, Barons of Bergavenny, and afterwards by purchase to John Pakington. Humphrey Pakington, his son, was seated at Harvington, a hamlet of the parish, and left by his wife, Abigail Sacheverell, two daughters co-heirs: Mary, who inherited Chaddesley, was married to Sir John Yate, Bart., of Buckland, Berks, and Anne to Sir Henry Audeley, of Bere-Church, in Essex. Lady Yate died 12 June, 1696, aged 86, and was buried in the Lady Chapel of Chaddesley Corbet church, where may be seen a quaint epitaph by her daughter Apollonia. She built and endowed three almshouses for widows. She was a strong supporter of the Roman Catholics, and sent a village lad, Sylvester Jenks, to Douay, who in 1686 returned to Harvington as missionary priest, and was made Chaplain to James II. In 1688 a "Protestant mob" from Kidderminster attacked Harvington Hall; but the drawbridge was up, and they could do little damage. The old Hall is still standing, though its glory has departed, and soon it will become a complete ruin. At the top of a fine old oak staircase is "Lady Yate's Nursery," which communicates by a latticed door with an inner chamber, formerly decorated with foliage, vine stems, and pomegranates. This was the chapel, from which a narrow doorway gives an outlet to the roof and many little secret rooms, providing a refuge for the priest, and where even now one could play a good game at "hide and seek." Under the boards was a small secret closet for the sacred vessels. On the first floor was a large banqueting-hall, lately despoiled of its oak wainscotting. By lifting up a step in the staircase, entrance is gained to another hidden room, 5ft. 9in. by 5ft., and 6ft. high. On its floor lies to this day the self-same thick sedge mat bed on which the hidden priests lay. Air was admitted by a curious contrivance in the roof; and in a small cupboard close at hand was a chink through which a message or food could be passed.

In 1743 a new chapel was built, much used by the foreign artisans of Kidderminster and Stourbridge. This became a school-room, and was replaced by the present chapel, opened May 29, 1825.

Father Wall had charge of Harvington for 12 years: he was taken prisoner at Rushock, tried at Worcester for high treason by Judge Atkins, and suffered death 22 Aug., 1679. His body was buried in St. Oswald's churchyard: his head is kept at Douay in the cloister of the English Friars. In 1879 a memorial crucifix was erected in the graveyard at Harvington. Charles Dodd, D.D. (Hugh Tootle), wrote his *Church History*, in 3 vols., at Harvington. He died Feb. 27, 1744. The sweet sedge *(Acorus Calamus)*, used formerly for strewing upon the floors of halls and chapels, grows abundantly in the moat of Harvington. Sir N. W. Throckmorton, Bart., the lord of the manor, is descended from Mary Yate, granddaughter of Lady Yate, who married Sir Robert Throckmorton, of Congleton, Warwickshire.

The church of St. Cassyon at Chaddesley is very fine, and contains some good Norman and Decorated work. The font is very ancient. There is a recumbent figure of a Crusader, supposed to be a Corbet; also a brass to Thomas Forest, keeper of Dunclent Park, his wife, and eleven children. There is no date, but by turning back to the will (page 68) it would appear to be about 1511.

William Beauchamp, Lord Bergavenny, gave to the collegiate church of Warwick, of his ancestor's foundation, the advowsons of the churches of Spellesbury and Chaddesley Corbet. At the dissolution of religious houses the tithes were granted to the Corporation of Warwick, in whom they continue.

HARTLEBURY.

URHRED, King of the Mercians, gave Hartlebury to the see of Worcester about 850. It is thus described in the Domesday survey:—" The Church of Worcester holds Huerteberie with six berewicks. There are 20 hides, and in demesne four ploughs, and 24 villeins, three bordars, and a priest ; among them all they have 21 ploughs. There are 12 bondmen and 3 bondwomen, and two mills worth four shillings and 10 seams of corn. A wood one lewe long and half a lewe broad. In Wich five houses paying five mitts of salt. In the time of King Edward it was worth sixteen pounds, now thirteen pounds and ten shillings."

Bishop Walter de Cantilupe, a supporter of Simon de Montfort, began to fortify the Castle, which was embattled and finished by his successor, Godfrey Giffard, 1268. The gatehouse was added in the reign of Henry VI. by Bishop Carpenter.

In 1646 the Castle was strongly fortified and held for the King by Captain Sandys and Lord Windsor, with 120 foot soldiers and 20 horse, and had provisions for twelve months. When summoned by Colonel Morgan for the Parliament, it surrendered in two days without firing a shot. The Parliamentary Commissioners seized the Castle and manor, and sold them to Thomas Westrowe for £3133 6s. 8d. At the Restoration they were given back to the Bishop. The avenue of limes in the park was planted by Bishop Stillingfleet. Bishop Pepys made a present of the deer, which had been kept here from time immemorial, to Queen Victoria. The library was built by Bishop Hurd, who also presented to it the choicest works from the libraries of Pope and Warburton. The copy of the *Iliad* from which Pope's translation was made is among them. Some of the Castle moats have been filled up and laid out as flower gardens.

In November, 1269, Bishop Giffard consecrated the church of St. James the Apostle. Bishop Sandys, in 1575, erected the present tower, and the chancel was rebuilt by a late Rector, the Rev. Samuel Picart, early in this century. The rest of the church was rebuilt in the Early English and Decorated styles in 1836, from the designs of Mr. Rickman. In 1877 the church was partially restored and refitted. In the churchyard is a stone coffin lid with floriated cross, supposed to be that of John de Rodeborewe, Rector in 1290, who founded a chantry in honour of the Blessed Virgin Mary, and endowed it with lands in Waresley, Whittying, Stone, and Shenston, in this manor. The communion plate is of gold, being the gift of good Bishop Lloyd and his wife in 1714. The font belonged to the old church. The Registers are interesting, and commence with 1540. In them is this entry:—" A.D. 1553. Bishop Hooper was called before the Privy Council, August 22. He was sent prisoner to the fleet, September 1. 1555, February 9, burnt. Richard Patey, whom ye Pope has made Bishop in 1534, was now restored."

The Rev. James Stillingfleet, when Rector in 1700, built the present parsonage house, a good specimen of the Queen Anne style. Among the Rectors have been some famous men, including Miles Smith, one of the translators of the Authorised Version of the Bible, Richard Bentley, the famous critic, &c. In the churchyard are the tombs of three Bishops of Worcester, Richard Hurd (1808), Robert James Carr (1841), and Henry Pepys (1861). A pretty half-timbered mission church was presented to the parish in 1882 by the present revered Bishop, for which Mrs. Philpott provided the interior fittings. The Rectory of Hartlebury, in the patronage of the Bishop, is now held by the Rev. D. Robertson, Rural Dean of Kidderminster, who has a very interesting collection of portraits of former Bishops of Worcester.

The Hartlebury Grammar School is mentioned as early as Richard II.; but was refounded by Queen Elizabeth, who granted it a charter in 1558.

In a secluded part of one of the glebe meadows is a curious hermit's cell, 18 feet by 12 feet, cut out of the rock.

APPENDIX.

Domesday Book, A.D. 1086.

Rex Willielmus tenet in dominio CHIDEMINSTRE, cum xvj Berewiches, Wenuerton, Trinpelei, Worcote, Frenesse, et alia Frenesse, Bristitune, Harburgelei, Fastochesfelde, Gurbehale, Ribeforde, et alia Ribeford, Sudtone, Aldintone, Mettune, Teulesberge, Sudwale. In his terris, simul cum Manerio, sunt xx^{ti} hidæ. Hoc Manerium fuit totum wastum. In dominio est j caruca et xx villani et xxx bordarii cum xviij carucis et adhuuc xx^{ti} carucæ plus ibi possunt esse. Ibi ij servi et iiij ancillæ et ij molini de xvj solidis et ij salinæ de xxx solidis et piscaria de c. denariis. Silva de iiij lewis. In hoc Manerio tenet Præpositus terram unius Radchenistre et ibi habet j carucam et molinum de v. oris.

Ad hoc Manerium pertinet una domus in Wich et alia in Wirecestre reddentes x denarios. Totum Manerium T.R.E. reddebat xiiij libras de firma. Modo reddit x libras et iiij solidos ad peis. Silvam hujus Manerii posuit Rex in foresta. De terra hujus Manerii tenet Willielmus j hidam et terram unius Radchenjstre et ibi habet j villanum et viii bordarios habentes iiij carucas et dimidiam. Valet xj solidos. De eadem terra tenet Aiulfus unam virgatam. Ibi j caruca et ij servi. Valet ij solidos.

Charter of King Henry the Second.

Henricus Rex, Dux Normanniæ et Aquitaniæ, Comes, Archiepiscopis Episcopis Comitibus, Baronibus, Vicecomitibus, Ministris, et omnibus fidelibus suis, Franciæ et Angliæ salutem. Sciatis me dedisse concessisse (in fœdo) et hereditate Mansero Bysset dapifero meo, pro servicio suo in Worcestershere, Kedemynster pro xx*li*. in Wiltes, Combe pro xxvii*li*., in Gloucestershire Wikewood pro x*li*., in Hampshire Dounreston pro viij*li*. et Burgagium de Rokebon cum Hundredo et cum omnibus suis pertinentiis pro xl*li*. et pertinentiis de Lechedesham. Et præterea dedi Wadersey que reddebat matri meo *(sic)* per annum xxs. scilicet in Wichenford. Quare volo et firmiter precipio quod ipse Manserus et heredes sui has terras predictas habeant et teneant de me et heredibus meis, bene et in pace, et honorifice, et hereditarie, in bosco, in plano, in pratis, pascuis, in viis et semitis, et in omnibus locis, cum soca et saca, et tol et them, et infantethef et outefantethef, et cum omnibus libertatibus et liberis consuetudinibus, cum quibus aliquis Baronum meorum Anglie melius et quietius, (et) honorificentius tenet. Teste me ipso, Thoma Cancellario, Reginaldo Comite Cornubiæ, Willelmo Comite Leicestriæ, Henrico de Essex Constabulario, R. de Ham, Roberto de Lacy, Warraino filio Barnard, Joselino Barrete, Roberto de Donstapell. Apud Cant u_ariam.

The Registers.

" The Regester Boke of Weddings Christenings and Buryings made and kept in the parish Church of Kidderminster, from and beginning in January in the year of our lord 1539 unto this present yeare of our lord 1614 newly written at the speciall Commandment of the right reverend father in god Henry Parry then Lord Byshopp of Worcester, John Colombine Clerke then being Viccar ther, John Clymar, John Peersall, Thomas Crane and Robert Hawkins, Churchwardens."

[The entries of baptisms, weddings, and burials are all mixed up together, just as they happened to occur. Our fixed rules of spelling were not then in force. We first give a list of the surnames occurring in the registers in the period from 1539 to 1565. The figures after the name show the date of its *first* entry. Few families could have been living here in the above time without the birth, wedding, or burial of some one or other of their members. Probable variations in the spelling of a name are indicated by brackets.]

N.B. As these names are arranged according to the alphabet, they will not be repeated in the Index.

Aslow	.. 1540	[Bucknell]	.. 1541	Brincklow	.. 1542
Arche	.. 1540	[Bucknyll]	.. 1546	Bradburne	.. 1542
Agraven	.. 1540	Betenson	.. 1539	Bolas	.. 1542
Allen	.. 1540	Blount	.. 1539	Brooke	.. 1543
Agborow	.. 1541	Butler	.. 1540	Barnard	.. 1545
[Abarowe]	.. 1542	Boucher	.. 1540	Brodwey	.. 1546
Alchurch	.. 1542	Bennett	.. 1540	Bowyer	.. 1546
Arthure	.. 1543	Browne	.. 1540	Bocher	.. 1546
Apen	.. 1543	Barnisley	.. 1540	Brushwood	.. 1547
Adams	.. 1545	Barbor	.. 1540	Ballard	.. 1550
Avery	.. 1548	Burfield	.. 1540	Burnell	.. 1550
Amys	.. 1550	Burlton	.. 1540	Bradeley	.. 1550
Ayre	.. 1552	Bytham	.. 1541	Blysse	.. 1551
Abintone	.. 1559	Badger	.. 1541	Bourne	.. 1553
[Abbington]	.. 1565	Bancks	.. 1541	Bache	.. 1560
Aston	.. 1559	'Banks'	.. 1547	Bradford	.. 1560
Astley	.. 1559	Brotherton	.. 1541	Bayleis	.. 1560
Alridge	.. 1560	Barret	.. 1541	Benton	.. 1561
[Albridge]	.. 1563	Buckman	.. 1541	Brocke	.. 1563
Allden	.. 1563	Burdnyll	.. 1541	Blassard	.. 1563
Bowky	.. 1539	Baker	.. 1541	Blythe	.. 1563
Buckenyll	.. 1539	Benbowe	.. 1542	Burrows	.. 1564

APPENDIX. 205

Barnes	..	.. 1565	Dawley	..	.. 1539	Gossard	..	.. 1542
Cowp..	..	.. 1539	Dolman	..	.. 1540	Goodman	..	.. 1543
Clymer	..	.. 1539	Doolittle	..	.. 1540	Goppe	..	.. 1544
Carpenter..	..	.. 1540	Dawks	..	.. 1540	Greene	..	.. 1545
Cowall	..	.. 1540	Dallow	..	.. 1541	Gorst..	..	.. 1546
Clemens	..	.. 1540	Dunclent	..	.. 1541	Gerye..	..	.. 1547
Cooke..	..	.. 1540	[Duncklen]	..	.. 1542	Garnat	..	.. 1549
Cownde	..	.. 1540	Dison..	..	.. 1541	Gyles..	..	.. 1560
Chapman	..	.. 1540	Denson	..	.. 1541	Gosnell	..	.. 1560
Clarke	..	.. 1540	[Denston]	..	.. 1551	Gouldsmith		.. 1560
[Clearke]	..	.. 1545	Deane..	..	.. 1542	Gest	..	.. 1563
Crompe	..	.. 1540	Dike	..	.. 1543	Glover	..	.. 1563
Combes	..	.. 1540	Dyplowe	..	.. 1543	Gurden	..	.. 1564
Capullwood		.. 1541	Dangland	..	.. 1545	Grayshill	..	.. 1564
Comber	..	.. 1541	Delph..	..	.. 1545	Gillam	..	.. 1565
Colbe..	..	.. 1541	Dicke..	..	.. 1548	Hayley	..	.. 1539
Collett	..	.. 1541	Dedicote	..	.. 1550	Hill	..	.. 1539
Costen	.	.. 1542	Dunston	..	.. 1553	Hoggeson	..	.. 1540
[Coston]	..	.. 1545	Done	..	.. 1559	Howseman		.. 1540
Clent	..	.. 1542	Dennis	..	.. 1559	Hoggins	..	.. 1540
Cloyter	..	.. 1542	ap David	..	.. 1564	Hey	..	.. 1540
Coke	..	.. 1543	Davies	..	.. 1565	Hurtill	..	.. 1540
Comberbach		.. 1545	Elyatts	..	.. 1539	[Hurtyll]	..	.. 1546
Colle	..	.. 1546	Eyre	..	.. 1540	Hancox	..	.. 1540
Clemeford..		.. 1546	ap Evans	..	.. 1540	Hulley	..	.. 1541
Carme	..	.. 1546	Egeley	..	.. 1541	Hondye	..	.. 1541
Cowden	..	.. 1546	[Eugeley]	..	.. 1545	Handye	..	.. 1550
Compayne..		.. 1546	Edmonds	..	.. 1560	Heath..	..	.. 1541
Colyns	..	.. 1547	Foxsall	..	.. 1539	Holymau	..	.. 1542
Clare ..	..	.. 1547	[Foxall]	..	.. 1541	Haskett	..	.. 1542
Churchyard		.. 1547	Fisher	..	.. 1540	Hadley	..	.. 1542
Cully ..	..	.. 1547	Fyndon	..	.. 1540	Hassould	..	.. 1542
Cokesey	..	.. 1547	Fox	..	.. 1540	Harries	..	.. 1543
Crakeford	..	.. 1547	Fearne	..	.. 1541	Holmer	..	.. 1544
Clemson	..	.. 1547	Fleminge	..	.. 1543	Hockham	..	.. 1545
Calvert	..	.. 1547	Foster	..	.. 1544	Hadgley	..	.. 1545
Chaunce	..	.. 1548	[Forster]	..	.. 1550	Hastings	..	.. 1546
Crane..	..	.. 1552	Fowler	..	.. 1547	Hullam	..	.. 1546
Cocke..	..	.. 1559	Fayrefield	..	.. 1550	Hope ..	..	.. 1546
Cagier	..	.. 1559	Freestone	..	.. 1559	Hyweye	..	.. 1546
Coppe..	..	.. 1560	Fartlowe	..	.. 1561	Hewett	..	.. 1547
Cutler	..	.. 1560	Fawkner	..	.. 1565	Haswell	..	.. 1548
Corbett	..	.. 1563	Grigorye	..	.. 1540	Hall	..	.. 1550
Cley	..	.. 1563	Gryffith	..	.. 1540	Higgins	..	.. 1550
Cauke..	..	.. 1564	Gryffyne	..	.. 1541	Hannsor	..	.. 1551
Churchman		.. 1565	Gnowsall	..	.. 1541	Hawke	..	.. 1552
Cawdry	..	.. 1569	Garden	..	.. 1542	Holbecke	..	.. 1559

206 A HISTORY OF KIDDERMINSTER.

Harrisone ..	.. 1559	Lyrrocke ..	.. 1560	Pyggyne ..	.. 1547
Hayles ..	.. 1559	Lyncall ..	.. 1564	[Piggine] ..	.. 1551
Hansett ..	.. 1560	Myson ..	.. 1540	Pyle ..	.. 1547
Hardye ..	.. 1560	Mill ..	.. 1540	Parker ..	.. 1548
Hullbye ..	.. 1560	Mershe ..	.. 1540	Pickthorne	.. 1548
Hopton ..	.. 1561	Mychell ..	.. 1540	Pyke ..	.. 1548
Hanburye ..	.. 1563	ap Morgan	.. 1541	Patricke ..	.. 1550
Hynston ..	.. 1563	Moore ..	.. 1541	Page ..	.. 1552
Hardwicke	.. 1563	[More] ..	.. 1550	Person ..	.. 1560
Horneblower	.. 1563	Mylls ..	.. 1541	Portman ..	.. 1560
Hulkey ..	.. 1564	Malpas ..	.. 1541	Payton ..	.. 1561
Heyes.. ..	.. 1564	Manning ..	.. 1542	Player ..	.. 1561
Heminge ..	.. 1565	Monnynge..	.. 1542	Parkins ..	.. 1564
Heyld.. ..	.. 1565	Moundye ..	.. 1543	Rice ..	.. 1539
Insall	.. 1548	[Monndy] ..	.. 1546	Rawlynes ..	.. 1540
Jennyns ..	.. 1539	Manneringe	.. 1553	Russell ..	.. 1541
Jones	.. 1540	Mathew ..	.. 1559	Rose ..	.. 1541
Jewks	.. 1540	Mason ..	.. 1559	Robins ..	.. 1542
Jorden ..	.. 1541	Middlehoppe	.. 1560	[Robynnes]	.. 1549
Johnson ..	.. 1543	[Middleshopp]	.. 1564	Riddle ..	.. 1542
Jokine ..	.. 1549	[Middlesop]	.. 1565	Raibold ..	.. 1542
Jerves.. ..	.. 1564	Machyne ..	.. 1563	Radford ..	.. 1542
Kynnerton..	.. 1540	ap Maddocke	.. 1564	Rogers ..	.. 1542
Kempstowe	.. 1540	Maynard ..	.. 1564	Richardsone	.. 1543
Kyles	.. 1545	Mather ..	.. 1565	Rugg	.. 1548
Kynrowe ..	.. 1545	Morris ..	.. 1565	Rowland ..	.. 1549
Kysone ..	.. 1547	Overton ..	.. 1559	Richmond ..	.. 1559
Kyrrye ..	.. 1548	Ap Powell ..	.. 1539	Ratcliffe ..	.. 1561
Kelleye ..	.. 1551	Pirry	.. 1539	Reynolds ..	.. 1564
Kyteley ..	.. 1549	Potter.. ..	.. 1540	Ryste	.. 1564
[Kiteley] ..	.. 1551	Parkes ..	.. 1540	Sharratt ..	.. 1540
Kinderdale	.. 1559	Penson ..	.. 1540	Skyler ..	.. 1540
Knotsfoord	.. 1559	Perkes ..	.. 1541	Sturnye ..	.. 1540
Kirkmans ..	.. 1560	Parkeyate ..	.. 1541	Stone	.. 1540
Karolynes ..	.. 1564	Penn	.. 1541	Smyth ..	.. 1540
Lyle	.. 1539	Pytt	.. 1542	Shelley ..	.. 1540
Longmore ..	.. 1540	Pereson ..	.. 1542	Stampes ..	.. 1540
Leycet ..	.. 1540	Pardoe ..	.. 1543	Stanley ..	.. 1541
Latwey ..	.. 1540	Purslowe ..	.. 1543	Serjeant ..	.. 1541
Lee	.. 1540	Pynner ..	.. 1545	Scott	.. 1541
Lache.. ..	.. 1540	Pralle	.. 1545	Stowre ..	.. 1542
Lowe	.. 1540	Pargett ..	.. 1545	Shingleton..	.. 1542
Lyndon ..	.. 1542	Plevey ..	.. 1545	Sherwood ..	.. 1542
Launder ..	.. 1545	Parsone ..	.. 1546	Sowthall ..	.. 1547
Lydeyate ..	.. 1547	Pellett ..	.. 1546	Somerfeild .	.. 1547
Lovell.. ..	.. 1550	[Pillet] ..	.. 1551	Sebright ..	.. 1549
Lake	.. 1559	Pope	.. 1547	Sadler ..	.. 1551

Stanfield	.. 1552	Tyrer ..	.. 1545	Vynsham	.. 1543
Stanford	.. 1553	Tyncker ..	.. 1559	Whyte	.. 1542
Sare ..	.. 1559	Thatchem ..	.. 1559	Warton	.. 1543
Sampson	.. 1559	Tymkins ..	.. 1560	Willmotts ..	.. 1543
Smalle	.. 1560	Trussell	.. 1563	[Wolmott	.. 1546
[Smale]	.. 1564	Toy ..	.. 1563	Wilcoxe	.. 1543
Symonds ..	.. 1561	Underhill ..	.. 1548	Wilkinsone	.. 1545
Standishe ..	.. 1563	Vernam	.. 1546	Wakeman ..	.. 1545
Symkes	.. 1563	Vaughane ..	.. 1559	Whytnyll ..	.. 1545
Stapull	.. 1563	Ware ..	.. 1539	Woodward	.. 1545
Skytt ..	.. 1564	Wryte	.. 1539	Wyckins ..	.. 1548
Sanford	.. 1564	[Write]	.. 1541	Whyttell ..	.. 1548
Sutton	.. 1565	Warroll	.. 1539	Whytaker ..	.. 1550
Tyllyate	.. 1539	Wilks ..	.. 1540	Watkys	.. 1550
[Tyllet]	.. 1551	Wannerton	.. 1540	Wall ..	.. 1550
Thomyns ..	.. 1539	Wordle	.. 1540	Waynwright	.. 1550
Tyler ..	.. 1539	[Woordyll	.. 1546	Waringe ..	.. 1559
Thruston ..	.. 1540	Whytefoot..	.. 1540	Whytmore	.. 1557
Taunton	.. 1540	Wynyatt ..	.. 1541	Whytfeild ..	.. 1560
Tayler	.. 1540	Weston	.. 1541	Welshman..	.. 1561
Togood	.. 1540	Walker	.. 1541	Woldnall ..	.. 1563
Tudge..	.. 1541	Walton	.. 1542	'Oldnall'	.. 1540
Turner	.. 1541	Wood ..	.. 1542	Whystone ..	.. 1564
Troughton..	.. 1542	Wats ..	.. 1542	Wawyne	.. 1564
Towneclarke	.. 1542	[Watts]	.. 1543	Yorksheire	.. 1543
Thatcher	.. 1543	Wynsham ..	.. 1542		

[Previous to the adoption of the Gregorian or New Style in England in 1752, the legal year began on March 25th.]

1539. January vi buried Johane the daughter of Thomas Hayley
xxxi maried John Bowky and Eme Buckenyll
Feb. xv. buried John the sonne of Michell Betenson
xvii buried Margret Jennyns widow
March xvii buried William the son of Thomas Blount

1540. Feb. v maried John Combes and Joyce Blount

1541. October iv buried Sr. John Barret, preist
xv ,, Sr. Nicholas write,* preist
Nov. xv maried John Bucknell and Joane Burdnyll

1542. Aug. xxv buried Sr. Thomas Alchurch, pst
Oct. i maried Thomas Jenyns and Agnes Benbowe

---

* Sir Nicholas Wright was appointed Chaplain of St. Mary's Chantry, June 27th, 1499. The patrons were Sir John Mortimer, Thomas Jenyns, bailiff, William Colsell, and other " more worthy " parishioners of the Church of " Kydermyster " He appears to have held the Chaplaincy only till 1515

A A

A HISTORY OF KIDDERMINSTER.

1543. April xx buried Sir Philip pardoe, preist
Feb. xix buried Sir James Pirry,* preist

1547. Aprill xvi was buried Mrs. Joane Blunt
June xvii maried Mr. Simon Clare and Mrs. Agnes Blounte
July xviii cristened John the sonne of Thomas Jenyns
Oct. xii buried William Cokesey

1548. Sept. viii maryed Kenellme Channce and Agnes Betenson
March iii christened Dennis dr. of John Bucknell

1549. May vi christened Elizabeth dr. of William Woodward
,, xvii ,, Agnes dr. of George Kyteley
Sept. xxvii buried Dame Agnes Blount †
March v christened Agnes dr. of Humphrey Sebright

1550. March xxx buried Sr. William Thomyns ‡ preist late Vicar of Kitherminster
Nov. vii buried Gilbert Clare gent
March i christened Myrable dr. of Thomas Mytton

1553. August the xxiij day was christned Alexander the sonne of Sir William Spittle, preist §

_____

[From September 24th, 1553, until June 24th, 1559, the record is blank.]

_____

In and from the xxvth day of June in the first yeare of the Raigne of our late Soveraigne Ladye Queen Elizabeth.

1559. The xxvth day of June was maried John Clymar and Joane Hodgetts
August xii buried Humfry Sebright
Sept. 1 buried Edward Blount Esquier
October xxviij christened Arthure the sonne of Nicholas Betenson
Feb. xxi maried John Bucknell and Amye Best

1560. July xxviij christened Agnes dr. of Robert Edgley.
Feb. xvi christened Thomas son of William Jennyns

_____

* Sir James Pyry was presented to the Chaplaincy of St. Mary, Trimpley, by Sir John Atwode, April 29th, 1501, and held it till his death.

† On the 20th of June, 14 Henry VIII (A.D. 1523), the rectory of Kidderminster was leased to Sir Thomas Blount, Agnes his wife, Edward Blount and Joan his wife, for 97 years.

‡ Sir William Thomyns was instituted to the Vicarage of Kidderminster on the presentation of Maiden Bradley Convent, July 12th, 1535. In 1542, June 6th, he was also presented by Henry VIII. to the Chaplaincy of St. Mary's Chantry. There is clearly no break in the continuity of the Church at the Reformation.

§ Curate of the Parish Church.

1561. May xi christened Richard son of John Bowyer of Trimpley
Sept. v christened Mary the dr. of Thomas Blount Esquier
Sept. vii christened Thomas son of Richard Potter

[Another blank occurs from Feb. 22nd, 1561, to October, 1563.]

1563. October xxvi maried Edward Crane and Joane Gryffyne
Nov. xii christened Gabriell son of John Brocke
Jan. xxix maried Edward Toy and Marget Goston

1564. Aug. 31. c. Nicholas, s. of Nicholas Freestone and Joane
1565. Apr. 20. b. W. Jennyns
  ,, 29. b. Joane, d. of John and Alice Fawkner
June 8. c. and b. John, s. of George and Joane Blount
1566. Feb. 3. b. Margery Ley, wyddow
1567. Aug. 6. c. Elizabeth, d. of Elize Cheltnam, and of Margery
1568. Sept. 21. c. Wm., s. of Thomas and Joane Dolittle
Dec. 2. b. Thomas Blount, Esquier
1570. Nov. 10. b. Richard Wilks, a bachelor from Mytton
Mar. 3. b. John Madeley, clerk
1571. Feb. 1. b. Joane and Joane, the drs. of Thomas and of Joane Whyttell
Sept. 23. b. William Hornblower, of Netherton
1572. June 21. c. Henry, s. of Thomas and Agnes Toy, from Mytton
1573. April 14. b. Gods creature,* the sonne of John and Jane Glazzard
May 9. b. Edward Newman Surgion a Londoner inhabiting with William Allen
Nov. 17. c. John, the sonne of Ralph Smyth, viccarr, and of Alice
1574. April 24. m. Thomas Webb of the Rock and Thomasin Hill, widdowe
Dec. 21. b. Henry Kempstowe, whoe was then high Baylife of Kidderminster
1575. April 19. was John Ball, of Carbee, in the County of Northampton and Margery his wife, passing through Kidderminster, when the said Margery was delivered of a man child, whose name was John, wher he was both baptized and buried

---

* This expression has given rise to much debate. It doubtless refers to the practice, common at that time, of lay baptism, so strongly objected to at the Hampton Court Conference of 1604. Compare the following entry in the Elmley Lovett Registers:—" 1588 Bu. Creature the daughter of Robert Briges being christd by the midwife was buried the xith day of December."

1575. May   4. b. Mrs Ann Clare, widdow
      Aug. 15. b. Sir Nicholas Compton, Vicar of Stone
      Jan. 28. b. Blanch, the wyfe of......St. Warborowes pishe in Westchester

1576. Apr. 24. m. Hugh Evans and Magdalenn Symcocks
      Dec. 16. b. A poor Welshwoman from Wrignall
      ,,   26. b. Richard, the sonne of Rd. Ingram, gent., wch child borded at Thomas Evesans, in Kidderminster
      Jan. 1. b. Joyce, the wyfe of Xtofer Cooke, from Haberley, and a creature of God, her sonne
      Feb. 14. b. John Hill, weaver
      Mar. 16. c. and b. John, s. of Thomas, a millner of the How Myll

1577. April 24. was christened and buried a Creature of God the daughter of Philip Whytefoot
      June 6. married Robert Smyth of Bwimingchamis Aston to Anne Lane of the parish Ketherminster with Willm Gosnell
      ,,   7. buried John Sergeant one of the high Baylifes of Kitherminster
      ,,   23. married Thomas Pytt and Clare Clare
      July 3. buried John Mason the fuller
      ,,   25. b. on........A. powell a scholler of Oxford drowned at Severne in Wrignall
      Dec. 23. c. Gilbert son of John Bourne and of Alis

1577. Feb. 26. bd. Alice wyfe of Raphe Smyth viccar of Kitherminster
1578. June 18. bd. Wm sonne of Nicholas Bettison which perrished by a fall out of the bell seller in the steeple and fell through all the flowers to the ground.
      July 6. md. Rowland Blunt and Alice Wilmot
      ,,   17   bd. Alice wyfe of Edward Sebright of Horstone
      Sept 20   b. Julyan Clowde from Mr. Coles of the Talbott

1579. Apr. 23. b. Lawrence Cromwell, a poore man
      June 13. b. a child from Roberts the welchmans in Coventry Street
      Aug. 11. b. Thomas Churchyard with the Crooke legg
      Nov. 23. b. old Joane a poore woman of the Church Hill out of the Chamber next to Mr. Blount's house
      ,,   30. b. Edmund Jurden of Worcester being drowned by misfortune

1580. June 12. m. Xtofer Symcocks unto Joane Holmer
      July 23. b. Symon Clare Esquier Justice of Peace and Quorum in the county of Worcester
      ,,   29. b. Agnes the wyf. of the said Symon Clare Esquier
      Aug 16. b. Robert Jervice one of the nomber of the highe Baylifes

1581.	June	10.	m. Thomas Dawxe unto Alice Doolittle
	Feb.	26.	b. one John Stevens A stranger and an inhabitant of A pishe in Lancashire called Armestirke (? Ormskirk), a surgion by professione
	Mar.	12.	b. Richard Rysse
1582.	Apr.	30.	b. John Hawwoth of Wymstowe his wyf Margrett being at his buriall
	Aug.	27.	b. Margrett the wyf of John Serjeant Highe Baylife
1583.	Apr.	12.	c. Thomas the sonne of Roger Hurtyll and Margerye
	May	3.	b. Mrs. Alice Dawks the wife of Mr. Henry Dawks
	Dec.	30.	b. Margarett a poore wench
	Mar.	13.	c. Magdalen the dr. of Mr. Edmond Burfeild and of Anne
1584.	Sept.	9.	c. John son of John Costen
	Nov.	11.	b. John Nott from the Crowne
1586.	Apr.	4.	b. John Burlton, Tanner from Wribnall
	May	30.	c. Richard son of Symon Clare and Joane
	July	20.	b. Alice wyfe of Thomas Jennings
	Aug.	28.	b. A man from Blackestone that was drowned
	Oct.	4.	b. Davy a welsh boy.
	Dec.	8.	b. A woman that was found dead in Burlashe by Mr. Edward Blount Esq. and vewed by vi honest men
1587.	June	10.	m. Evan ap Powell and Marye ap Meredith
1588.			b. Magdalen dr. of Edmond Burfeild, Clearke
	May	4.	b. Raphe Smyth viccar of the Towne
	Aug.	12.	c. Alice dr of Nicholas ffayroyeare, Clearke
	Mar.	18.	b. Anne wyfe of Mr. John Hassoll
1590.	June	16.	c. Thomas son of Thomas Doolittle
	Aug.	8.	c. Merriall the daughter of Sir ffrauncis Clare, knight
1591.	Mar.	6.	c. John son of Nicholas Freestone
1594.	July	30.	b. John Legg from Heythey Myll
1595.	Nov.	2.	b. Mrs. Margerye Blount
	Feb.	13.	b. a fondling from Wrignall
1596.	Apr.	30.	b. Mrs. Merrell dr. of Mr. Francis Clare, Esquier
	Aug.	21.	m. William Stooke and Margaret Mason
	Nov.	8.	m. Nicholas Allyne of Wakysbery Court and Anne Woldnall.
	Dec.	20.	m. Mr. John Dawks and Anne Aston of Tewxburye
1597.	Mar.	2.	c. * John son of John ffreestone.
	April	25.	b. owld Elizabeth Damice one of the Alms Howse

* John Freestone was nominated the first Bailiff of Kidderminster by the Charter of King Charles I. 1637.

1598.	Jan. 22.		bd. Wm. Rayson of Worcester clothworker from the Bow (?) Myll at Nethermytton
1599.	Feb. 24.		A lycence of eating flesh made the xixth day of the same moneth for Nicholas Bowyer the younger for recovery of his health his said sickness still continuing was recorded according to the statute
			* Willm Smith Curate Thomas Pytt Churchwarden
1600.	Feb.	6.	cd. John son of John Radford of the porche
	Feb.	8.	bd. Ezechiell the sonne of John Stuard the Jockye
1601.	Oct.	13.	b. Hughe boucher of Puckstone
	Oct.	22	b. Rowland Blount
	Feb.	5.	m. Mr. John Acton to Mrs. Anne Clare
	Mar.	6.	b. Joane wife of Thos. Jenens
1602.	June	15.	m. Thomas Jenens and Eliz. Edgley
	Aug.	12.	b. John Raybold servant with Humfrey Doolittle in Worcester Street
	Oct.	31.	c. Edward that found at the Lee
	Nov.	17.	m. John Wildgoose and Alice Blount
1603.	Feb.	15.	b. Nicholas Betenson Deacon of the Church of Kitherminster
1604.	Ap.	30.	b. Anne the wife Philip Flanders and John his sonne of the sicknes †
	May	5.	b. Nicholas Lowe and his mother of the sicknes
	May	26.	b. Mr Rd Child Highe Baylife
1607.	Dec.	13.	c. Lettice d. of Edward the Singer
1610.	Ap.	4.	b. Wm. Sebright
	Jan.	20.	b. Mr John Gower gentleman
1612.	Mar.	28	b. Mr Gilbert Blount Esqre
	May	13.	b. Mr Thos Dawks one of the hihe Baylifes
	Sept.	14.	b. Mr Thomas Pytt one of the hihe Baylifes
	Sept.	28.	c. Anne d. of Mr Walter Blount
1614.	Oct.	26.	b. Margrett Collyns a poore wench yt went from Connstable to Connstable to wrignall.
	Dec.	11.	b. a creature of Christ the daughter of John George from Mytton
1615.	Dec.	5.	b. John Denson, A poore man that came from Bewdley to bee conveyed to Belbroughton and died by the way with a certifficate from Mr Milson Baylife in the yeare 1615

* An Act for the increase of fishermen and mariners, 5 Eliz. (1563). Any person eating flesh on Wednesdays, &c., shall pay a fine of £3 or suffer three months' imprisonment.

† The Plague (Gaol Fever) of 1604 ravaged all England. 115 died at Bewdley in 5 months. In London with a population of ~150,000 it is computed that 30,000 perished.

1616.	Ap. 10.	m. Thos. Doolittle and Margaret Bowyer
	July 17.	c. Jane d. of Edward Dawks and Ales his wife
	Oct. 24.	b. Sorobabell the son of William Seelee
	Feb. 9.	b. Parnell the wyf of Richard Bucknell
	Feb. 15.	m. John Heath* preacher of gods word and Mary Houlden
1617.	Nov. 14.	m. John ffrestone and ffrancis Pytt.
	Feb. 10.	b. the honorble ladye Madame Mary the wyfe of Sr. Edward Blount knight †
1618.	June 12.	m. Thomas Wyldye of Worcester and Ursula Soley of Bewdley
	June 22.	was Mr. John Odwell inducted viccar of Kidderminster The same day buried John Davids A freemason
	Oct. 18.	c. Thomas son of Henry Sergeant and Bridgett
	Mar. 23.	b. Andros from Lickhill within the libertie of Mitton
1619.	May 16.	b. Wiliam Child one of the low bailiffs
1620.	Julye 16.	c. Frauncis the dr. of Rowland Hill and of..........his wife
	Nov. 26.	c. John the sonne of Richard Somers
1621.	April 2.	c. Dorothie dr. of Thomas Woodward of the Angell
	May 27.	b. Margarett dr. of Mr. Thomas Blount of Astley
	Nov. 1.	m. Henry Dyson of Inkeberow Gent and Jane Fownes widdow
	Nov. 13.	b. Muriell lady Clare ‡
	Jan. 23.	b. John Woodward of the Green being drowned
	Jan. 30.	c. Elizabeth dr of Xtofer Wade Citizen of London and of Elizabeth
1622.	April 24.	Thomas Causten had a certificate for marriage at Worcester
	April 26.	b. Mr. Thomas Acton from Comberton
	May 8.	b. Abraham Woolverley killed at Habberley
	Julye 30.	b. olde Edward Crane of Haberley
	Sept. 24.	b. Henry son of Henry Baker and of Alice his wyf from Blackestone
	Feb. 7.	b. one Griffyne Powell supposed a straunger and wandering person found dead in a barne at Wribenhall whoe died as is supposed about St. Andrewstide before, whoe was afterward knowne to be maried and dwelling in Ludlow, and by his mother a woman of good estate, and his brother with her of the pishe of......neer Ludlow, caused him to be taken up, whome haveing soe viewed shee acknowledged him to be her sonne

* Incumbent of St. Anne's, Bewdley.
† Lady Mary Neville, sister of Lord Abergavenny : one of the two ladies in alabaster, now lying near the tower entrance of the Church
‡ Wife of Sir Francis Clare, and mother of Sir Ralph Clare.

A HISTORY OF KIDDERMINSTER.

1622.	April	1.	c. Margarett the dr of Rd Hickotts of the pishe of St. Chadde in Shrewsbury and of Mary his wife brought to bedd at Widow Stevens in Wribbenhall comeing up Severne in a trow with her husband
1623.	June	12.	m. Thomas Balamy and Elizabeth Cowp
	June	30.	b. an abortive the sonne of Cesarr Hawkins Esquier and of Priscilla his wife
	Aug.	6.	b. Alice Edgley widdow from Parke Attwood
	Sept.	22.	b. owld Mr. James Taylor
	,,	23.	a boy from Netherton being a stranger and wandering beggar owt of Chesheir
	Dec.	6.	b. owld Thomas Walker of the well in Worcester Street
	Dec.	24.	m. Simon Potter and Dorrytie Wall by lycence at the Rock
	Jan.	3.	b. Anne......a poore girle called blacke Anne
	Jan.	29.	b. a poore wandering beggar man a stranger unknowne who died in a Barne at Netherton
1624.	May	20.	b. a servant dwelling at the Bull
	June	24.	b. owld father Symcoxe
	July	8.	c. Mary dr. of Richard Sommers and of Joyce his wife
	Aug.	4.	b. Mr. Symon Clare batchelor
	Nov.	5.	c. John son of Nicholas Pearsall and Alice
	Mar.	19.	c. John the sonne of Thomas Lea and of Jane his wife
1625.	July	3.	Richard Baker had a certificat for marriing of Jone Marice at Dowles
	Oct.	12.	c. Honora dr of Richard Harding Esquier and of Catherine
	Jan.	18.	c. John the sonne of Edward Pytt and of Mary
	Mar.	17.	b. Richard ffreestone, Deacon
	,,	20.	c. Elizabeth dr. of Captaine Edmund Woodward
1626.	Aug.	26.	b. Joyce the wyfe of Richard Sommers low bayliffe
1627.	June	19.	m. Mr. Willm. Glasbrooke and Anne Longmore at Worcester by Lycense
	Oct.	19.	b. John Snowe a poore impotent man travailinge from the the Councell in ye Marches of Wales dyed at Blakestone
	Nov.	15.	b. Mr. John Odell vickar
	Nov.	30.	Thomas Lee had a certificate to marry with Mary Mowle of the pishe of St. Peters in Droytwitch
	Jan.	29.	m. Mr. William Smith and Mrs. Anne Odell
	Mar.	17.	c. Jozias a childe founde neere the Whooe brooke
1628.	Mar.	25.	c. Mary dr of Elizabeth Foster a poore walking woman
	May	10.	m. Thomas Willmott and Elizabeth Shenston
	June	14.	c. Marryan dr of Rowland Hill and Mary

APPENDIX. 215

1628.	June	18.	b. Symon Brotherton
	July	24.	m. Michaell Betenson and Margarett Cheltnam
	Aug.	29.	c. John son of Mr. William Glasbrooke and Anne
	Jan.	5.	c. Jane dr. of Mr. Rd. Barbar and Katheryne from Blakestone
1629.	July	14.	b. Mrs. Alice Dawkes Widdow
	Oct.	20.	b. a poore traveilling child out of Mr. Burton's barne
	Dec.	20.	c. Edward son of Alexander Caple A mountebank
	Dec.	25.	b. Hugh Stevens that was drowned at Bewdley in Severne
1630.	July	8.	b. Margery dr of David Jones an extravagant and of Margarett Meredyth bastard
	Nov.	18.	b. Sir Edward Blount Knight
	Feb.	24.	b. the child wch was found drowned at wrignall being made away by the mother of it whose name was Joane Lylley for wch fact she suffered at Worcester the 4th of Aprill next after the Gaole Delivery
1631.	Aug.	17.	b. Humfrey Grove of the Chaunter house neere Alveley servant to Mr. Humfrey Burlton of Wrignall
	Oct.	27.	b. Symon Smith bellman
1633.	May	9.	b. Mrs. Alice the wyfe of Mr. John Daukes one of the High Bayliffs
	June	18.	were marryed Henry ffylldust and Joane Hodgetts ye wch marryed Mr. Samuell Attwoodd Esq. Elisabeth Baskervill by lycense
	Jan.	30.	c. Mary dr. of Stephen Bache
1634.	May	24.	b. Newporte son of Mr. John Stepkin and of Judyth
	June	8.	c. John son of John Baskerville and of Mary
	Jan.	24.	b. Thomas Hill Clothworker
	„	31.	b. Rd. Raynolds who was starved to death in the snowe
	Feb.	1.	b. Thos. Wells starved in the Snowe
	Mar.	21.	b. Anne wife of Mr. Thomas Bray doctoure of Phissicke
1635.	Ap.	30.	b. John son Symon Potter
	Aug.	26.	b. Welch John
	Oct.	6.	c. Sissillia dr. of Mr. Daniell Dobbins Esquier and of Ursula his wife
	Oct.	14.	c. William son of Josephe Amphlett and of Johane
	Dec.	13.	b. Richard Cleeve clericus ecclesiæ
	„	29.	b. Anne dr. of Mr. ffrauncis Clare and of Anne
	Feb.	14.	b. Mr. Symon Pitt one of the High Bailiffs
	Mar.	21.	b. Edward son of Phillip Flaunders

At the end of Volume. 1 is engrossed " A true Copie of the letter of that Worthy and Charitable christian William Sebright of London Esquier expressing for his Guift of Thirteen Pence weekly in wheaten bread &c.'

" Forasmuch as certain pishioners of Kidderminster whose names are subscribed have by the consent of the Viccar and Churchwardens for the tyme being newlie enlarged nyne seats next unto the middle Alley of the Church at their owne pp. Costs and charges, amounting to the some of fowerty shillings or thereabouts : It is concluded and agreed that the said nyne persons shall have convenient Roome in the said Nyne seats soe by them repaired as shalbe fytting for them the better thereby to heare divyne service, and the word of God read and preached unto them, soe that they may from tyme to tyme resorte thereunto without the lett molestation or disturbance, of any the rest of the pishioners that would displace them and seat others therein. For wytness whereof we the said Viccar and Churchwardens have hereunto set our hands this present Aprill the eighteenthe Anno Dni 1620."

[Names cut out.]

VOLUME II.

1636. This Register Booke was begun on the first day of June 1636

    June 24, c. Hanna dr. of John Wallis and Susanna
    November b. Frauncis the sonne of Henry Baker the xxth. day whoe was drowned at the Callis Bridge in a greate floude by a fall of a horsebacke the xiiith day of the same moneth and not found until the sayd xxth day
    Dec. 21, c. John the sonne of Elizabeth Tyllam filius populi
    ,, 28, c. Anne dr. of Mr. Frauncis Clare and of Anne
    ,, 29, c. Candida dr. of Mr. William Welsh and of Elizabeth.
    Feb. 27, c. Mary dr. of Joseph Amphlett and of Johane

1637. April 13. c. Ursula dr. of Daniel Dobbins Esquier and of Ursula
    June. William the son of Mr. James Kyrle somtyme sojourninge at Mr. Danyell Dobbins whoe went to Beawdley schoole was there drowned in Severne by bathinge himselfe and was buried on the 14th day
    Sept. 8. b. Thomas Sutton of the sicknes
    [In October 60 deaths from the "sicknes."]
    Oct. 20. The searching woman buryed the same day of the sicknes.
    [In November 1637 there were 62 deaths from the sickness. In November 1636 there were the average number of 7, which included one by drowning]
    [In December 47 deaths from the plague.]
    Feb. 14. b. Robert Morris servant to Sir Raphe Clare Kt
    ,, 18. c. William the son of Thomas Lea and of Jane
    Mar. 1. c. Mary dr of Thomas Wylkes and of Joane by Mr. Turner of Mytton

APPENDIX.

1638.	July	1.	c. Nicholas son of Nicholas Pearsall and of Alice
	,,	25.	m. Symon Clymer and Anne Hassold
	Sept.	1.	c. Elizabeth dr of Mr. Nathaniell Eston cl and of Elizabeth
	Dec.	5.	b. Marmaduke Corbett
1639.			c. Thomas son of Thos. Cheltnam and of Mary
	July	26.	b. William son of Richard Bradeley deceased
	Jan.	1.	b. Elizabeth dr of Francis Holloway and of Jane
	Feb.	13.	c. Elizabeth dr. of John Cholmeley Esq. and of Anne
1640.	April	13.	m. John Baskervile and Alice Baker
	,,	,,	m. Thomas Bucknell and Florance Pryce
	May	20.	c. Ursula dr. of Thomas Dannce and of Ursula uxor
	June	7.	m. Moses Mason and Annie Sufild
	Aug.	16.	c. Dorothy dr of Daniell Dobbins Esq and of Ursula uxor
	Sept.	3.	c. Thomas son of Bartholomew Perrins and of Margaret
	Oct.	18.	c. Cordilla dr of Humphrey Pagett and Alice
	Nov.	3.	m. Frauncis Bradeley and Elizabeth Peeters
	,,	21.	b. a Cripple wch dyed in the prison
1641.	May	28.	b. Elizabeth dr. of John Chomley Esquier and Anne
	Nov.	25.	m. Richard Bucknell & Margarett Malpas
1642.	Mar.	2.	b. John Burnham Master of Arts and Schoolemaster
1643.	Nov.	31.	c. Alice dr of Andrewe George a walkinge body
1644.	June	15.	b. a pliament souldier
	,,	21.	b. a souldier
	Aug.	22.	b. James Phewtrell a souldier
	Mar.	11.	b. John Windie alias Walker whoe was slain at Cawdwall
	,,	15.	b. Samuell Taylor a ragman drowned in ye well in Coventry Streete
1645.	July	1.	b. a strainge woman wounded at ye battell in Leicestershiere
	July	7.	b. Rd. the son of Rd. Pitt gent. & of Joice his wife who bathinge himselfe in Stower was there unfortunately drowned
	Nov.	8.	b. a souldier belonginge to Sr Thomas Aston slaine at Trimpley
	Nov.	11.	b. John Vygons a souldier under Captaine Dunghill
	Nov.	14.	b. another of his souldiers one Giles both slain in ye towne
	Mar.	13.	b. Captaine Charles Dungham and Richard Kerby one of his souldiers
1646.	April	19.	b. John Jones a pliamt souldier slaine at the skirmish at Worcester
	Dec.	28.	c. John ye sonne of a wanderinge woman from fraynch
	Jan.	17.	c. Thomas ye sonne of Thomas Doolittle & of Anne
1647.	Aug.		b. Mr Samuell Attwood Esqr

1649. Aug. 6. b. Elias Harryts, Mary his wife their sonne and daughter all slayne by the fall of a tree
      Dec. 1. m. James Pitt & Elizabeth Cooper at Dowles
1650. April 25. b. Guendoline ye wife of James Tolbutt
1651. June 22. b. Mistress Margrett Merricke widdow gent
      July 14. b. Mary Cheltnam whoe was scalded in Rd. Clarkes Furnace
      July 24. m. John Pearsall and Rebecka Bellarmy
      Feb. 3. m. Mr. Richard Sericant and Mtris Hannah Burnham at Cosson in ye parysh of Woorfield
      Mar. 4. b. Mr. John Pitt scoolmaster
      ,, 22. c. Sarah dr of Mr. Rd. Sericant & Hannah
1653. July 25. m. Thomas Pardoe and Sarah Naysh by Mr. Osland of Bewdley
      Aug. 15. b. Alyce dr. of Richard Bough Esquire who dyed at Mr. Danyell Dobbins his house
      Sept. 11. b. ould John Hill a pfessed doctor
                A true and pfett Register of all *births* of children, weddings and burialls on and after the 29th Sept. A.D. 1653 by Edward Climar late before chosen and elected Register by the Vote of the townesmen and pryshoners at a publique meetinge, and afterwards Sworne by Mr. Lawrence Pearsall then Justice of the Peace according to an Act of Pliament of the 24th of August.
1653. Oct. 14. b. Thomas Crane ye Eldar from Spennylls. The 6th, 13th, & 20th days of this instant November was an intention of marryge published in the church accordinge to ye Act of pliament at the clause of the morninge Exercise betweene Edward Climar the sonne of John Climar weaver And Cicillie the dr. of Richard Raynolds dyer none excepting against it by me Edward Climar Registar.
      Dec. 3. day was marryed Edward Climar abovementioned and Sycillie & pronounced husband and wife by Mr. Thomas bellamy then High Bayliffe and Justice of the peace and quorum
               m. William Warren and Elizabeth Attwood of Wolverley.
1654. July 13th &c. m. William Kendrick of the —— Chaddesley Corbett to Ann Amphlett of Elmley Lovet widow of Wm. Amphlett, of Ambersley
      Oct. 17. Samuel Whitefoote of Woolverley and Ursula Kettle of Kingsnorton came to Kidderminster with 2 certificates under the hand of Mr. Thos. Baldwin and Mr. Francis Pottar and married by Mr. Nycholas Pearsall High Bayliffe.

APPENDIX.

1654.	Feb. 26.	William Cardall of Hagley & Mary the dr of Mr. Nycho. Addenbrooke of Ould Swinford came with certificates from Mr. Gervace Bryan & Mr. Bartholomew Kettle &c. Upon sight whereof they were joined in marriage by Mr. Thos. Bellamy.
	30 Aprill 1655.	Cornelius Holland and Jane Rushmore (?) of the payshe of oulde Swinford came &c. and were joined in marriage by Mr. Lawrence Pearsall High Bailiff
1655.	Mar. 23.	Roger Shakespeare and An Davis both of Dudley came &c
1656.	April.	published the intention of marriage in our market place of kiderminster at the season appointed by the late Act of pliam't between William Thomason of Wolverley &c
	July 24th	&c. in our mkett place Wrofe Rogers of the Cittie of Hereford Esquier and Mary Sallway Spinster the dr. of Mtriss Dorothie Sallway of Kidderminster &c
1656.	Sept. 13.	b. ffraunces the wife of John Carpenter junior beinge the firste Corps the greate belle was runge for after he was caste
	Oct. 26.	b. Mr. William Speerels at Stone church
1657.	June 25.	b. Waltar Hardman whoe was slaine by blankley
	Oct. 23.	William Read of Mamble gent and Elizabeth Dyckins of Bobbington brought a certificate under the hand of Mr. John Boroston pryshe Register of Bewdley in wh he certified that by his appointment the intention of marriage had been published in their Market place of Bewdley without exception &c. Declared &c. by Mr. Wm. Mountford Justice of the Peace
1658.	Mar. 28.	*baptised* Thomas son of Mr. Lawrence Pearsall & Joan
	June 13.	c. Joseph & Benjamin sonns of John Hill
	Aug. 22.	c. Aquila and Priscilla children of Thomas Simon
1659.	July 12.	m. Waltar Yarrington of Astley and Margrett Myllton of Stower brydge by Mr. Samuell Bowatter
	July 3.	c. Eliz dr of Nevill Simonds
	,, 12.	Mtris Roberta Dyson was carried to Inkberough and ther buried
	,, 24.	b. Mr. John Rowden
	Aug. 30.	b. Ann George whoe poysoned herself found Guiltie of hir own death by the Jurors then chosen
	Aug. 15.	Thomas Woodward and Mary Richards were joined in marriage by Mr. Richard Baxtar minister
1660.	June 26.	m. Edward Baxtar of Layton, Salop joynar and Joyce Browne of this pryshe by Mr. Waldron
	May 24.	Mr Thomas Bawldwin minister of Gods word and Mtriss Elizabeth Solev were joined in marriage by Mr. Richard Serieant minister of Stone

1660. July 22. c. John s. of John Baskarvield and Katherine
      Sept. 1. b. Mrs Marie Thomas wyddow late wyfe of Mr. John Thomas late minister at Over Arley
      Mar. 5. b. a creature of Christ the sonne of Edward Walker apothecarie
1661. May 20. c. Abigaile dr of Mr. Rowland Spencer
      Oct. 23. b. Marie wife of John Clare
      Dec. 27. b. Margrett wife of Richard Bucknell of fraynsh
1662. April 9. m. John Baskarvield to Isable Johnsone
1663. Nov. 8. b. Joyce the wife of Mr. Francis Clare
      Feb. 1. b. Joane Yarrenton wid
1664. Aug. 22. c. Mariell dr of Mr. Francis Clare & Mary uxor
      Oct. 20. b. Mr. Abraham Plymley
1665. June 30. c. John son of John Beuchampt & Judith
      Mar. 20. b. Elizabeth wife of Mr. George Dance Vicar
1666. Oct. 26. b. Edward Burton who was kild at ye walke mill at Broadwaters
      Dec. 4. b. a welshman from the bell
      Mar. 5. b. Thomas Harcot kild with a cart coming from Bewdley
1667. April 3. b. Mary dr. of John Rosse who came with a passe
      Nov. 23. b. a Innocent a dr. of Thomas Hawkes
      Mar. 23. c. Henry son of Henry Addenbrooke
1668. Jan. 23. c. Joseph the son of John Williams and Joane ux
      Feb. 21. b. Winifred Wilmot widow
      Sept. 17. b. M{tris} White widow
1669. Oct. 15. c. Thomas the son of Thomas Leah & Eliz. uxor
      Feb. 12. c. William the son of Thomas Lea and Grissell uxor
      Mar. 1. c. Ann the dr. of Thomas ffoley Esqre & Elizabeth
1670. April 23. b. Sr Ralph Clare
      Sept. 3. c. Thomas s. of Thomas Perrens and Mary uxor
      Nov. 3. b. Richard Aumphlit
      Nov. 11. c. Ralph s. of Mr. Francis Clare & Mary
      Dec. 1. b. Humphrey Whittell
      Jan. 7. b. John s. of Thomas Hancox and Mary
1671. Mar. 1. b. Nicholas Penn of Trimpley
1672. April 15. m. Christopher Humphries & An Proudly
      May 5. c. Thos. son of Robert Vernon and Mary of Ribbenhall
      Dec. 4. c. Daniell s. of Beniamine Broome & Margery ux
1674.   This Register Booke was bought by Thomas Perins & Edward Walter churchwardens for the Burrough & Wm. Bowyer & John Crane churchwardens for the floreigne in the yeare supradicto Pretium £1 15s. 0d.
1673. June 28. b. Mrs. Dorothy wife of Mr. Adam Hough.
      Nov. 12. c. Thomas the sonn of Thos ffoley Esq. & Elizabeth
1675. Sept. 24. m. Mr. Charles Bowyer and Mary Cooper
      Oct. 27. c. John son of Benjamin Broome and Margery

APPENDIX.   221

1675.	Jan.	4.	Remember betweene 7 and 8 aclock at night an earthquake
	Jan.	11.	b. Mr. Wm. Kent an exciseman
	Jan.	13.	m. Richard Hill & Eliz. Amis
1676.	April	6.	m. Thomas Hill & Anne Tilt
	July	13.	m. Ralph Cheltnam & Eliza Bradley
	July	31.	m. George Patchett and Clariencha Geligoe
	Aug.	18.	m. Stephen Lea & Margaret Callow
	Sept.	23.	c. Edward sonn of Thomas ffoley Junior Esqnire & Elizabeth ux
	Dec.	9.	c. Simon s. of Simon Deage Esq. and Mary
1677.	June	7.	c. Stephen s. of Stephen Lea and Margaret
	Dec.	29.	m Mr Thomas Baldwin & Elianor Bennett by licence
1678.	May	9.	c. Elizabeth a childe that was founde in the common water lade in the Mill strete
	Aug.	20.	b. Margaret wife of Edward Crane in woollen *
	Dec.	31.	c. Richard s. of Mr. Rd. White Vicar & Mary
	Feb.	11.	m. Robert Willmott and Sarah Willton by lycence
1679.	Aug.	27.	c. John s. of Thos. Hill and Ann feltmaker
	Mar.	11.	borne Martha d. of Thomas ffoley Esq. & Eliz
1680.	April	4.	b. John Broome in wollen
	Aug.	1.	c. Richard s. of Rd. Bottlestaff & Alice
	Feb.	19.	borne Rd. son of Thomas Foley Esq. & Eliz
	Mar.	1.	borne John s. of Mr. Thomas Baldwin & Elionar
	,,	5.	b. Francis Clare Esquier in woollen
1681.	Aug.	13.	m. Elias Artch and Mary Rowley
	Dec.	25.	b. Robert Fleming who died in the heath goeing to Bewdley
	Dec.	31.	m. Joseph Housman & Prudence Clymer
1682.	May	12.	b. Alice (who was slayne by her husband in Kidderminster) dr of Thomas Hornblower & of Alice
1683.	June	24.	b. Moses Mason in woollen
	Sept.	2.	m. Edward Rouse and Mary Clare by banes
	Oct.	23.	b. Rd. son of Mr. Walter Thatcher
1684.	Sept.	24.	b. Richard Holloway in woollen
	Nov.	6.	m. Jonathan Lea and Mary Sale by bandes
	Mar.	22.	c. Ann dr. of Allen Breaknell and Susannah
1686.	Mar.	30.	c. Joane d. of Edward Rouse and Mary
	Oct.	26.	b. Mr. John Reynolles Schoolmaster
1687.	Sept.	17.	b. John Mathews Mr. Packwood's man
1688.	May	9.	b. Thos. s. of Mr. Abell Attwood and Ann
	Nov.	13.	m. William Lea and Alice Hole
1689.	Jan.	6.	c. Thomas found at Hoge hill barne
1690.	May	28.	borne Frances d. of Francis Preene & Mary

* The Act was passed to encourage the woollen manufacture.

Bailiffs of Kidderminster.

1381	Nicholas Polton
1388	{ William Hulpole / John Sugge
1400	{ John Pryntour / John Horewode
1574	Henry Kempstowe
1576	Hugh Wantner
1577	John Sergeant
1578	Henry Benton
1579	William Fearne
1580	Robert Jervice
1585	Henry Dawkes
1591	— Hassoll
1598	John Dawkes
1604	{ Richard Fearne / Richard Child
1608	John Radford
1612	{ Thomas Dawkes / Thomas Pitt
1615	Nicholas Bowyer
1616	Thomas Woodward
1619	William Child
1623	{ Geoffrey Hornblower / Francis Perry
1626	Richard Somners
1630	Thomas Lake
1633	John Dawkes
1635	Simon Pitt
1636	John Freestone
1637	William Best
1638	Richard Potter
1650	John Elsmore
1653	Thomas Bellamy
1654	Nicholas Pearsall
1655	Lawrence Pearsall
1657	William Mountford
1675	John Pearson
1683	William Lewes
1707	Allen Brecknell
1712	William Hill
1716	William Silk
1721	William Silk
1723	John Harris
1743	Thomas Lea
1753	Charles Knocker
1755	William Wallis
1756	Richard Colley
1757	Joseph Baker
1759	Joseph Baker
1763	Joseph Lea
1764	Joseph Lea
1765	William Lea
1766	Thomas Perrins
1767	William Oldnall
1768	Thomas Perrins
1769	William Oldnall
1770	Joseph Callow
1771	{ Edward Crane (dec^d) / William Wallis
1772	Stephen Miles, jun.
1773	Henry Bird
1774	John Newcomb
1775	John Yearsley
1776	Samuel Harris
1777	William Lea
1778	Henry Bird
1779	John Newcomb
1780	William Lea
1781	Henry Perrin
1782	Josiah Lea
1783	Henry Perrin
1784	Josiah Lea
1785	Timothy Crump
1786	Joseph Pardoe
1787	Robert Shirley
1788	Joshua Moreton
1789	Timothy Crump
1790	Joseph Pardoe
1791	Joshua Moreton
1792	Robert Shirley
1793	James Cole
1794	William Thorn

APPENDIX. 223

1795	..	*Richard Colley, jun.	1811	..	John Newcomb
		William Thorn	1812	..	William Boycott
1796	..	George Gower	1813	..	John Roberts
1797	..	James Cole	1814	..	Joseph Newcomb
1798	..	William Thorn	1815	..	William Nichols
1799	..	*George Gower	1816	..	John Roberts
		*Richard Colley, sen.	1817	..	William Boycott
		*John Newcomb	1818	..	Winter Frost
		*Henry Perrin	1819	..	Joseph Newcomb
		*Josiah Lea	1820	..	William Nichols
		*Robert Shirley	1821	..	James Sprigg
		*James Cole	1822	..	Thomas Jones
		William Thorn	1823	..	James Sprigg
1800	..	*Richard Colley, sen.	1824	..	George Hallen
		*John Newcomb	1825	..	Thomas Jones
		Henry Perrin	1826	..	Samuel Beddoes
1801	..	Josiah Lea	1827	..	George Hallen
1802	..	Robert Shirley	1828	..	Samuel Beddoes
1803	..	James Cole	1829	..	George Custance
1804	..	George Gower	1830	..	John Gough
1805	..	John Roberts	1831	..	Thomas Bradley
1806	..	George Gower	1832	..	John Gough, jun.
1807	..	William Boycott	1833	..	Samuel Beddoes
1808	..	Joseph Newcomb	1834	..	Thomas Bradley
1809	..	James Newcomb	1835	..	Thomas Bradley
1810	..	William Nicholls			

Mayors.

1835	..	†William Butler Best	1847		William Boycott, sen
1836	..	William Butler Best	1848		William Boycott, sen.
1837	..	George Hooman	1849		William Roden, M D
1838	..	George Talbot, jun.	1850	..	William Boycott, jun
1839	..	Charles Talbot	1851	..	William Grosvenor
1840	..	Henry Brinton	1852	..	Joseph Kiteley
1841	..	Joseph Newcomb	1853	..	Joseph Kiteley
1842	..	William Henry Worth	1854	..	Henry Saunders
1843	..	James Morton	1855	..	George Turton
1844	..	William Butler Best	1856	..	Joseph Kiteley
1845	..	George Hooman	1857	..	James Batham
1846	..	William B. Best	1858	..	Henry Jecks Dixon

* Refused to serve. As a result bye-laws were constituted 7 July, 1801, imposing fines for refusal, viz., Bailiff £12, Alderman £6 5s., Councillor £10 10s

† Elected Dec. 31st

224   A HISTORY OF KIDDERMINSTER.

1859	..	Henry Jecks Dixon	1876	.. Thomas Tempest-
1860	..	George Turton		Radford
1861	..	Pemberton Talbot	1877	.. James Joseph Harvey
1862	..	William Roden	1878	.. William Cowen
1863	..	William Roden	1879	.. Joseph Naylor
1864	..	William Roden	1880	.. Henry Richard Willis
1865	..	Alfred Talbot	1881	.. James Binnian
1866	..	Charles Edwd. Jefferies	1882	.. George William Gros-
1867	..	Charles Edwd. Jefferies		venor
1868	..	William Cowen	1883	.. Daniel Wagstaff
1869	..	William Cowen		Goodwin
1870	..	Samuel Tovey	1884	.. William Green
1871	..	William Boycott	1885	.. George Holdsworth
1872	..	William Green	1886	.. Thomas Tempest-
1873	..	Henry Dixon		Radford
1874	..	Daniel Wagstaff	1887	.. Michael Tomkinson
		Goodwin	1888	.. Edward James Morton
1875	..	Thomas Tempest-	1889	.. Edward James Morton
		Radford		

High Stewards.

1636	..	Sir Ralph Clare	1802	.. Thomas Lord Foley
		. . . .	1833	.. Thomas Henry Lord
——	..	Thomas Lord Foley		Foley
1766	..	Thomas Foley, Esq.	1870	.. William Earl of Dudley
1778	..	Thomas Lord Foley	1888	.. William Humble Earl
1793	..	Hon. Edward Foley		of Dudley

Recorders.

.——		John Viscount Dudley	1789	.. William Viscount
		and Ward		Dudley and Ward
1774	..	John Viscount Dudley	1823	.. John William Viscount
		and Ward		Dudley and Ward

Town Clerks.

[1487]	..	Thomas Kynfare, alias	1826	.. Thomas Hallen
		Taillour	1836	.. Thomas Hallen (re-
1764	..	Gregory Watkins		elected)
1788	..	James Pinches	1856	.. Henry Saunders
1801	..	George Hallen	1867	.. James Morton

BRIEF GENERAL INDEX.

Abergavenny, family of, 35-38
Appropriation of Church, by Bp. Simon, 109; by Bp. Bransford, 111; by Bp. Tideman, 113; by Bp. Clifford, 113.
Archery, 61, 62
Arthur Prince, ordains love and concord between Bewdley and Kidderminster, 69
Auxeville, Ralph de, gets knight's fee in Kidderminster, 14; gives land to Maiden Bradley, 15, 16

Bailiffs, antiquities and duties of. 20; privileges of, 55; list of, 222
Baptist Chapel and Ministers, 138
Beauchamp, William de, his Charter, 17
—— Sir John, made Baron of Kidderminster, 31; gets charter from Richard II, 31; beheaded, 32
Benefactors, 146-149
Bewdley, its prosperity, 69; quarrels with Kidderminster, 69
Biographies of — J. Withers, 113; Bishop Harley, 114; G. Dance, 115; Baxter, 117; White, 121; Butt, 121; Dean Onslow, 122; Bishop Claughton, 123; Dean Boyle, 124; Canon Claughton, 124; Abbot Kidderminster, 150; Jervyes, 150; Sir R. Clare, 150; John Somers, 152; R. Cooper, 152; Waller, 153; Yarranton, 153; Lord Foley, 154; Williams, 155; Pearsall, 155; Baskerville, 156; Greaves, 156; Job Orton, 157; Dr. Johnstone, 157, 158; T. Wright Hill, 158; Dr. Lant Carpenter, 159; Sir Josiah Mason, 161; Sir Rowland Hill, 162; Archdeacon Lea, 166; Rev. H. Price, 167; Rebecca Swan, 167; G. Griffith, 168; Helmore, 168; Bradley, 168; D. W. Goodwin, 169; Simcox, 170

Biset family, 13, 28-32; pedigree of, 32
Blackstone, hermitage at, 128
Blount family, 46-49; pedigree of, 49
Brinton Park, 149
Bulls (papal), 104, 105, 194
Burnell, family of, 33-35
By-laws (1330), 56-60 (1640), 75-77

Carpet-making, introduction of, 182; factories, 183-187
Chantries, St. Mary, 35, 39, 40, 44, 67, 94, 95, 97, 99, 100, 101; St. Katharine, 42, 97, 99, 100, 101; Trimpley, 95-97, 99, 100; Hartlebury, 202
Chaddesley Corbet, short history of, 198
Charles I., Charter of, 72-75
Charters of. Henry II., 13, 203; Richard II., 31; Henry VIII., 38; Elizabeth, 13; Charles I., 72-75; George IV., 82
Civil War, 77, 78
Clare family, 44, 45; pedigree of, 45; Sir Ralph, 150
Clent, short history of, 189
Cokesey, family of, 38-43; monument of, 42; brass of, 41; pedigree of, 43
Corporation, constitution of, 82; ornaments of, 83
Churches: All Saints, architecture of, 86, 87; bells of, 89; plate of, 90; goods of, 98, 99; monuments in, 91, "process" of, 101-113; Vicars of, 113-126; St. George, 129, 130; St. John, 131, 132; St Barnabas, 132; St. James, 132; Trimpley, 132; Mytton, 126-128; Wribbenhall, 128, 129; Clent, 191; Wolverley, 195; Hagley, 197; Stone, 198; Chaddesley Corbet, 200; Hartlebury, 201, 202.
Churchyard Cross—see addenda

Court of Requests, 80, 81

Danes, ravages of, 7, 8
Deneberht, his agreement with Kenulph, 6
Domesday Book, Kidderminster, 10, 203; Hagley, 196; Chaddesley, 198; Clent, 190; Hartlebury, 201; Wolverley, 193; Stone, 197

Earthquake, 78
Enclosure Act, 61

Final Concords, 64-67
Foley, family of, 49-51; pedigree of, 51
Frankpledge, 56
Freedom, growth of, 20, 25, 26, 58, 63, 67

Grammar School, 74, 141

Habberley Valley, 149
Hagley, short history of, 195
Harmanville, Maud, brass of, 41
Hartlebury, short history of, 201
Harvington Hall, 199
Henry III, at Kidderminster, 16
High Stewards, list of, 224
Husbandry, old system of, 18, 19, 20

Infirmary, 148

Kidderminster, etymology of, 9, 10; population of, 12, 85; fairs, 17, 29

Leland, his description of Kidderminster, 70

Maiden Bradley Convent, founded 28; its connection with Kidderminster, 101-113; suppressed, 45
Mayors, list of, 223
Markets, Regulations of, 57-60, 72
Members of Parliament, 54, 84
Mitton, 16, 107; monuments in church, 127. See also addenda

New Meeting, 135, 136
Newspapers, 82

Offa's settlement, 5, 6
Old Meeting, 134-136

Pedigrees of, Biset, 32; Burnell, 35. Cokesey, 43; Clare, 45; Blount, 49; Foley, 51; local families, 53
Phelip Sir John, 40, 41; brass of, 41
Plagues, 25, 26, 71, 72
Population in 1086, 12; in 1563, 1776; 1793, 71; in 1801, &c., 85. See corrigenda

Recorders, list of, 224
Registers, names in, 204, &c.; extracts from, 207
Rentals of manors, 21, 25
Riots, 82, 167
Roman Catholic chapels and priests, 139, 199, 200
Roman remains, 1

Schools; Grammar, 74, 141; Parish Church, 142; Potter's, 143; Pearsall's, 143; Art, 145; Science, 145; Board, 143, 145; voluntary, 144
Stone, short history of, 197
Town clerks, list of, 224
Trades in olden times, 71
Trade Tokens, 78, 79

Valuation of benefice, 106-109, 115, 116
Villeins, their condition and duties, 10, 11, 19, 20; lists of, 21-24; their houses, 27
Volunteers, 80, 82

Ward, Baron, purchases Kidderminster, 50; a benefactor, 52; memorial of, 52
Weavers, Society of, 174, &c.
Wesley, at Kidderminster, 137, 138
Wills, of Coton, 67; Forest, 68; Hyheway, 68; Hill, 68
Witches, 167
Woolcombers, 181
Wolverley, short history of, 193
Wribbenhall, Christchurch, 128; All Saints, 128

INDEX OF NAMES.

[See Page 204.]

Abberley, 18
Abergavenny, 34, 35, 36, 38, 47, 67, 70, 72, 75, 95, 100, 128, 196, 198, 199, 200, 213
Abraham, 68, 69
Acheborn, 15
Acton, 44, 81, 99, 121, 212, 213
Adam, 184, 185
Addenbrooke, 66, 149, 219, 220
Aegelsi, 189
Aevic, 189
Agborow, 10, 22, 25, 98, 100, 109
Aiulf, 11
Alchurch, 207
Allom, 139
Allyne, 211
Alured, 171
Amphlett, 215, 216, 218, 220
Andrews, 51
Ansculf, 11, 196
Apen, 100
Arley, 1
Argyle, 124
Artch, 73, 115, 221
Arthur (Prince), 69
Arundel, 33, 35
Ashbourne, 124
Ashe, 51
Ashurst, 118, 119, 143
Astley, 66, 153, 213
Aston, 217
Atherstone, 87
Attwill, 147
Attwood, 55, 56, 64, 95, 96, 194, 215, 217, 218, 221
Audeley, 109
Austin, 81

Auxeville, 14, 15, 16, 20, 21, 25
Avignon, 105, 194
Axminster, 182

Bache, 215
Bacoun, 95
Bagger, 67
Baker, 62, 66, 81, 125, 129, 198, 213, 214, 216, 217, 222
Baldwin, 119, 121, 128, 135, 219, 221
Ballamy, 79, 81, 214, 218, 219
Balle, 16, 24, 25, 209
Banbury, 75
Banks, 81, 134
Bannister, 90, 187
Barbar, 215
Barbour, 96
Bardolph, 41
Ba'ford, 81
Barker, 147, 180
Barnett, 67
Barrett, 135, 207
Barton, 65, 185, 186
Baskerville, 156, 194, 213, 217, 220
Basset, 28, 32
Batham, 223
Bathe, 130
Batten, 82
Baugh, 129
Baxter, 40, 78, 91, 115, 117, 118, 119, 120, 121, 123, 125, 135, 138, 143, 151, 167, 176, 180
Baylly, 65
Beauchamp, 17, 31, 32, 34, 35, 36, 47, 64, 65, 95, 97, 152
Beaconsfield, 153

Beck, 17, 62, 81
Becket, 14
Beddoes, 223
Belbroughton,87,104,212
Belenger, 95
Bell, 137
Bellamont, 143
Bellamy, 222
Benbow, 83, 207
Benedict XII., 104, 105
Bennett, 66, 221
Bennie, 187
Bentley, 202
Benton, 141, 147, 222
Berewyke, 104
Bergavenny (see Abergavenny)
Bernard, 62
Best, 73, 80, 81, 82, 83, 84, 91, 93, 135, 138, 142, 208, 222, 223
Betenson, 100, 125, 207, 208, 210, 212, 215
Beterton, 68
Beuchampt, 220
Bewdley, 46, 47, 48, 61, 64, 68, 69, 74, 77, 78, 117, 119, 137, 139, 150, 153, 172
Bigelow, 183
Bill, 180
Binnian, 224
Bingham, 129
Birch, 72
Bird, 55, 81, 100, 222
Birmingham, 156, 158, 161, 162
Biset, 13, 14, 16, 17, 28, 29, 30, 32, 36, 55, 56, 70, 95, 101, 102, 103, 125
Black, 86, 87, 104, 125
Blackmore, 130

Blackstone, 128
Blake (see Black)
Blakewell, 7
Blanchford, 136
Blaze (Bp.), 181
Bleke, 62
Blomfield (Bp.), 123
Blount, 44, 45, 46, 47, 48, 49, 72, 74, 98, 100, 115, 125, 141, 146, 207, 208, 209, 210, 211, 212, 213, 215
Blunt, 84
Blurton, 152
Bocher, 98, 100
Boraston, 81, 90, 129, 219
Bordesley, 198
Boscobel, 7b
Boscode (see Attwood)
Bosel, 2
Boteler, 26, 39, 43, 64, 196
Botetourt, 34, 190, 196
Bottlestaff, 221
Boucher, 211
Bough, 218
Bourne, 210
Bowater, 219
Bowyer, 66, 134, 143, 147, 167, 186, 209, 212, 213, 220, 222
Boycott, 82, 83, 84, 223, 224
Boyle, 124, 126, 134
Bradford-on-Avon, 171
Bradley, 119, 121, 168, 169, 217, 221, 223
Bradshaw, 94, 135
Bransford (Bp.), 111
Bray, 215
Brecknell, 81, 143, 148, 221, 222
Brede, 62
Bredon, 86, 110
Brentford, 5
Bridgman, 92, 148
Bridges, 48, 115, 113
Bridgnorth, 34, 117
Brindley, 51
Brinkworth, 14
Brinton, 82, 84, 142, 143, 149, 184, 186, 223
Bristol, 100
Bristow, 84
Brittol, 93
Broad, 72, 146, 198
Brock, 121, 166, 209
Bromley, 196

Brommore, 30
Bromyard, 155
Bromsgrove, 62, 63, 173
Brooke, 77
Brookes, 81, 139
Brooksbank, 92
Broom, 190, 191
Broome, 81, 87, 167, 182, 183, 187, 220, 221
Brotherton, 94, 100, 215
Brough, 82
Browne, 66, 73
Bruges, 143
Brugge, 125
Bryan, 219
Bucksbie, 98
Bucknall, 67, 88, 147, 207, 208, 213, 217, 220
Burfeild, 211
Bund, 66
Burcher, 52
Burford, 7
Burhred, 7, 193, 201
Burlish, 14, 111
Burcher, 52
Burlton, 53, 148, 211, 215
Burnham, 217, 218
Burnynson, 100
Burnell, 33, 34, 35, 190
Burton, 66, 93, 142, 147, 215, 220
Butcher, 146, 186
Butler, 79, 80, 92, 100, 137, 147, 190
Butt, 88, 121, 122, 126
Button Oak, 1
Butts, 61

Caldecote, 125
Caldrigan, 54
Caldwell, 38, 39, 63, 70, 77, 107, 109
Calixtus, 102
Callow, 80, 221, 222
Cameron, 122
Cantilupe, 17, 102, 201
Carpenter (Bp.), 87
Carpenter, 159, 160, 161, 201, 219
Carslegh?, 104, 105, 110, 111, 125
Carter, 79
Cartwright, 81
Ceadde (Chad), 2, 9
Cedd, 2, 9
Ceolfrith, 4, 6,
Cergan, 100

Chaddesley, 1, 6, 9, 68, 87, 102, 198, 199, 200
Chaddaleswyche, 64
Chamberlin, 79
Chambers, 90
Chaucer, 41
Chauncc, 97, 99, 100, 101, 208
Charlton, 80, 121, 126, 155
Charouse, 95
Chellingworth, 81, 132
Cheltenham, 128, 209, 215, 217, 221
Chesshire, 124, 129
Child, 81, 135, 147, 152, 212, 213, 222
Children-Hanley, 64
Chiroton, 104, 105
Cholmeley, 217
Church, 130
Churchill, 66
Churchley, 96, 99
Churchyard, 66, 210
Churton, 124
Clare, 43, 44, 47, 49, 53, 64, 65, 66, 67, 74, 75, 80, 100, 139, 147, 150, 208, 210, 211, 212, 214, 215, 220, 221, 224
Clarke, 66, 98
Claughton, 52, 90, 123, 124, 126, 131
Cleeve, 215
Clement (Pope), 194
Clent, 1, 66, 189, 190, 191, 192, 195
Clifford (Bp.), 113
Clifton, 7
Clymer, 204, 208, 217, 218, 221
Cobham (Lord), 95, 197
Cockin, 142, 169
Cocks, 152
Cokesey, 38, 39, 40, 42, 43, 62, 64, 65, 70, 95, 97, 208
Cole, 81, 210, 222, 223
Coleshill, 153
Colley, 65, 80, 81, 222, 223
Collins, 129
Colsell, 95, 207
Columbine, 125
Combe, 13, 46, 49, 71, 207
Comberton, 14, 15, 16, 23, 25, 26, 46, 48, 64, 109, 153, 162, 213

INDEX. 229

Complagu, 100
Compton, 210
Conder, 134
Cooke, 100, 142, 146
Cookley, 6, 7, 193
Cooper, 63, 81, 82, 92, 145, 152, 218, 220
Cowen, 224
Cowp, 214
Cowper, 81
Corbet, 18, 87, 199, 200, 217
Corrie, 91
Coston, 55, 66, 100, 211, 213
Coton, 67
Cotton, 78, 95
Cottrell, 81
Courtenay, 139
Coventry, 44
Cowell, 137, 138
Cox, 93, 198
Craddock, 139
Crane, 53, 67, 80, 81, 93, 146, 149, 157, 185, 209, 213, 218, 220, 221, 222
Craven, 127
Creak, 114, 125, 136
Croft, 45, 49, 70
Croome, 44
Crossley, 184, 186
Crowther, 187
Crump, 185, 222
Custfield, 77
Custance, 168, 223
Cyniberht, 4, 9

D'Abitot, 18, 44, 197
Dalby, 87
Dalmahoy, 127
Danes, 7, 8
Dance, 115, 116, 117, 120, 125, 217, 220
Darby, 81
Darell, 64
Davies, 81
Dawkes, 66, 72, 89, 100, 147, 211, 212, 213, 215, 222
Deanes, 97, 98
De Burgh, 52
Deerhurst, 2
Degge, 93, 221
De la Donne, 110, 111, 125
De la Lade, 103, 125
De la Mere, 40, 95, 103, 125

Deneberht, 6, 193
Dennington, 40
Deorham, 1
Despencer, 34, 35, 47
Dixon, 82, 184, 185, 186, 188, 223, 224
Dobbins, 48, 66, 153, 215, 216, 217
Dobson, 81, 184
Dodd, 200
Doddridge, 157
Doharty, 56, 80, 88
Doolittle, 69, 73, 81, 100, 118, 134, 148, 209, 211, 212, 213, 217
Douglas, 40, 124
Dounreston, 13
Dowies, 1
Downall, 130
Downes, 139
Droitwich, 11, 54, 55, 72, 154, 166, 173, 199
Dudley (see Northumberland)
Dudley, 54, 117
Dudley (Lord), 52, 88, 126, 145, 184, 224
Dudley (Lady), 52, 148
Duffory, 182
Dunclent, 55, 56, 64, 72
Dungham, 77
Dyckins, 219
Dyson, 213, 219

Eastham, 7
Eaton Constantine, 117
Eddeve, 198
Edgbaston, 159
Edgeley, 83, 97, 101, 208, 212, 214
Ednam, 51
Elkington, 161
Elmley Lovett, 44, 103
Elsmore, 174, 222
Elyot, 65
Englefield, 65
Erdington, 161, 162
Eridge, 38
Essex, 102, 103, 125
Esthope, 81
Estlin, 160
Eston, 217
Ethelbald, 4, 7
Ethelred, 7
Evans, 81, 130, 137
Evelyn, 48, 153
Evesham, 18, 54, 72, 77, 78, 139, 173
Exeter, 159

Eymore, 108, 109, 110

Farr, 93
Fawcett, 80, 135, 138, 155, 184
Fawkner, 209
Fayreyeare, 211
Fearne, 222
Feckenham, 62, 95
Ferne, 97, 98, 100, 101
Fewsterell, 101
Filewood, 129
Fincher, 137
Finian, 2
Fish, 137
Fisk, 139
Fitzalan, 35, 51
Fitzwalter, 34
Fitzwith, 31
Flanders, 172, 212, 215
Flemyng, 67
Foley, 18, 20, 21, 38, 48, 49, 50, 51, 53, 80, 89, 117, 125, 126, 127, 129, 154, 155, 198, 220, 224
Folliott, 80, 127, 197
Forest, 38, 67, 68, 198, 200
Forster, 97, 98
Fortescue, 124, 132
Franche, 10, 23, 25, 55, 62, 132, 144
Frankley, 87
Fraser, 77, 84
Freeman, 136
Freeston, 66, 73, 147, 181, 209, 211, 213, 214, 222
Frome, 104
Frost, 70, 223
Fry, 81, 137
Furnivall, 41, 42
Fylldust, 215

Galabank, 157
Garet, 67
Garmson, 115
Garnett, 100
Geligoe, 221
Gentleman, 137
Gething, 145
Gibbons, 124, 130, 155
Gibbs, 197
Gibson, 137, 184
Giffard, 136, 201
Gilbert, 95, 143
Gilis, 68
Gisborne, 84

Glasbrooke, 214, 215
Glynn, 148
Godiva, 7, 193
Godson, 84, 142
Goodwin, 82, 83, 145, 169, 224
Gough, 185, 188, 223
Gower, 147, 185, 212, 223
Grafton, 63
Grant, 84
Granville, 50, 51
Gray, 143
Greaves, 94, 148, 156, 157, 180
Green, 74, 187, 195, 224
Greenfield, 136
Greville, 42, 43, 95
Grey, 101
Grice, 97, 98
Griffin, 100, 139, 147, 209
Griffith, 168
Griffiths, 81, 161
Grosvenor, 145, 169, 185, 186, 223, 224
Grove, 66, 126, 215 29
Gunhilda, 7
Gurney, 129
Gyldon, 97
Gyll, 100

Habberley, 10, 19, 21, 25, 62, 64, 149, 213
Hacun, 7
Hagley, 1, 55, 56, 66, 195, 196, 197
Hale, 65
Hales Owen, 34, 87, 126, 190, 191
Hall, 135, 137, 139, 146, 147
Hallen, 81, 82, 129, 167, 223, 224
Ham, -
Hanbury, 48, 66, 93, 143, 150
Hancocks, 81, 169, 194, 195, 220
Handlo, 34, 35
Hankys, 95
Hanley Castle, 36
Harding, 214
Hardman, 136, 138, 139, 219
Hardwicke (Earl), 152
Harley, 35, 114, 125, 143
Harmanville, 41, 43
Harper, 80

Harris, 81, 222
Harrison, 161, 187
Hartlebury, 18, 68, 78, 99, 100, 112, 201, 202
Harvey, 130, 224
Harvington, 199, 200
Harward, 66
Hassall, 129, 211, 217
Hassoll, 222
Hastings, 36
Hawkins, 214
Haye, 66
Hayle, 62
Hayley, 207
Heath, 128, 138, 213
Heathy, 55, 56, 62, 109
Heathored (i. p.), 5
Helmore, 136, 140, 168
Hemming, 128, 129
Henleghe, 17
Henry II., 13
Henry III., 16
Henster, 65
Herdson, 97
Hereford, 35, 69
Heryng, 62
Hickes, 195
Hickeson, 62
Higgins, 147
Hill, 24, 65, 68, 81, 95, 132, 135, 137, 158, 159, 162-166, 210, 213, 214, 215, 219, 221, 222
Hinton, 81
Hoare, 143
Hoarstone, 18, 48, 66
Hobday, 66
Hodgetts, 51, 208, 215
Holcroft, 198
Holdsworth, 83, 224
Hole, 221
Holla d, 139, 219
Holloway, 217, 221
Holmes, 186
Holt, 95
Hook, 159
Hookham, 142
Hooman, 130, 167, 184, 185, 223
Hooper (Bp.), 202
Hopkins, 88, 195
Hore, 65
Horewode, 62, 222
Hornblower, 81, 209, 221, 222
Hough, 48, 66, 80, 93, 220
Housman, 135, 155, 221
How (Bp.), 124

Howard, 51, 80, 125, 142, 158
Huddlestone, 84
Hughes, 186
Hulpole, 62, 222
Humphries, 184, 187, 220
Hunsworth, 136
Hunt, 66, 81
Hurcott, 10, 25, 26, 46, 48, 67, 101, 106, 112, 153, 187, 188
Hurd (Bp.), 201, 202
Hurtill, 53, 100, 115
Hussey, 143
Hyheway, 68

Ibery, 101
Ingram, 50, 81, 91, 122, 210
Inkberow, 213
Ivens, 18, 52

Jambertus, 5
Jefferies, 81, 93, 121, 180, 224
Jekyll, 152
Jenks, 199
Jennings, 62, 83, 91, 95, 98, 100, 114, 119, 125, 207, 208, 209, 211, 212
Jernaule, 182
Jervice, 222
Jervyes, 150, 210
John (King), 15
Johnstone, 80, 157, 158
Jolly, 81
Jones, 81, 129, 139, 155, 223
Jordan, 125
Jukes, 53, 100, 127

Kempsey, 102
Kempstowe, 209, 222
Kendal, 65
Kenelm, 189, 192
Kenirick, 218
Kent, 55, 56, 62, 221
Kenulph, 6, 193
Kershaw, 132
Ketelbern, 171
Kettle, 106, 218, 219
Kewley, 132
Key, 130
Kidderminster Abbot, 150
Kimberline, 139
Kineton, 86

INDEX. 231

Kinlet, 46
Kinsale, 127
Kinver, 4, 6, 64
Kinwarton, 86
Kiteley, 132, 208, 223
Knight, 194, 195
Knocker, 222
Knowles, 90
Kynfare, 224
Kyre. 7
Kyrle, 216

Lacon, 74
Lacey, 66
Lake, 222
Langton (Abp.), 102
Lamb, 97
Lane, 137, 210
Lant, 159
Laud (Abp.), 115
Laweher, 87, 95
Lea, 19, 22, 25, 81, 82, 84, 90, 91, 92, 129, 134, 143, 148, 149, 162, 166, 184, 187, 214, 216, 220, -21, 222, 223
Le Hunt, 125
Leland, 43, 61, 70, 173
Lechmere, 55
Leitleye, 64
Lewes, 146, 222
Lewis, 66, 137, 187
Ley, 206
Lichfield, 121
Lickhill, 65, 127
Lihtfot, 54
Lindridge, 122
Lincroft, 96
Lister, 81, 138
Lloyd (Bp.), 92, 142
Lloyd, 187, 202
Logwardyne, 106
Longmore, 66, 100, 214
Lorde, 62, 63
Lowe, 64, 84, 98, 212
Ludford, 155
Ludlow, 117
Lugg. 127
Lunn, 137
Lutley, 66
Lye, 68
Lygon, 101, 113
Lyle, 185
Lyttelton, 77, 95, 143, 157, 190, 195, 196, 197

McCave, 6, 139

Maddocks, 97
Madeley, 209
Madstard, 117
Maiden Bradley, 15, 16, 20, 21, 26, 33, 36, 45, 46, 70, 101, 104, 105, 110, 112, 113, 125, 171
Makins, 84
Mal, 62, 125
Malpas, 62, 66, 95, 217
Marsden, 136
Martin, 80, 92, 142, 158
Martineau, 160
Mason, 161, 162, 210, 211, 217, 221
Matthews, 56, 81, 142
Mauger (Bp.), 102
Maunsell, 98
Maydeston (Bp.) 86
Maynard, 198
Mears, 82, 90, 182
Mellone, 137
Meredith, 83
Merrick, 218
Miles, 81, 129, 142, 222
Milred (Bp.), 4
Mills, 139, 147
Miniae, 90
Mitton, 10, 12, 14, 16, 19, 21, 23, 24, 25, 65, 66, 71, 85, 98, 103, 107, 108, 109, 110, 114, 116, 120, 126, 127, 128, 171, and addenda
Moncrieffe, 51
Montacute (Bp.), 106, 109
Morgan, 142, 201
Morley (Bp.), 115, 120
Moore, 17, 149
Morrell, 140
Moreton, 222
Morton, 82, 90, 131, 184, 185, 195, 223, 224
Mortymer, 95
Moseley, 117
Moses, 90
Mossop, 82
Mottram, 130
Mountford, 79, 125, 219, 222
Mountjoy, 48
Mundye, 100
Mustell, 55, 64
Mydlopp, 100
Myll, 67
Myllton, 219

Mytton, 208

Nash, 72
Naylor, 187, 224
Needwood, 167
Nelme, 65
Netherton, 22, 25, 98, 148
Newchurch, 122
Newcomb, 81, 131, 222, 223
Newland, 125
Newman, 125, 209
Newnham, 80
Newton, 70
Nevill, 14, 36, 47, 49, 72
Nichols, 223
Niger, 21, 22, 86
North, 71
Northampton, 159
Northumberland (Duke of), 45, 46, 114
Noake, 136
Notgrove, 122
Nott, 211
Notynham, 95
Noy, 72

Oakhampton, 64
O'Connor, 88, 139
Odell, 115, 125, 126, 213, 214
Odhams, 66
Offa, 5, 6
Offmore, 107, 110
Oky, 62
Oldefelde, 62
Oldington, 10, 14, 15, 16, 18, 20, 21, 23, 24, 25, 26, 46, 65, 66, 111, 112
Oldland, 187
Oldnall, 53, 63, 68, 146, 221, 222
Onslow, 122, 126, 130
Orton, 80, 81, 94, 151
Ossulton (Lord), 152
Oswald, 2
Oxford, 114

Packington, 65, 66, 199
Paganel, 196
Page, 90
Pagett, 115, 217
Pardoe, 53, 184, 185, 208, 218, 222
Parkes, 68
Parlour, 65
Parr, 158

Parry, 82, 137, 143
Paston, 77
Patchett, 221
Patrick, 81
Pauncefote, 32
Payne, 125
Penda, 2
Pearce, 81, 137
Pearsall, 66, 72, 73, 79, 81, 115, 137, 155, 159, 181, 182, 214, 217, 218, 219, 222
Pearson, 164, 222
Pedmore, 96, 98
Peel, 124, 130
Peinton, 64
Penda, 2
Penley, 142
Penn, 62, 81, 93, 95, 148, 160, 220
Pennell, 167
Pepys (Bp.), 131, 201, 202
Perrin, 222, 223
Perrins, 81, 217, 220
Perry, 161, 222
Pershore, 54
Phelip, 40, 41, 43
Phillipps, 44, 64, 67
Phillips, 84, 124, 125, 126, 143
Philpott, 121
Phipps, 122
Picart, 202
Pickerell, 97, 98
Pinches, 224
Pipard, 64
Pirry, 96, 208
Pitt, 45, 55, 79, 100, 136, 142, 210, 212, 213, 214, 215, 217, 222
Plessetis, 29, 30, 33, 36
Plimley, 147, 220
Poer, 171
Pole, 34, 41
Polton, 62, 222
Ponet, 62
Pope, 97, 100
Portes, 64
Porter, 125
Porto d'Anzio, 160
Portway, 1
Potter, 66, 73, 95, 142, 187, 209, 214, 215, 222
Powes, 70
Powell, 81
Power, 18, 139
Powys, 66

Poyntz, 70
Pranke, 96
Preene, 221
Preston, 149
Price, 138, 167
Priestley, 159, 161
Pritchard, 132
Pritty, 79
Pryntour, 62, 222
Purdey, 187
Puxton, 10, 22, 25, 62, 64
Pykenham, 114, 125
Pymp, 64

Quinzehides, 34

Radford, 66, 73, 79, 134, 147, 211, 222
Rammohun Roy, 160
Ramyston, 100
Ratsey, 65
Ray, 145
Rayson, 212
Reade, 79, 81, 119, 134, 146, 147, 219
Reve, 97
Reynolds, 93, 218, 221
Ribbesford, 6, 8, 10, 64, 65, 169
Ricardes, 95
Ricardo, 84
Rice, 44, 45, 65, 68, 94
Richard II., 26
Richardson, 81
Ripariis (see Rivers)
Rivers, 29, 30, 32, 36, 103
Roberts, 81, 223
Robertson, 202
Rock, 64, 65
Roden, 143, 224
Rodeborowe, 202
Rogers, 63, 219
Rokebourne, 13, 101
Ross, 136
Romsey, 30, 31, 32, 33, 65
Rouse, 48, 118, 221
Rowden, 79, 219
Rowland, 195
Rowley, 221
Rudhall, 90
Rugge, 63
Rupert Prince, 77, 78
Rushock, 96, 100
Rushout, 198
Russell, 43, 98
Ryppel, 95

Sacheverell, 199
Sadler, 79
Sale, 221
Salter, 97
Salwarpe, 153
Salway, 219
Santon, 65
Sandbourne, 92, 107, 109
Sandford, 30
Sandys, 201
Saunders, 195, 223, 224
Savage, 72
Sawyer, 66, 99
Scott, 126
Sebright, 53, 74, 95, 146, 194, 208, 210, 212, 215
Seckley, 193
Seelee, 213
Selwood, 104
Sergeant, 66, 101, 210, 211, 213, 218, 219, 222
Severn, 137
Severne, 152
Severn Stoke, 152
Seymour, 124
Shakespeare, 219
Sheldon, 45, 98
Shenston, 214
Shepherd, 139
Sheppard, 142, 170
Sherman, 68
Sherwood, 121
Shirley, 222, 223
Silk, 222
Simmons, 79, 118, 143, 219
Skey, 92
Skinner, 185
Simcox, 170, 184, 210, 214
Snel, 21, 24
Soley, 53, 66, 91, 127, 143, 213, 219
Smith, 66, 100, 114, 125, 134, 137, 139, 185, 202, 209, 210
Somers, 94, 152, 213, 214
Somery, 190, 196
Sommers, 222
Smiles, 154
Southall, 81
Sparry, 147, 150
Speerels, 219
Spencer, 81, 220
Spicer, 53, 64

INDEX.   233

Spilsbury, 93, 94, 135
Sprigg, 223
Spring Grove, 61, 92
Spyttell, 98, 208
Stacy, 29
St. Albans, 124
Standish, 100
Stanhope, 51
Stanley, 121
Stapleton, 42, 43
Steill, 136
Stephens, 139
Stephyn, 66
Stepkin, 215
Steynor, 81
Stillingfleet (Bp.), 201
Stokes, 81
Steward, 53, 212
St. Leger, 190, 196
St. Pierre, 40, 43
Stooke, 137, 211
Stringer, 81, 95
Strode, 51, 155
Stourton, 70
Stoughton, 121
Stratford, 71
Stretton, 90, 149
Sugge, 62, 222
Sutton, 1, 10, 22, 25, 51, 63, 125
Stone, 64, 68, 102, 166, 197, 198
Stour, 8, 12, 24, 171
Stour-in-Usmere, 4, 5, 6, 7, 9, 193
Stourbridge, 1, 77, 78, 150
Stourport, 18, 21, 85, 137, 138, 144, 187
Stafford, 63, 190
Stanford, 121, 122, 155
Symonds, 63, 95
Syner, 73

Taillour, 224
Talbot, 14, 64, 81, 82, 84, 137, 218, 223, 224
Tanner, 6, 8
Tarring, 134
Taverner, 47
Taylor, 64, 81, 90, 92, 129, 135, 137, 214
Tempest-Radford, 52, 83, 224
Templeton, 185
Tenbury, 7
Tewkesbury, 2, 36, 155
Thanet (Lord), 143
Thatcher, 79

Thomas, 55, 81, 97, 220
Thompson, 52, 134
Thomason, 219
Thornborough (Bp.), 117, 126
Thorn, 222, 223
Thornycroft, 143
Throckmorton, 65, 200
Thursfield, 82
Thurston, 100
Thynne, 124
Ticknell, 91
Tillyatt, 100
Timmins, 158, 159
Tombes, 119, 138
Tomkinson, 52, 90, 132, 142, 144, 184, 185, 224
Tompkins, 66
Tomyns, 95, 99, 100, 125, 208
Tovey, 224
Townclarke, 101
Townshend, 53
Toye, 53, 66, 93, 209
Trimpley, 10, 23, 25, 34, 48, 63, 77, 95, 96, 97, 108, 110, 132
Tucker, 145
Turner, 80, 82, 91, 126
Turton, 223, 224

Ubeton, 104, 125
Upton, 102, 114
Urban IV., 103
Uriconium, 1
Usmere, 4, 193

Vernon, 53, 220
Villiers, 130
Vincent, 66

Wacna, 69
Wade, 66, 213
Wadersey, 13
Waite, 136
Wakeman, 63, 82, 95, 100
Waldron, 93, 148
Walker, 66, 98, 214, 220
Wall, 66, 200, 214
Waller, 48, 153
Wallis, 80, 81, 216, 222
Walter, 220
Walters, 137
Wannerton, 10, 53, 58, 66
Wantner, 222
Ward, 48, 51, 88, 94, 124, 126, 131, 137, 185, 198

Waresley, 66, 130
Warm', 18
Warminster, 155
Warner, 124, 129
Warren, 46, 218
Warrington, 160
Warton, 129
Warwick, 30, 35, 100, 198, 200
Wassell, 2, 77
Watkins, 80, 224
Watt, 98
Watson (Bp.), 154
Watson, 81, 82, 148
Webb, 200
Weaver, 66
Wenlock, 180
Werefrith, 7
Wesley, 137, 138
Westbury, 95
Westminster, 10, 196
Westrowe, 201
Wharton, 77
Wheatley, 139
Wheeler, 80
Wheler, 66
White, 65, 81, 84, 121, 125, 145, 220, 221
Whitefoote, 218
Whitehouse, 52
Whiting, 148
Whitnell, 147
Whittall, 186, 187, 209, 220
Whytock, 183
Whyston, 100
Wiccii, 2, 5
Wich, 10, 11, 171
Wichenford, 13
Wickens, 126
Wickstead, 117
Widder, 136
Wiggan, 81, 129
Wigmore, 49
Wike, 18
Wikewood, 13
Wilberforce, 124
Wilder, 128, 187
Wilde, 53
Wildgoose, 212
Wilkes, 66, 126, 209, 210
Willets, 66
Willey, 137
Williams, 80, 135, 136, 155, 220
Willies, 68
Willis, 166, 186, 224
Willoughby, 114, 125

Wilmot, 49, 53, 78, 127, 210, 214, 220, 221
Wilson, 81
Wilton, 182, 183
Wiltshire (Earl of), 190
Winchcombe, 150
Winchester, 16
Winford, 66
Winnington, 50, 131, 155
Winter, 43, 70, 100
Wintour (see Winter)
Witfield, 54, 55
Withers, 113, 114, 125
Witley, 39, 40, 50
Wodehouse, 129
Wolseley, 75
Wolverhampton, 162, 164

Wolverley, 6, 7, 8, 54, 95, 96, 100, 102, 122, 193-195, 213
Wood, 93, 100
Woodfield, 94, 141
Woodward, 81, 90, 119, 131, 167, 184, 185, 186, 208, 213, 214, 219, 222
Worcester, 1, 7, 10, 11, 17, 33, 34, 36, 39, 41, 44, 54, 55, 67, 72, 77, 78, 100, 105, 108, 114, 122, 124, 136, 137, 139, 143, 157, 158, 169, 173, 180, 194, 200, 201
Worth, 184, 186, 187, 223

Wribbenhall, 6, 10, 18, 20, 23, 25, 38, 48, 65, 66, 128, 144, 213
Wright, 81, 95, 139, 185, 207
Wroxeter, 1, 117
Wulstan (Bp.), 7
Wyld, 74, 100
Wyldye, 67, 213
Wynde, 81
Wyre Forest, 172
Wysham, 32

Yarrington, 66, 126, 153, 219, 220
Yate, 199, 200
Yates, 73, 81
Yearsley, 81, 222
Yonkers, N.Y., 185

www.ingramcontent.com/pod-product-compliance
Lightning Source LLC
Chambersburg PA
CBHW031929230426
43672CB00010B/1870